Also by Marshall Loeb

PLUNGING INTO POLITICS
(*with William Safire*)

MARSHALL LOEB'S
Money Guide

MARSHALL LOEB'S
Money Guide

Marshall Loeb

Managing Editor of Money *Magazine*

LITTLE, BROWN AND COMPANY • BOSTON • TORONTO

LIBRARY OF CONGRESS CATALOGING IN PUBLICATION DATA

Loeb, Marshall.
  Marshall Loeb's money guide.

  Includes index.
  1. Finance, Personal.   I. Title.   II. Title: Money guide.
HG179.L555   1983   332.024   83-16186
ISBN 0-316-03132-1

MV
*Published simultaneously in Canada
by Little, Brown & Company (Canada) Limited*

PRINTED IN THE UNITED STATES OF AMERICA

For
Peggy, Michael and Margaret
and
Edward L. Jamieson

Preface

THIS book is based largely on the work of my colleagues — the writers, reporters and editors of *Money* — and to them it is dedicated. One part of my job as managing editor is to choose articles from the magazine, abridge and sometimes rewrite them, and then present them on the CBS Radio Network in two daily broadcasts, titled "Your Dollars" and "Your Money Minute." I have revised, re-edited and updated a selection of those scripts to create the chapters in the book.

Readers of *Money* have benefited from the rare insights of such journalists as Jerry Edgerton, Allan Sloan, Patricia A. Dreyfus and the late Charles Rolo, writing on various investments; Augustin Hedberg and Tyler Mathisen on computers; Richard Eisenberg on taxes and government policy; Marlys J. Harris and Carrie Tuhy on a host of consumer affairs; Candace E. Trunzo on financial planners; Malcolm N. Carter on careers; Suzanne Seixas on travel; and Robert Runde on housing — among many other subjects. I hope that I have been able to preserve and convey their main points.

Let me express my appreciation to the *Money* staff members, present and past, whose work is reflected here:

Greg Anrig, Jr., Kate Ballen, Gail Bronson, Sarah E. Button, Malcolm N. Carter, Julie Connelly, Joseph S. Coyle, Judith Daniels, Caroline Donnelly, Katharine B. Drake, Patricia A. Dreyfus, Jerry Edgerton, Richard Eisenberg, Valerie W. Gerry, Jordan E. Goodman, J. Howard Green, Marlys J. Harris, Augustin Hedberg, Keith R. Johnson, Landon Y. Jones, Peter Kadzis, Robert J. Klein, Leslie Laurence, Flora S. H. Ling, Lani Luciano, Richard A. Lynch, Susan J. Macovsky, Jeremy Main, Michael B. Martin, Tyler Mathisen, Frank B. Merrick, Lisa Redd, Charles J. Rolo, Robert H. Runde, Edward E. Scharff, Suzanne Seixas, Michael Sivy, Allan Sloan, Pauline Tai, Denise M. Topolnicki, Candace E. Trunzo, Carrie Tuhy, and Clint Willis.

A quite special note of thanks belongs to Leslie Laurence. She has been my associate, reporter and researcher throughout the preparation of this book. Without her organizational skills, fact-checking and constructive criticism, it would have been a much lesser — and later — work. She is an excellent young journalist with a first-class future.

My deepest appreciation as well to Anne Gut, *Money*'s highly talented and dedicated administrative assistant, who has been so very helpful in so many ways.

Ray Roberts of Little, Brown, an editor and a gentleman, worked wonders to bring this book to publication.

William M. Kelly, Jr., *Money's* Publisher, gave the project enthusiastic support. Marilyn Sahner and Patricia A. Straus, invaluable colleagues at Time Inc., made it possible for me to broadcast material from our magazine on the CBS Radio Network. At CBS, my particular thanks go to Richard Brescia, Frank Miller and Frank Murphy.

Let me express my gratitude to Henry Grunwald, Time Inc. Editor-in-Chief, who has always inspired me and who made it possible for me to edit *Money*; to Ralph Graves, Time Inc. Editorial Director, who encouraged me in this work and who has done so much to make *Money* an editorial success; to Ray Cave, Managing Editor of *Time*, who has taught me more about being a managing editor than he will ever know; and to Edward L. Jamieson, Executive Editor of *Time*, my friend, mentor and boss for the better part of twenty-five years.

Contents

[xiii]

[xv]

[xvii]

MARSHALL LOEB'S
Money Guide

Introduction

A LOOK AHEAD TO THE NEXT TEN YEARS

In an era of uneven growth, the rich opportunities for investments and careers will be in technology, services and resources.

OIL from Saudi Arabia cost $2.60 a barrel. Inflation was roaring along at 3½%. A new Chevy Malibu set you back $2,891, and the median-priced new house was $26,900, with mortgage rates just under 7½%. Unemployment ran a fearsome 5½%. But there was encouraging news, too. A recession was ending, an ebullient recovery was beginning, and the Dow Jones industrials were heading toward their awesome closing high of 1051.7. Meanwhile, President Richard Nixon, having distanced himself from a third-rate burglary, was en route to re-election by a landslide.

The world is quite a different place from that time — scarcely a dozen years ago. In the intervening period, Americans have experienced four Presidents, three recessions, two bouts of double-digit inflation and one frightening flare-up of interest rates that pushed the prime beyond 20%. Just consider what is now common that only then did not exist: money-market funds, low-cost commodity funds and tax-exempt bond funds; Individual Retirement Accounts and bond unit trusts; stock futures contracts, universal life insurance and asset-management accounts. In that almost ancient age, had any casual pal asked you about your very intimate experiences with your savings or mortgage rates, stocks or Treasury bills, you would have thought him gauche, gross or slightly mad. Now that money matters have come out of the closet, such subjects are the most intensely discussed topics among consenting adults.

People who consistently have anticipated and kept up with the turns in these and other subjects of personal finance have usually managed to cope, and even prosper, better than those who have not. In the present mercurial era, when the only certainty is change, nobody can anticipate precisely what the next ten years may bring. But after weighing current trends and realities, one can make a fair estimate of the probable shape of some future developments.

We know, for example, that the 76 million American baby boomers are now aged 20 to 38, and over the next decade they will be passing through the time of life when people invariably spend the most for cars, houses, books, diapers and almost everything else. So, demand for consumer goods stands to rise. We know that these young adults, millions of whom have re-

[3]

cently entered the labor force as raw beginners, will gain more experience and become more skilled as time goes on. Consequently, America's productivity stands to increase. We know that far fewer people will be turning 18 and going to work in the next ten years than in the past ten. Thus, the labor problem of 1994 may not be unemployment but shortages of many kinds of trained employees.

And there are other, broader developments that you can discern, developments that perhaps you can act upon to increase your earnings, improve your investments and enhance your career.

One trend in American society that seems likely to accelerate is the rise of the quality market. We Americans lately have come to appreciate, as Europeans and Japanese have long appreciated, that less can be more, and smaller can be better, if the goods and services one buys deliver real value for money. We are driving smaller, more fuel-efficient automobiles; we are living in smaller, better-insulated houses; we are buying fewer but better clothes and other goods.

In every marketplace, Americans are increasingly quality-conscious. They are not necessarily picking the fancy designer labels or paying the highest price, but they are showing a new, sophisticated awareness that high quality is more efficient and therefore more economical in the long run. Thus the goods that are selling well are those that deliver reliability and lasting value. When looking for opportunities to invest or launch a new enterprise, one might conclude that companies that serve the quality market will do notably well.

Companies will also prosper if they serve the needs of, and fully employ the talents of, America's fast-rising majority: its women. Over the past ten years, the women's movement has become a real revolution, one that is still in its infancy. In this past decade, the proportion of women among M.B.A. students has almost quadrupled, from one in fifteen to one in four; among law students it has nearly tripled, from one in eight to one in three. Women will continue to climb to increasingly higher positions of influence and decision-making, as well as higher affluence. This will substantially expand America's pool of talent and give us a significant edge in the intensifying global economic competition of the next ten years.

The rise of working women portends that future recessions will be milder and briefer than they otherwise would have been. If one member of a working couple loses his or her job, there will be a better than 50% chance that yet another person in the household will be bringing in full-time earnings. So family income, and spending, will remain relatively high.

Because they suddenly find themselves rather affluent, young women who are members of two-income families have a motivation to economic conservatism. It is not unusual for college-educated couples in their late twenties or early thirties to be earning $35,000 or much more. They are the New Elite — people who find themselves with assets that they want to conserve

[4]

against the twin depredations of high taxation and oppressive inflation. So, while women will remain a liberal force on social issues, they very likely will become a more conservative force on economic issues.

The conservative trend in the U.S. and other nations seems likely to continue, because many people in many places for the first time also have acquired assets that they want to conserve. Despite the perception that the world is moving to the left, voters in a dozen free nations — as disparate as West Germany, Britain, Norway, Venezuela, Israel, Sri Lanka, Holland and Jamaica — have moved their economies from the left to the center.

Yet, simultaneously, there is rising doubt about the efficacy and simple fairness of the free economic system and the democratic political system. The harsh reality is that capitalism has failed to distribute its benefits equitably, so there are grave inequalities of income within nonsocialist societies. In the past, even low-income people were prepared to accept those inequities because they felt confident that they, or at least their children, had a fair, full opportunity to rise to the middle-income or even upper-income groups. That has been the American social compact. But when insidious inflation deprives them of that opportunity, they begin to question the free system, and they look for alternatives of both the left and the right, some of them extreme. Free societies cannot endure without basically free economies. Most likely, both will continue not only to survive but also to spread in the next ten years. But people who champion this free system would be foolish and irresponsible if they did not recognize the real threats to it.

Economic growth in the U.S. and much of the rest of the world stands to be relatively modest in the rest of the 1980s. Growth will indeed occur, but not at the prolonged real annual rates of 5%, 6% and more that so many western societies enjoyed in the quarter-century after World War II. The great birth rates and bursts of demand that fueled such exuberant rises are behind us. Also, growth will be retarded by the huge debts growing round the world and the continuing high prices for energy (in 1982, a year of "glut," the U.S. poured out more than $61 billion to import oil).

Not only will growth be slower but, more important, it will be spottier. Some regions and enterprises are poised to do notably well, particularly those associated with the fast-expanding high-tech and information industries, as well as energy development. Meanwhile, other regions and enterprises probably will lag, notably those linked with older, heavier, import-sensitive industries, such as basic metals and big machines. More than in past eras, people who work in or invest in the fast-growth areas will do better than those in the slow-growth areas.

In the next ten years, the computer's middle-age spread will revolutionize our job opportunities and the way we work. As demands increase for services, notably information delivery, the economy's shift away from heavy manufacturing will accelerate. Jobs by the millions will be created for computer programmers, systems analysts and other service workers as disparate

[5]

as secretaries and lawyers, financial advisers and nurses. Demand will be intense for the skilled — whether they wear white, blue or pink collars — but many unskilled assembly-line workers may have to step down to the lower rungs of the services, accepting jobs as fast-food workers or janitors. Increasingly, knowledge will be power: power to earn big, to advance fast, enjoy autonomy, make decisions. And the computer will become the great weapon to convey knowledge: to teach the old three Rs to schoolchildren and new skills to workers.

Industries based on resources — everything from agriculture to energy — have been battered lately. But as the western economies recover from the global recession in the months ahead, rising demand will revive many resource-based industries and the regions dependent on them. Thus we may well be entering a period in which the major growth areas will be not only high technology and services but also energy and other resources, notably that ultimate energy: food. The countries, the regions and the companies that possess those resources, or have the technology and capital to develop resources, stand to prosper economically and dominate politically.

One consequence will be a marked shift of power within the U.S. Already under way is a historic migration of jobs; and with them, a movement of people; and with them, a swing of economic and political power. They are leaving the smokestack industry capitals of the Northeast and the North Central regions. They are decamping to the West and South, where the rich opportunities are. The fastest-rising regions over the next decade probably will be the Southwest, the Intermountain West and California for high-tech and energy; and the Midwest farm belt for grain and cattle.

The problem is that the U.S. is rapidly, and perhaps dangerously, becoming two countries. Two countries in terms of its regions, its races and its economies. In many parts of the West, the Southwest or the Southeast, one finds attitudes quite different from those in the northeastern quadrant of the U.S. In Phoenix and Atlanta, in San Diego and Kansas City, in Denver and Houston and numerous other places west of the Mississippi and in the South, local economies continue to do much better than the national norm. But in Toledo and Detroit, Cleveland and New York, and many another once proud city of the old industrial-commercial belt, the picture is much bleaker.

Socially we are also becoming two countries. Recession and inflation exacted their cruelest price on the poor, the citizens who are least prepared to cope. The educated, the skilled people can take care of themselves. They ride the crest. They get jobs in the new technologies; they move to the booming regions; they invest in those still high-yielding money-market funds or exotic tax shelters, and their lives grow better. But as technology becomes more complex, opportunity increasingly eludes the unskilled. For them, the good life, the American dream becomes more elusive. Quite possibly American society in the next decade will divide into two classes: those

[6]

who can master (or comprehend) the computer — and those who cannot.

One of the nation's most basic challenges over these next ten years — and beyond — will be to find innovative ways for the American underclass to lift itself out of its economic and emotional depression. Even liberals concede that most of our social programs and institutions have failed to accomplish what we expected. In many communities, our public schools have created a generation of semi-literates. Our public housing has produced public slums. Our public welfare has fathered dependence, despair and hopelessness among millions.

Because nothing else has worked well enough, it is quite likely more of the task of lifting the underclass will be turned over to private companies. Working with government tax incentives, credits and guarantees — financed perhaps by a new tax on consumption — corporations will have to take on more and more of the job of razing and rebuilding the slums, creating the factories and offices, employing and training the people and even providing some of the basic services.

In the increasingly interdependent global economy, the U.S. and many other developed nations will face a ticking time bomb: the huge international debts that are being built up by developing countries, notably those that must borrow to import oil. Their debts have grown to the incredible sum of more than $700 billion, and they are swelling by a frightening $70 billion a year. Much of this credit has been extended by private banks in North America and Europe. Many of these imprudent institutions have perilously large shares of their assets tied up in questionable foreign loans. Nobody knows how countries as disparate as Zaire, Rumania, Turkey, Tanzania, Togo, Zambia, Sudan, and, of course, Brazil, Mexico, Argentina and Poland ever will pay off their growing debts. So the bankers just keep rolling over those debts, which grow larger and take increasing shares of the debtors' scant export earnings.

Default on these twelve-digit loans and bankruptcies of whole nations are no longer unthinkable, but the consequences are still unknowable. At the very least, powerful private banks could come up short, and governments might have to bail them out, meaning that taxpayers ultimately would have to pay the bill.

None of us can fully protect himself against such calamities, but all of us have to watch economic turns very closely and be prepared to move our savings and investments very quickly. Nobody can consistently guess what the Dow Jones industrial average or the prime rate will be even a few weeks from now, but all of us can educate ourselves to the basic economic and political tides that influence those all-important numbers. To do that, all of us will have to become armchair economists and educated readers of the financial news.

Despite these obvious problems, there will be plenty of opportunities to prosper through personal investments. The best investments may well be

[7]

common stocks. Even after the market's recent leaps, shares remain extremely low. The Dow Jones industrials, adjusted for inflation, were in mid-1983 still some 60% *below* their levels of 1966. Stocks will benefit from the recent reductions in America's income and capital-gains taxes, as well as the many steps taken by corporations during the recession to reduce bloated overhead and enhance efficiency. A sound course for the investor who does not constantly monitor his stocks would be to entrust his money to a mutual fund family. Such families allow you, easily and inexpensively, to switch your money around from stock funds to bond funds to money-market funds as changing conditions motivate you.

What about other investments? Real estate has built more fortunes than any other investment throughout American history, but prices have surged so extravagantly that real estate profits over the next ten years stand to be lower than over the past ten. Precious metals? Gold will boom — if the world falls apart. It is unlikely to do so. Commodities? Since it's difficult to outguess Mother Nature about climatic conditions and crop yields, four speculators lose money for every one who profits from commodities. Gems? Most of the sparkle has gone out: prices of investment-grade diamonds are much lower than two years ago. Collectibles? Prices of many — from stamps to Tiffany lamps — have turned flabby, in part a reaction to the binge of recent years. But if you do buy, buy the best of its class. The prices of the best always stand up best of all.

Your investments in securities probably will be enhanced because leaders of both U.S. political parties will be speaking out more for policies to curb inflation and to stimulate investment. The U.S. indisputably has fallen behind many of its political allies and economic competitors over the past 10 years. So many of its steel, auto and rubber plants, so much of its infrastructure and urban landscape are outmoded, decaying, inefficient. The reason is clear. In 1976, the President's Council of Economic Advisers concluded that, just to keep up with its global competitors for world markets, the U.S. every year would have to plow 12% or more of its gross national product into capital investment for new or improved plants, tools, automation. In fact, we reinvested less than 11% of our GNP over the past decade. Meanwhile, the Japanese were investing 16% and the West Germans 20% of their GNP.

Now the U.S. has more than $300 billion of backlogged demand and need for capital projects. If we can find the will to adopt policies that would unleash that investment, we could experience a capital boom in the next 10 years that would lift America to new peaks of material prosperity and geopolitical strength.

A remarkable new consensus has developed among economists about what needs to be done to free up that investment. Spend less personal income today in order to save more for tomorrow. Reduce the money drained off by government activities in order to increase the capital available for private investment. Decrease the billions flowing out for energy imports and expand the sums put into developing domestic energy sources — of all kinds.

Many senators and governors advocate a series of economic moves that only ten years ago would have been considered radical. Among them: Expand the tax incentives to save and invest, and make up the lost revenue by putting a tax on consumption. Limit the long-term increase in federal budget transfer payments and subsidies to the size of the real increase in the GNP. Eliminate all controls on energy prices, a move that would stimulate conservation of known resources and exploration for new ones.

The next ten years will provide more dangers and yet more opportunities than the last. In negotiating this period, it might be wise to recall history's lesson: this country has a unique capacity to change and to amaze. The nation also has the human and material sources necessary to make life better.

During the 1980s and 1990s, there will be five ingredients for the economic, the political, the social success of a nation:

First, a rich, a modern, a highly productive agricultural base, giving a country the capacity not only to feed its own people but also to export — for economic gain, occasionally for political leverage, certainly for humanitarian purposes.

Second, an abundant base of energy-bearing raw materials — not only oil and natural gas but also coal, uranium, hydroelectric power, geo-pressured methane and all the rest.

Third, a vital, a strong base of other raw materials — iron ore, copper, lead, phosphate, zinc and the like — significantly including the secondary and tertiary sources, which will become more and more important because we will have skimmed off the cream in the world.

Fourth, an advanced, a modern, a computerized, a highly developed technology and industry.

Fifth, and most important, an educated, a well-motivated, a skilled, a highly sophisticated population.

There are three — only three — nations in the world that have all five. They are Canada, Australia and, of course, the United States. So, despite all of our immediate and very visible problems, if we Americans adopt sensible policies of capital formation, of government deregulation, of energy development and energy conservation, then the economic, the political and the social future of the United States in the next ten years should be absolutely dazzling.

— Marshall Loeb

[9]

Adoptions

WHERE TO FIND A CHILD

IF you're childless — and not by choice — you will find that you have many new options in adoptions. Today almost anyone can adopt a child, but it may be a rather special one.

Only a decade ago public and private adoption agencies had a surplus of healthy American-born babies. Now they are in short supply. The reason, of course, is the wide availability of birth control devices and abortion. Also, unmarried mothers are more willing to keep their children.

Many would-be parents are having to adopt foreign children, principally from South America and South Korea. Couples are also much more interested in adopting kids whom social workers categorize as "hard to place" or as having "special needs." They include youngsters with physical, mental or emotional handicaps, as well as nonwhite children, older children of all races, and brothers and sisters whom adoption agencies do not want to split up. Such youngsters account for nearly all the 150,000 to 200,000 children now available for adoption in the United States.

Agencies are finding it easier than ever to place these special-needs kids, often with people who formerly did not qualify as adoptive parents. Now single, handicapped and low-income people — even couples in their 50s and 60s — are allowed to adopt.

About 75% of all parents adopt through agencies; the rest get children through doctors or lawyers. Public adoption agencies, operated by state and local governments, generally do not charge fees. Private agencies, commonly sponsored by religious and charitable groups, charge as much as $5,000. But fees are often reduced or waived for parents who adopt hard-to-place children. In addition to the agency fee, if any, you will usually have to pay from $200 to $500 to an attorney for preparing adoption papers.

Almost all states have subsidy programs for parents who adopt hard-to-place kids. Moreover, a fairly recent federal tax law allows parents who adopt these youngsters to deduct up to $1,500 of their expenses. A growing number of companies also offer to help employees who adopt children with one-time payments of up to $2,200.

Your city or state department of social services can give you a list of licensed adoption agencies in your area. For help in finding special-needs children in other states, write to The National Adoption Exchange, 1218 Chestnut Street, Philadelphia, Pennsylvania 19107.

If you want to adopt a healthy child fairly fast, you can seek help from

American agencies that specialize in foreign adoptions. To get their names and addresses look in your library for a copy of the *National Directory of Intercountry Adoption Service Resources,* published in 1980 by the then Department of Health, Education and Welfare. Your local social services agency also might have a copy.

The cost of adopting a foreign youngster can run as high as $5,000, but the wait is usually no more than eighteen months.

Another way to avoid waiting years to adopt a child is through private placement — that is, adoption without an agency's help. Typically, private placements cost between $3,000 and $5,000, including lawyers' fees and the mother's hospital bills. Adoptive parents who choose this way instead of using an agency run a slightly higher risk of losing their child if the biological mother changes her mind.

If you decide to adopt an American-born youngster through private placement, tell all of your friends. They may know of available infants. Ask your gynecologist or obstetrician if he has a patient who is pregnant and does not want her child. Also mention it to your lawyer. He may have a client who wants to give up a baby for adoption — or know of another lawyer who does.

Air-Conditioners

REBATES FROM UTILITIES

A RE you planning to shop for a room air-conditioner? Consult your utility company first. Many are offering rebates to encourage customers to buy energy-efficient machines from appliance stores.

To qualify for this rebate, your air-conditioner's energy-efficiency ratio — which is a rating that ascends from 5 to 11 — must exceed a certain minimum level. Typically that's 8 or 9. The higher a machine's cooling capacity — measured in BTUs—the bigger the rebate. That's because utilities are especially eager to steer people who are shopping for energy-gobbling large machines toward the most efficient ones.

Both energy-efficiency ratings and cooling capacities are listed on the labels of air-conditioners, so you can easily figure out your rebate before you buy. For example, Texas Electric Service has two rebates for machines rated 8.5 or better: $80 for those with less than 12,000 BTUs of power and $120 for more powerful ones. Rebates or credits also are given by Public Service Electric & Gas in New Jersey, Northern States Power in Minnesota and Houston Lighting and Power, among others.

No matter what the rebate, you should not buy an air-conditioner with a capacity larger than the space it is to cool. It will not adequately control humidity, and even with the rebates, small machines are less expensive to buy and operate than large ones.

Airlines

HOW TO GET THE BEST, CHEAPEST RIDES

Soaring airline fares have scared off many would-be vacationers, but there is some good news, too. Deregulation of the lines has created fervid new competition, and this provides passengers with bargain fares on some routes and an occasional free ride.

If you travel often, it pays to become a steady customer of one airline. That way you can earn free trips. One example: American Airlines awards anyone who logs 12,000 miles a first-class seat for the price of one in coach. The plan progresses in stages to the grand prize of two first-class round trips almost anywhere that American flies, including Mexico and the Caribbean, for passengers who accumulate 75,000 miles. United, TWA, Eastern, Pan Am and many other airlines have similar offers.

Once you have found the best price for a flight, buy your ticket right away. You then will avoid any fare increases before your departure date. Fares can and do go up overnight, sometimes sharply.

Several of the airlines reduce their prices for night flights, usually beginning at 9 p.m., but sometimes earlier than that, so be sure to check with the airlines. You then can get a first-class seat for what you'd pay for coach during the day. And coach fares at night are 20% to 30% less than in the daytime.

Whatever you pay, you can get the most for your money if you make some plans in advance.

Wise travelers always try to reserve their airplane seats well before the flight. If you've already bought your ticket, you can pick your seat as much as one year ahead of time. You will have a smoother flight if you avoid the rear of the plane. Tail winds cause the most turbulence there. On rear-engine planes like the 727 or DC-9, you also will escape engine noise and vibration by sitting as far forward as you can.

On any plane, you will get the most leg room by sitting in the seat next to an emergency exit, since there must be enough space in that area to permit easy exiting from the plane. Sitting in the row just behind the bulkhead also gives you more room above the waist because there is no seat in front of yours that can suddenly recline and slant back into your face.

In the coach section, a most desirable seat is in the first row, behind a bulkhead. You usually have extra leg room and a good view out the window that is unobstructed by the wing. You also tend to get a smoother ride in the

[13]

front end of coach than back in the bumpier rear. And you avoid the crowds when you leave the plane. Being one of the first out the door can speed you on your way — provided you have only hand baggage and don't have to wait for checked luggage.

There's no foolproof way to avoid being bumped off an oversold plane. A good plan is to call the airline the night before your flight and ask how full the plane is. If it's 60% full, don't worry. If it's more than 75% full, and you absolutely have to make that flight, get to the airport at least an hour early.

Of the 292 million people who flew domestically in 1982, a few more than 100,000 were bumped. But if your plane is overbooked, don't fret. Before bumping anyone, the airline must ask for volunteers who are willing to give up their seats. The carrot may be cash or a later flight at no charge — basically anything you and the airline can agree to. If only a little money is offered, you may be able to bargain for more. And a free ride can be well worth a few hours' wait.

If there are not enough volunteers, the airline must get you to your destination within an hour of your originally scheduled arrival time. If it can't, it must pay you a penalty equal to your one-way fare up to a maximum of $200 and still fly you to your destination. If the airline can't get you there within two hours on a domestic flight and four hours on an international one, the penalty doubles to a maximum of $400.

Every airline has its own "contract of carriage," in which it spells out its responsibility to you. You can get a copy simply by asking for it at the ticket counter or by writing to the airline.

You also can improve your plane food — or at least get more choice — if you order a special meal by calling the airline at least a day in advance. Quite a few lines offer a remarkable array, from pasta to pastrami, but many veteran fliers say that you get the best deal — and the freshest food — by ordering salad or a vegetarian plate.

Annuities

SAVINGS WITH A TAX SHELTER

F OR safety-minded people with sizable sums to invest for retirement, annuities can offer welcome tax relief. An annuity is really a savings account sponsored by an insurance company. It's sold by brokers and insurance agents, who charge fees ranging from nothing to 5% of your investment. Most contracts require an initial deposit of $5,000 or $10,000.

The earnings accumulate untaxed until sometime in the future, usually after you retire. Then you can "annuitize" — that is, start receiving monthly payments that will continue over a fixed period or for the rest of your life. Each payment is considered to be partly a return of principal, and you are taxed only on the portion that's considered income.

Say, for instance, a 35-year-old put a $10,000 inheritance into an annuity that paid an average 8% interest over the years. By the time he reached 65, the tax-deferred buildup would total $100,600. If he then took monthly payments for life, he might get $1,100 each month from an insurance company with a reasonably generous pay-out schedule.

Annuities from well-established companies are safer than almost any other investment except Treasury securities and federally insured bank certificates. But annuities have one big advantage because taxes on interest from these other investments are due immediately.

Different insurance companies pay widely different monthly rates. Among various insurers, the lifetime payment for a man aged 65 recently ranged from $7.50 to $12.50 a month for each $1,000 of capital. Rates are adjusted periodically. Usually they're changed every year, but some companies guarantee rates for up to five years. In recent years the rate has approximated the interest on long-term Treasury bonds. In mid-1983, that was about 10%.

Some company sponsors consistently outperform others in the Lipper Analytical Survey of annuities. Routinely at the top of the rankings are American General and Guardian/Value Line.

Antiques

DO-IT-YOURSELF HEIRLOOMS

With antique furniture becoming scarcer and costlier, you can save money by putting together your own reproductions. You can build fine copies from kits and pay about 60% less than if you had bought comparable furniture at a store.

Kits vary widely in price and style. You can get a simple candlestand for $34 from Cohasset Colonials in Cohasset, Massachusetts. Or you can pay almost $1,500 for a formal Queen Anne highboy from the Bartley Collection in Lake Forest, Illinois. About 40 retailers and manufacturers are listed in *The Kit Furniture Book* by Lynda Graham-Barber (Pantheon, $9.95).

Start with a simple and inexpensive kit. Look for one that is true to the designs of the period. You will not need sophisticated tools. A hammer and screwdriver generally will suffice. Make sure your kit is complete and that no wood is damaged. And take a dry run before fitting and gluing the pieces permanently. For example, you might assemble a pine drying rack modeled after ones used by colonists for food and clothing. Even a neophyte kit builder can put together this piece in under an hour. Assembling parts takes about 20% of your time; sanding, staining and finishing consume the rest.

You also can buy good, assembled replicas of antiques from several nationally known furniture manufacturers — Kittinger, Kindel and Baker are among the best. Or you can get them from independent cabinetmakers, who turn out one-of-a-kind pieces in backyard workshops and barns. The lone craftsman who sells his products directly to customers charges as much as 50% less than big-name companies that must market their wares through stores and decorators.

Finding these individual furniture makers isn't easy. A few craftsmen advertise in magazines such as *Country Living* or *Antiques*, which you can get on some newsstands and in libraries. You can find an extensive list of cabinetmakers in the *Third Old House Catalogue*, published by Collier Books at $9.95. Sometimes you can locate a woodworker at a crafts fair or through a museum's restoration department or by getting in touch with art or vocational schools that teach furniture-making.

The best reproductions closely resemble the originals, not only in their appearance but also in their construction; they are made of solid wood. Fortunately, reproductions are more durable than genuine antiques. But, unlike an original, a reproduction is neither a limited first edition nor historically significant. So it won't appreciate in value as the years go by.

Appraisers

HOW TO FIND ONE

An appraiser can be a very important person in your financial life. If you are buying insurance to cover your jewelry or silverware, you will probably need an appraiser to certify their value. And you very likely will want to hire an appraiser if you are buying or selling a house — or merely refinancing it. Countless people call themselves appraisers, but finding a knowledgeable and reliable one requires some effort.

To locate a real estate appraiser, ask your banker, lawyer or insurance agent for recommendations. Get the names of several candidates and then call each one. Ask him about his background and fees. Find out if he belongs to one of several appraisal associations. They include the American Institute of Real Estate Appraisers, the Society of Real Estate Appraisers and the National Association of Independent Fee Appraisers. Members tend to be trustworthy and experienced because each of these organizations screens and polices them to some degree. That is important because few states license real estate appraisers.

For personal property appraisers, once again seek advice from your banker, lawyer or insurance agent; museum curators can suggest names, too. The two major associations are the American Society of Appraisers and the Appraisers Association of America. For jewelry alone, you might consider a member of the American Gem Society.

Appraisers use two measures to establish the value of your possessions. One is the replacement cost, which is what you would have to pay to replace the item. Usually you insure the property for the replacement cost. Then there is fair market value — it's the price a willing buyer would pay a willing seller. The fair market value is used for settling an estate, dividing property for a divorce or donating a work of art for a tax deduction.

The fair market value is usually only half the replacement cost. That's because a dealer's markup is often 100%. An appraiser might tell you to insure a Chippendale highboy for $10,000 because it would cost that much to replace one. But if you wanted to sell the highboy, a dealer might pay you only $5,000.

An appraisal must be precise and explicit to back up an insurance or tax-loss claim. For jewelry, it should note size and weight of stones and their settings, as well as clarity, purity and color. Art and antiques should be evaluated for age, condition and any special factors, such as rarity.

What should you pay for an appraisal?

A real estate appraisal will cost you a flat fee of $125 to $250 or perhaps more. The price depends on the size and condition of your house, and on how long it takes to compare your property with others in your neighborhood.

To assess your jewelry, artwork or furniture, you should hire only an appraiser who charges by the hour or by the job. Most professionals believe that it is unethical to base fees on a percentage of the value of your goods, since there is an obvious temptation to overstate their worth. You also should avoid anyone who offers to appraise your belongings and buy them too. In that case, the appraiser may deliberately underestimate.

The cost of a personal property appraisal depends on how long the job takes, which can be from less than one hour to several days. For simple pieces of jewelry, you may pay $20 to $50 an hour. But a gemologist, who is best qualified to judge valuable jewelry, can charge up to $125 an hour.

When a personal property appraiser comes to your house to evaluate your furniture, silverware and other property for insurance purposes, he will check each item's condition. He may also photograph your valuables. If he does not, then you should take photos yourself, including close-ups of any significant details.

Keep your appraisals up to date. The prices of jewelry, antiques and other collectibles fluctuate so sharply that you should have your insurance appraisals updated every two years.

Send one copy of your appraisal to your insurance agent. Keep all other copies and photographs of your belongings in a safe-deposit box or your lawyer's office or another place that is fireproof and theftproof. One appraiser tells of a client who stored in his dining room sideboard a list of the values and locations of his most prized possessions. A thief found the list and neatly checked off the items as he loaded them aboard his truck. He then scrawled on the list, "thanks for the appraisal." It was just about the only thing he left behind.

Art

INVESTING IN ART

Works of art by such big names as Chagall, Monet and Andrew Wyeth once seemed glamorous and reliable investments. Today they sometimes sell for a fraction of what they commanded a couple of years ago. So, for the buyer on a budget, opportunities for investing in art could not be greater.

The trick of intelligent investing is to shy away from the junk and seek out works that were not overvalued during the market boom of 1978 through 1981. They may be excellent buys now.

Three fields are particularly promising for beginning collectors: prints, photographs and contemporary works of painting and sculpture by little-known artists. Some of them may become tomorrow's great stars. Fine pieces in these fields may be had for as little as a few hundred dollars. Buyers on limited budgets do not have to settle for obscure artists. For example, some of the 4,000-plus lithographs by 19th-century French social satirist Honoré Daumier can be had for less than $200 each.

A factor that has nothing to do with an image's beauty can boost the price of a print or photograph. People sometimes pay 100% more for a work that has the artist's signature on it. For less affluent collectors, the absence of a signature is a small price to pay for the opportunity to acquire a superb print for little money.

Among the most reputable sources of prints are major auction houses and the galleries that belong to the Art Dealers Association of America. For their names and addresses, write to the Art Dealers Association at 575 Madison Avenue, New York, New York 10022.

To find the best sources of photographs, write to the Association of International Photography Art Dealers at 60 East 42nd Street, New York, New York 10165. If you buy its $3 booklet, *On Collecting Photographs,* AIPAD will send you a free copy of its membership directory.

In assembling a collection of contemporary paintings and sculpture, it's sometimes fun to try to discover new talent on your own. But the safest path for the neophyte is to develop long-term relationships with professional dealers who are closely associated with emerging artists. These dealers can offer much expertise and advice.

The major galleries and auction houses are concentrated in New York City, still the undisputed capital of the U.S. art trade. If you can't make fairly regular trips to New York, then seek out local dealers as your agents to establish relationships with other dealers and auction houses.

The place *not* to buy works by lesser-known contemporary painters and sculptors is at an auction. Auction houses rarely offer such works anyway because they sell poorly there.

By contrast, auction houses are often excellent sources of prints and photographs. First, go to dealers to see what the prices are. Then, if something you want comes up at an auction, you may be able to get a better price.

When you are ready to buy, deal only with galleries and auction houses whose directors and employees have well-established reputations for honesty. Make sure they're willing to disclose all the facts about the art they sell. No reputable dealer should object to your consulting other experts before you make a purchase.

When buying from a dealer, it's customary to *negotiate* the prices. Many dealers routinely add 10% to their asking prices for bargaining purposes. But don't badger a dealer who insists that his price is firm. Many dealers allow buyers up to a year to pay, interest-free, and sometimes even longer than that.

Even though you are buying art on a low budget, there are some so-called bargains you will want to avoid. Stay away from World War I and World War II posters that are more interesting as historical curiosities than as art objects. Also avoid any contemporary prints that were produced in huge numbers and photographs that are neither rare nor of high quality. And remember: nothing is a good buy, unless you really want it and have a passion for it.

Art

INVESTING IN FOLK ART

EVERYTHING from diamond rings to oriental rugs has declined in value from the peaks of several years ago, but one family of collectibles that has held up well — and even risen — is American folk art. But it is a crazy-quilt world with whirlygig prices, so you have to love it — or leave it alone. Not even the experts agree on what domestic folk art is, and nobody can say for sure what it is really worth. Generally, American folk art can include any tangible rudiment of daily life in the 18th, 19th and even 20th centuries that has been enhanced by a touch of art — everything from a gravestone to an old rag doll.

Indeed, 19th-century weathervanes can cost more than the average meteorologist earns in a year, and some patchwork quilts are so rare and valued that no one would ever dream of sleeping under them. Yet a number of experts view the current boom in folk art as a bubble that will shortly burst. They charge that dealers started pushing the stuff when they ran out of reasonably priced antiques in the 1960s. Much of it — such as worn-out baskets, tattered quilts and some hideous paintings — will have nowhere to go but down.

Even so, two other things are true: the best examples of American folk art will continue to command high prices, and you can still get good buys now. There is plenty of investment-grade American folk art to be had for less than $500 — and even more that is just fun to own, for much less than that. Above all, the best folk art buy is something that truly delights you, aesthetically and personally. It should figure as a wise investment only secondarily.

A reliable guide to the shops, auctions and regions where a fledgling collector might begin looking for American folk art is the *Maine Antique Digest*. It costs $23 a year. Its address is P.O. Box 358, Waldoboro, Maine 04572.

If you want to buy folk art, it's wise to concentrate on a particular category. That will help you to establish a sense of confidence and expertise.

Among the safest and fastest-rising investments are quilts. That's partly because there is a strong international demand for them. When buying for investment, look for the quilt with complex, intricate stitching and with unusual features, even a one-of-a-kind pattern. Top-quality old examples range from $2,000 to $5,000. However, handsome contemporary quilts that you can actually sleep under without depreciating your investment are available for less than $300.

When buying a basket, check the bottom to see if it is still strong. But if the rest of the basket looks well-worn, yet the bottom has hardly been scuffed, that's a sure sign of a forgery. The best investments in baskets are those with unusual forms or those with hand-painted decorations. It's hard to find one in good condition for less than $100. To get bargains, avoid shops with expensive business cards, and head for stores and auctions in the back hills. There you sometimes can come across an oak splint basket from the late 19th century for as little as $75.

With a weathervane, older is considered better. If wood, it should be dulled and weathered; if gold leaf, it should have lost much of its gilt; if copper, it should be green. A vane with a beautifully aged patina is worth considerably more than one that has been repainted.

When you buy a painting as an investment, be wary of heavy restoration. And an anonymous folk painting may be just as valuable as one by a recognized artist.

If you are buying furniture, rely on the eye of an experienced dealer to avoid counterfeits. Once you get home with your piece of furniture, stifle any ambitions that may arise in you to fix it up. One woman who bought an 18th-century painted chest a few years ago for $25,000 then proceeded to refinish the piece. As a result, it's now not worth more than a few hundred dollars.

Asset-Management Accounts

CHOOSING THE RIGHT ONE FOR YOU

COMPETING fiercely for your savings and investment dollars, more and more brokers and banks now offer one-stop services that let you combine your checking and savings accounts, your credit cards and your securities trading. They also give you a convenient monthly statement of what you have and put any spare cash of yours to work right away in a high-interest money-market fund.

Merrill Lynch pioneered with its highly successful Cash Management Account. Many other brokerage houses and banks have coined their own names, but they are commonly called asset-management accounts. To get one, you usually have to deposit certain minimum amounts in either cash or securities you may own.

In exchange for your letting them just hold onto your assets, most brokers provide a big bundle of services. With your single asset-management account, you can trade stocks and bonds, buy money-market funds, write out checks and use a credit or debit card that permits you to borrow more than usual. Bank-sponsored plans work much the same way.

Annual service charges for all the plans vary widely. Generally they range from $100 down to nothing. To start an account, you are commonly required to deposit anywhere from $5,000 to $20,000 in cash or securities. Most banks and brokers also insist that you maintain a minimum balance of $2,500 to $3,500. But the trend is toward steadily lower minimum initial deposits and lower annual fees.

You don't have to own stocks or bonds to open an asset-management account with a broker. You can do it by depositing at least the specified initial investment in a money-market fund sponsored by the firm. It is obviously the broker's hope that you will become an active stock and bond customer too. A nice plus is that any dividends or proceeds from the sale of securities are automatically reinvested in a money fund, where they earn market rates.

If you are shopping around for an asset-management account, don't be overly influenced by any extras that the sponsor dangles before you. Instead, ask yourself what your main reason is for opening the account.

If you are primarily interested in investing in stocks, then you should put the emphasis on finding an excellent broker. But if you are satisfied with the

[23]

broker you already have, stay with him. If his firm does not offer a cash management account, don't worry. It probably will do so soon.

The broker and bank plans are becoming increasingly competitive with each other. Both usually offer the same range of basic services: regular and tax-exempt money-market funds, interest-bearing checking accounts, lines of credit, and the like. In some of the plans any money that you deposit above a certain level, usually $2,500, flows into a money fund that pays you much higher interest than a NOW checking account. Whenever a check you have written arrives for payment, your money fund will be tapped for that amount.

In all but a few bank or broker plans, you can write checks against your money-market fund for any amount, no matter how small. That is an improvement on the usual money fund, which will not honor checks for less than $250 or $500. If you have securities in the account, you also can write checks for more than your cash balance. That's because your stocks and bonds serve as collateral for loans up to about half their value. And if you have a speculative bent, you can borrow against your stocks or bonds to buy additional securities.

All plans include an ordinary money fund, but most give you two other choices. They are a tax-free money fund for investors in top tax brackets and a fund invested wholly in U.S. Treasury securities.

One other tip: Traditional full-service brokers offer asset-management customers a standard array of research reports and advice. But investors who do not want to pay for brokerage house research can save a walloping 50% to 70% on commissions just by choosing a plan at a discount broker. (See also "Brokers: How to Choose One" and "Brokers: The Discounters.")

Auctions

BIDDING FOR BARGAINS

Shopping for artworks, antiques and other collectibles, more and more people are turning up at auctions in search of bargains. You don't have to be a high-roller or a big-time collector to get them. But the growing number of auction buyers has made those bargains harder to come by. Two places where you can still find them are at the charity auction and the old-fashioned country auction.

People who attend auctions held for charity or political fund-raising are often more interested in the cause than in the merchandise. As a result, bidding seldom becomes heavy, and you can get some real buys. Similarly, most of the bargain hunters who show up at country auctions of estates are local folks interested in the land, the stock or the machinery on the block. That leaves the field clear for you, the seeker of antiques and other collectibles.

Wherever you go, the rules are fairly simple. All auctions display the merchandise before the bidding begins, so don't bid unless you have inspected an item thoroughly. You can get an idea of what an item will go for by studying the auction catalogue, if there is one. It gives high and low estimates of each item's worth, and bidding usually starts at about 70% of the lower figure.

It's best *not* to bid at the first auction you visit. Newcomers often get caught up in "auction fever" and bid too high. You would be wise to begin by observing the auction process. Visit the pre-auction exhibit, decide how much you would pay for an item, and then see what it actually goes for. Watch who the other bidders are and keep track of the winning prices in the auction catalogue. That way, when you spot something you might want at a future sale, you will have the price history of a similar item for reference. Put that together with some knowledge of regular retail prices, and you'll know how far to go in your bidding.

At some auctions you will be given a paddle or a paper plate with a number on it. When the auctioneer calls out the price, just hold up the paddle, the plate or your hand if you want to bid. If you don't like the price, you can holler out something lower. Don't worry that you will wind up owning some large expensive whatnot because you scratched your nose or tugged your earlobe. That just doesn't happen.

Try to arrive early at an auction. Bidding at the start often is on the low

[25]

side as the audience and the auctioneer try to get the feel of each other. Before you bid on anything, set a mental limit on what you'll pay. And be careful that you don't bid against yourself. That is a mistake some beginners make. When the auctioneer calls for a higher price, they forget that the last bid was theirs.

Auctions,
Government-Style

BARGAINS FROM UNCLE SAM

Y OU can get some exceptional deals when the government auctions off its surplus property. In fact, you can buy just about anything at cut-rate prices, from a bronze statue of a Buddha to a seaside house, a down vest to a private plane.

A government auction probably is going on in *your* area every week. Several thousand auctions are held throughout the country each year by the General Services Administration, the Department of Defense, the Customs and Postal Services and the Internal Revenue Service. The sales raise money for the Treasury and clean out the government's attics. Meanwhile, you can save an average 50% off the retail price, and often much, much more. And the government doesn't charge state or local sales taxes.

Virtually any item the government has ever bought, used or confiscated goes to the auction block. The Pentagon offers more than 400 classes of property, from used guided-missile launchers to guard dogs. The GSA traffics in office and hospital equipment, cars from the government motor pool and even Coast Guard lighthouses. A stream of civilian property that has been abandoned, confiscated or lost goes under the hammer at Customs, Postal and IRS auctions.

The quality of the offerings varies radically. Goods at GSA and Department of Defense auctions usually have seen better days. But the property at Customs, Postal and IRS auctions is newer.

To find out about sales, write or phone the agency whose auctions you want to attend and ask to be put on the free mailing list. The government can pack your mailbox every day with its sales catalogues and auction notices, so be selective. Some mail-order firms advertise that for $20 they will notify clients of forthcoming sales. But all they do is pass your name along to the appropriate government agency.

Government auctions often pit the amateur against the professional dealer. You can avoid competing with dealers if you look for the odd item in an auction that is dominated by another category. Wholesalers and retailers are not as likely to show up for a few pieces of jewelry or some fishing gear if the sale consists mainly of electronic parts. And if you are willing to travel, you are likely to find better buys because fewer people show up for sales at hard-to-find warehouses and military bases. For the same reason, you should try to attend the auctions that are held on weekdays rather than weekends.

A sparse audience, however, does not mean that the government will part with its property to the lowest bidder. It sets a so-called upset price, below which the property will not be sold. That price is usually at the low end of what the bureaucrats who run the auction figure the property would be worth on the open market. But such people are not always the best judges of value. So you might be as lucky as the sharp-eyed bidder who for $15,000 bought an entire lot of 94 miscellaneous furs at a GSA auction. She kept one of the sables she found in the lot and sold the others for $50,000.

To learn when auctions and sales of government-surplus property will take place, here is where to write:

— General Services Administration. For personal property, primarily manufactured goods, write to the General Services Administration, Customer Services Bureau, Personal Property Division, in the region nearest to you. The regions are Atlanta (30303); Auburn, Washington (98002); Boston (02109); Denver (80225); Kansas City, Missouri (64131); New York (10278); Philadelphia (19107); San Francisco (95105) and Washington, D.C. (20407). Ask for a copy of *Buying Government Surplus Property*, which spells out the rules and procedures. Then ask to be put on the mailing list. Each region has its own.

The GSA also has a monthly catalogue listing all its real estate sales. Write to Properties, Consumer Information Center, Dept. J, Pueblo, Colorado 81009 and request a free publication called *Sales of Federal Surplus Real Estate*. If you want to be notified of real estate sales in a certain price range and location, ask for an application form from the Director of Real Property Sales, General Services Administration in Atlanta, Auburn, Boston, Chicago, Fort Worth or San Francisco.

— Department of Defense. Write to Bidders Control Office, Defense Property Disposal Service, Box 1370, Battle Creek, Michigan 49016 for a copy of *How to Buy Surplus Personal Property from the Department of Defense*. It tells how to get on all DOD auction mailing lists.

— U.S. Customs Service. Unfortunately, there is no general mailing list for the auctions held by 25 or so of the U.S. Customs Service offices. To find out which ones run public sales and to get on those lists, phone the customs office at the nearest large port or border crossing. Most branches conduct one auction a year, but New York will have 10, all in the basement of the World Trade Center, Building 6.

— U.S. Postal Service. Postal auctions take place in nine cities. For information about the sales nearest you, write to the U.S. Post Office, Claims and Inquiries Section, or to the Dead Parcel Office, Atlanta (30304); Boston (02109); Chicago (60607); Fort Worth (76101); Los Angeles (90098); New York (10001); Philadelphia (19104); St. Paul (55101) or San Francisco (94105). Include a self-addressed, stamped envelope.

If you are interested in surplus postal equipment, inquire at a local post office for the address of the nearest Procurement Services office where these sales are held. Postal vehicles, such as the jeeps used by letter carriers, are sold at fixed prices by the vehicle maintenance facilities of local post offices.

— Internal Revenue Service. If the seizure of his property does not lead a recalcitrant taxpayer to pay his back taxes, the IRS auctions it off. Write to Chief of Special Procedures, Collection Division, at whichever of 60 IRS district offices is nearest you.

Auto Clubs

CHOOSING AMONG THEM

Worried about being stranded in a disabled car on a snowy night, millions of motorists have sought reassurance by joining an auto club. If you or other drivers in your family have any doubts about coping with breakdowns on your own, the question is probably not whether you should join a club but which one to join.

All auto clubs claim to offer the same basic services, and their annual fees range from $25 to $64. But these charges are no indication of the quality of what they provide. In fact, two basic services — trip planning and accident insurance — should not be important considerations when you choose a club. Your choice should be dictated by the quality of an auto club's road service.

Three national clubs offer so-called dispatch service in metropolitan areas. That means members have only to call the club's number and wait for help to arrive. Those three are the American Automobile Association, Allstate and Amoco. If your club does not offer dispatch service, you will have to find help on your own.

Some other clubs provide a directory of affiliated service stations or a toll-free number for you to call to get the name of an approved station near where you've broken down. In most of these cases, the club pays for the emergency service, but that is usually limited to towing and minor roadside repairs, such as tire changing and battery recharging. Still other national clubs merely reimburse you for service you arrange on your own, which can be no boon to the panic-prone.

Whether the club pays directly or reimburses you later, the payments are often unrealistically low. For example, there is always either a dollar limit or a mileage limit for towing. The limit for road services generally ranges from $25 to $50, and if you exceed it, you pay the extra cost.

Be sure to read the fine print of any auto club's membership contract. Some demand an initiation fee and charge extra for a spouse, and others do not. Some clubs cover emergency service on any car you're driving; others limit coverage to cars you own or lease long-term. One tip: if you rarely travel far from home, you may find that regional auto clubs offer service equal to or better than many of the nationals.

Auto Mechanics

HOW TO FIND ONE

IF you are hoping for years of trouble-free driving, finding the right auto mechanic can be almost as important as finding the right car. The best way to discover a competent mechanic is through a growing network of reputable service stations that are identified and appraised by the American Automobile Association. This is done through its Approved Auto Repair Services program.

The AAA's program is the first nationwide effort to separate good repair shops from bad. It covers every kind, from franchised dealers to independent neighborhood garages. The program includes more than 3,500 garages in 25 states and is adding hundreds more each year.

Inspectors from the AAA apply rigorous standards. In fact, more garages fail than pass the first inspection. The repair bays, tools and mechanics' qualifications are checked. Then the AAA queries customers whose names an inspector takes from the shop's files.

You don't have to join the automobile association to take advantage of the program. Simply look for a garage with the AAA's red, white and blue sign and the inscription "Approved Auto Repair." Nonmembers can phone the local affiliated auto club for names of approved shops in the area.

One of the AAA's measures of a worthy shop is whether or not its mechanics are certified by the National Institute of Auto Service Excellence, or NIASE. The institute supports itself entirely from examination fees. To earn a certificate of competence, a mechanic has to pass a 2½-hour test and have two years of hands-on experience.

Shops lacking AAA approval may still do first-rate work. Ask whether the mechanics are NIASE certified. Or go one step further and have the mechanic show you if he has an NIASE certificate that says he is specially trained in repairing the system that you need to have fixed.

New-car owners are inclined to have repairs done by the dealer because that's where their warranty is honored. The dealer usually has good facilities and makes a special effort to please a customer who has bought one car and may buy another. But dealers tend to be expensive. For specific services, such as buying and installing a muffler, you may get the best price at a discount store, mass marketers such as Sears or Montgomery Ward or a specialty shop such as Midas. You could save 50% on a set of shocks by going to a specialist.

[31]

But don't let bargain prices take you away from an able general mechanic — if you have been lucky enough to find one. When you take a sick car to him, describe the symptoms in detail or even write them down. Request an estimate and ask him to call if something unexpected or expensive turns up. But don't offer your own diagnosis. That's *his* job.

Auto Theft

INSURING YOUR CAR

MANY states have drafted insurance companies into the war against auto theft. If you live in one of those states and you have installed special alarms or other antitheft devices, your premiums will be reduced. But there are many other steps that drivers everywhere can take to improve their insurance against auto theft.

If you have ordinary auto theft insurance, you might wonder why you should spend even a penny more for *extra* insurance against the loss of your car to thieves. Here is a good reason: though most auto insurance policies are written to cover all but $50 or $100 of your loss, actual settlements can fall far short of that. So it might be smart to buy extra coverage that will pay you the *full replacement value* of your car if it is stolen.

If you rent a car while waiting for the insurance settlement, you will probably have to bear some of that expense too. Most policies pay just $10 a day toward a rental car — for a maximum of 30 days. Renting is likely to cost you two or three times that much per day, and you probably will not get a settlement within a month. Thus, it is wise to buy a little-known rider that costs only $10 a year and boosts rental coverage to $15 a day. The rider also pays for transportation not only while your car is missing but also while it is in the shop for the repair of theft damage.

Your insurance coverage for the theft of accessories or possessions you have in the car may not be as extensive as you expect. Some insurance companies that classify removable radios as a portable accessory do not cover their theft. If you have resorted to toting your expensive stereo or radio around when you are out of the car, consider buying a disguise for it instead. For about $20, a plain plastic front gives your equipment the look of an ordinary factory-installed radio.

Neither your auto policy nor any extra coverage applies to other things that a thief might steal from your car, such as a $1,000 set of golf clubs or a $400 designer blazer. But you are probably covered anyway. Most homeowners' policies apply to anything taken by someone who breaks into your car. There is a hitch, though: you have to *prove* that the doors were locked at the time of the theft.

[33]

Auto Theft

PREVENTIVE DEVICES

PROFESSIONAL car thieves are so swift and experienced that policemen, insurance underwriters and even manufacturers of antitheft devices feel that it's hard to thwart them. But although alarms and other preventions are not foolproof, the right ones can save you anguish and expense.

If you own an expensive automobile and particularly if you live in a big city, your best protection against theft is never to leave your car on the street. Professional thieves are a match for almost any antitheft equipment. However, you should seriously consider buying alarms and locks to discourage joyriders and casual miscreants.

Antitheft devices now are so varied and sophisticated that you can outfit your car to do just about everything but roll over and play dead when it is attacked. One gizmo disengages the ignition and bolts the hood securely, another shuts off the fuel line and still others shriek if the car is molested. You can get these gadgets at stores that sell automotive accessories.

You are probably smart to start with an alarm because it will scare away the unprofessional thief. Typical alarm systems, such as those manufactured by General Automotive Electronics in North Brunswick, New Jersey, cost about $150 to $400 installed. The least expensive type sets off your car's horn at a variety of intrusions — for example, if someone bangs a window or jolts the car.

If you figure an alarm may not be enough to scare the professionals off, you probably should invest in a device that stalls the engine before a thief can drive far. Fuel cutoffs made by Cahs, of Mount Vernon, New York, start at $50 for a basic device and rise to $350 for one that shuts off your fuel and ignition, sounds a siren alarm, prevents towing, protects all the locks on your car and even includes a back-up battery. An ignition cutoff and hood lock made by Vaslock of Brooklyn, New York, costs $450 installed.

Less elaborate automobile protection devices also lock cars more tightly than usual. One of the best is the Medeco Super Lock, a heavy-duty ignition cylinder, also by Vaslock. It costs about $125 installed. However, a professional thief can bypass the ignition switch in most late-model cars. He also will not be put off by a cane lock, one end of which clamps to the steering wheel and the other to the brake pedal.

If what a thief wants is your wheels and tires, you can complicate his task by installing locking lugs. A set of four plus the special wrench needed to unlock them costs only about $15.

[34]

Bankruptcy

BUYING STOCKS OF BANKRUPT FIRMS

Business failures have been running at high rates, and that's a shame. But many investors are finding bargains in bankrupt firms. They buy up the stocks and bonds of big, bankrupt corporations at distress prices. These speculators hope that the companies will come out of their court-directed reorganizations slimmed down and comparatively debt-free, and that the increased value of their securities will amply reward investors for the steep risks they are taking.

Investors' eyes glisten at memories of the huge fortunes that were made on such bankrupt companies of the past as Penn Central and Interstate Stores, which later became Toys 'R' Us. Of course, many investors in bankrupt firms have lost considerable money: W. T. Grant is just one example.

The potential for gain springs from the nature of the bankruptcy laws. They are designed to give moribund companies a new lease on life, to let them work out a plan to pay off creditors. Among those creditors, bondholders have the first claim on a company's assets. Common stockholders' rewards are much less assured. They are entitled to whatever assets are left — if any — after the bondholders and other debt holders are paid.

So, bankruptcy investors tend to stick with secured debt. At times they will venture further down the pecking order to preferred or common stock. But usually they will do that only after a company has just come out of reorganization, shining with such virtues as a clean balance sheet, an accumulation of tax losses that can be carried forward to offset future earnings, and a talented management with definite ideas about where it's heading.

Investing in bankrupts is not for the faint of heart or short of pocket. Even situations that look promising often do not pan out. Since the bankruptcy investment game is dominated by the professionals, it would be foolhardy to sit in without coaching from the experts at such brokerage houses as Drexel Burnham, Bear Stearns or another of the firms that invest considerably in bankrupt companies. Two mutual funds that do the same are Mutual Shares (26 Broadway, New York, New York 10004) and First Investors Bond Appreciation Fund (120 Wall Street, New York, New York 10005).

Bargains

HOW TO GET THEM

IF you plan your shopping carefully, you can buy the best of nearly everything at the top stores in the country for 15% to as much as 75% off the original prices.

Everyone knows that department stores, specialty stores and manufacturers have sales from time to time. But the smartest shoppers track the sales systematically to learn in advance just which products and services will be discounted in just which months.

Seasonal markdowns now are likely to start earlier and last longer than they have in many years. The traditional white sale of household linens, for instance, often winds on for nearly two months. That's partly to justify the escalating cost of the accompanying catalogues and partly to counter competition from discount chains. Stores are under heavy pressure to turn over their merchandise quickly because high interest rates make it costly to carry it on the shelves. Retailers estimate that only 20% to 25% of the total sales of high-fashion clothes in department stores are made at the original retail prices.

If you want to cash in on bargains, make a calendar of sales in your area. Very often stores have sales at the same time, year after year. For example, fall is a good season to check for promotional sales of brand-name china, glassware and silver. Store-wide clearances of all kinds of merchandise regularly occur after Christmas, Easter and Independence Day. In department stores, men's clothing sales begin after Christmas and in late June, and last four weeks. Similarly, men's specialty stores schedule sales quite predictably — just after Christmas and Father's Day.

The most expensive brands of perfume, skin cream and cosmetics rarely go on sale in department and specialty stores. But promotional sales — for example, giving away a travel pouch with the purchase of a bottle of perfume — are common before Mother's Day and Father's Day, at Christmas and in the spring, when cosmetics houses introduce new products and colors.

One cautionary note: don't assume everything in a sale has been marked down for clearance. Even fancy stores stock special sale merchandise of inferior quality. And most stores have a stern policy of no refunds, no credits, no exchanges and no free alterations on sale items. If that blue silk tie has a greenish cast and the navy suit you hoped it would match runs to purplish, well, maybe Uncle John would like the tie for Christmas.

[36]

Bargains

DISCOUNTS BY MAIL

Y ou don't have to live in a big city with a lot of discount houses to get some terrific bargains. Instead, you can consult several new publications that list hundreds of discount mail-order catalogues.

The New Wholesale by Mail Catalog, published by St. Martin's Press for $7.95, lists vendors of such diverse items as reconditioned motorcycle parts and exotic coffees. The editors name more than 350 companies that trim 30% to 90% off suggested retail prices. For photo supplies, as an example, you are directed to 47th Street Photo (67 West 47th Street, New York, New York 10036), where the mail-order price of a Minolta X700 35 mm camera is about $217 with postage; you would pay close to $300 in, say, Tacoma. Many of the firms listed promise additional discounts for the book's readers.

Another guide is *The International Catalogue of Catalogues,* published by Harper & Row for $10.95. It lists all types of discount catalogues and identifies many discounters. One of its typical finds: a Pringle crew-neck cashmere sweater that costs $200 at a Manhattan department store is only $107, including postage and duty, when you order it through the mail from Scottish clothier W. S. Robertson (41 Bank Street, Galashiels, Scotland).

Discount America Guide is a bimonthly newsletter that names 80 to 100 mail-order discounters per issue and has cost-comparison charts so that you can weigh every penny of shopping expenses. It costs $9.95 a year, and you can subscribe by writing to 51 East 42nd Street, Suite 417, New York, New York 10017.

Better Business Bureaus

HOW TO GET THEM TO HELP

Now that the government is relaxing its regulation of business, where can consumers turn for help to settle their complaints against companies? More and more of them will be relying on the Better Business Bureau.

The nation's 157 Better Business Bureaus operate on funds contributed mostly by local businesses. All bureau members agree to respond promptly to consumer complaints, make fair adjustments when the customer has grounds for a gripe and advertise honestly. The most common complaints are against mail-order companies and auto dealers.

How much a Better Business Bureau can help varies widely from community to community. For example, the Manhattan office, with a large full-time staff and budget, is one of the country's most pro-consumer bureaus. But some bureaus spend little time on investigations.

Probably the best time to call for help is before you make a deal. The bureau can tell you whether people have complained about a store or company and, if so, whether that business handled the complaint. But Better Business Bureaus won't ever give you lists of complaint-free companies. That's because recommendations of any kind are taboo. People who think they have been swindled or misled may get help, but it probably will take weeks to settle the case. It's best to put complaints in writing to give bureau specialists time to check out the facts.

Increasingly, the Better Business Bureau is resolving disputes by arbitration. More than 150 bureaus offer this service free to buyers and sellers willing to accept the results as legally binding. Consumers who don't like an arbitrator's decision may have no further recourse. In some states, a small-claims court will decline to hear their case. But if you win in a Better Business Bureau arbitration and your adversary doesn't pay up, the award is enforceable by the courts.

Bonds

SIZING UP THE MARKET

Bonds used to offer secure income from interest, a safe harbor for your money and no excitement whatever. Oh, how that has changed. Jagged rises and falls in interest rates have sent bond prices plunging and leaping like a bronco with a burr under its saddle. Interest rates now fluctuate more in a day than they once did in a year. Since bond prices move as fast as interest rates, but in the opposite direction, the bond market is no longer a safe haven for the fainthearted.

Despite the uncertainties in the market, Americans have gone on a bond-buying binge. But the professionals who manage investments for banks, insurance companies and pension funds have held back on some buying of long-term bonds. They are afraid to commit money for decades ahead at fixed rates. To replace these fugitive institutions, bond dealers are turning to individuals.

What has the bond market on edge is worry that the U.S. Treasury must borrow so much to finance twelve-digit federal budget deficits that interest rates may shoot up again and bond prices will tumble. Of course, some other forecasters believe that the deficits will soon narrow and inflation will subside permanently, thus pushing interest rates lower.

Interest rates in general started heading down in 1982, and if they continue to do so, the prices of bonds will go up. In that case, the bond that you buy today, you can sell for a nice profit in the future. The risk you run, of course, is that interest rates could turn the other way around, and climb back up. In that case, the prices of bonds would fall — and if you ever had to sell before your bond matured, you would take a loss.

Bold investors who are willing to trade actively may be able to profit handsomely from volatile interest rates. The principles of trading in fixed-income investments are simple: to get the highest yields you should invest for as short a term as possible when interest rates are rising. Once you are convinced that interest rates have peaked, you should move into longer-term securities — to lock in those high yields and to reap any capital gains.

Prudence dictates caution in the bond market. But you can make sound use of bonds as long as you understand the risks. For in-and-out speculators seeking quick capital gains, trading can be as attractive in bonds as in

[39]

stocks. If you seek steady, reliable income, you can still find that old-time safety, perhaps by buying the bonds of reliable, major corporations that are now selling at deep discounts from their face values. And if you are willing to take a risk with your principal, there is an opportunity now to lock up 20 or 30 years of relatively high yields.

Bonds

HOW THEY WORK

IF you are thinking about investing in bonds, you have a vast smorgasbord of choices. You can buy ordinary, individual bonds, the way that Mother and Dad did, or you can buy into whole portfolios in the form of a bond fund or a unit trust.

A bond is a long-term IOU, and it pays a fixed rate of interest. Usually, you collect your interest checks every six months. Then, when the bond comes due, your capital is repaid in full. The far-off maturity dates and the fixed interest rates, however, are what make bonds risky.

Say you buy a new 30-year corporate bond at its face value of $1,000. Say also that it pays 10% interest, so you collect $100 a year, every year until the date when the bond matures, or comes due. But if long-term interest rates in the meantime rise — say, to 20% — your bond will fall in value. It will be worth only $500 in the open market, because that is the amount that makes your $100 annual return equal to a 20% yield.

On the brighter side, however, if interest rates fall below 10%, your bond is obviously worth more than $1,000. You may want to speculate on bonds if you think that interest rates will fall, thus pushing prices up.

When you buy a bond you should consider four different factors. First, there is the so-called coupon rate. That's the percentage of interest you collect. Second is the maturity date. That's the date when you will be paid the face value of the bond, usually $1,000. Third, there is the quality rating — AAA or B-minus or such — which tells you the financial soundness of the issuer. Finally, there is the tax status. The interest paid on bonds issued by government bodies is usually exempt from certain taxes.

The bond market provides some buying opportunities for many different kinds of investors. Most investors should stay with bonds that have a quality rating of A or higher. Indeed, U.S. Treasury securities are even safer than AAA bonds.

But adventurous buyers might consider lower-quality issues. You will find that a bond rated BBB offers a yield two or three percentage points higher than one rated AAA. And yields for so-called junk bonds — which are those rated lower than BBB — are still higher. But these low-rated bonds have real risks. While very few bond issuers have ever defaulted on the principal, interest payments could be deferred or the bond's quality rating could be lowered further, and that would depress the price.

Bonds

YOUR CHOICES

PROSPECTS for making money from bonds in the near future look reasonably good — provided you choose the right bond.

If you still have substantial amounts of cash tied up in a money-market fund or a bank account, perhaps you should consider switching some of it into bonds. Many bonds have been paying higher interest rates than the banks or the money funds.

If you want the richest yields, look to longer-term bonds. For example, in mid-1983, a three-year U.S. Treasury note was paying about 10.7% interest, but a 90-day Treasury bill was returning 9%. The trouble is, longer-term bonds are the riskiest; they have the most volatile prices. Yields on long-term Treasuries are lower than those on corporate bonds, but there is an important difference. When interest rates drop, private companies often "call" — that is, buy back — their high-yielding bonds. By contrast, 30-year Treasury bonds are "noncallable" for 25 years; all other Treasury bonds are totally "noncallable." So you can hold onto those yields for a long time — usually until the bonds mature — with no fear that the government will force you to sell out. When you buy any kind of corporate or municipal bond, you should check to see whether it can be called in early by the issuer. Some corporate bonds guarantee against calls for up to 10 years.

Speculators who aim for maximum capital gains — but are willing to take maximum risk, too — should consider convertible bonds. They are called convertible because they can be swapped for a stated number of shares of the borrower's stock. A convertible's price swings not only with interest rates, but also with the value of the company's underlying shares. If share prices rise or fall, so do convertible prices.

Then there also are low-quality bonds, those rated below BBB, which are rather affectionately called junk bonds. They reflect seemingly weak spots in the issuer's financial armor. In return for taking extra risk, the speculative investor might get 3½ to four percentage points more yield than from ultra-safe U.S. Treasury bonds. In mid-1983, some bonds of out-of-favor companies were yielding between 14% and 15%.

Junk bonds behave more like stocks than bonds. Their prices tend to rise in line with improvements in the economy or in the fortunes of the issuing company. So, if the economic recovery continues, fears of bankruptcy should lessen, and prices of low-rated issues should rise. In that case, if you add the price increase onto a 15% interest yield, you might get a golden profit from your junk bond.

Investors who yearn for that old-fashioned bond-market religion — that is, a faithful return without much risk — should buy a bond that is way down in price. These deep-discount bonds are securities that were issued 10 or 15 years ago, when interest rates were only 4%. Naturally, nobody would buy a bond today paying only 4%. So the prices of these bonds have gone down deeply in the market. The result is that you can go to a stockbroker and for much less than $1,000 buy a bond that will pay you back $1,000 some years from now — and in the meantime will pay you its regular, though low interest. Many analysts say that among the best deep-discount bonds are those issued by the telephone company.

For example, in mid-1983 you could buy $1,000 worth of AT&T's 3⅞% bonds maturing in 1990 for only $710. The interest that these so-called discount bonds pay is small, which is why they are cheap. But you can use a discount bond to build a college fund for the kids, and you will like the fact that at least 60% of any profit that you ultimately will make on the bond will be excluded from federal income tax. That's because the difference between what you pay for the bond now and what you collect when the bond matures some years from now — that is, your profit — will be taxed at the low capital gains rate.

A fairly new way to lock in a predictable return for the future is to buy zero-coupon bonds. They sell at really deep discounts. For example, for only $360, you could buy a corporate zero-coupon bond in mid-1983 that will pay you $1,000 in 1992; and for $160, you could get one that will pay you $1,000 in the year 2000. There are two problems. Zero-coupon bonds yield no interest in the meantime — that's why they're called zero-coupon — but you will have to pay income taxes on the interest you have not received. The way to escape this tax is either to buy tax-free municipal zero-coupon bonds or to buy corporate zero-coupon bonds for your tax-sheltered Individual Retirement Account or Keogh plan. If you own a zero-coupon bond, you are not confronted every six months with the problem of reinvesting interest income to maintain the high yield. So you make as few investment decisions as possible.

One cautious gamble may be to buy the A-rated bonds of electric utilities that are just now completing construction projects. When a new plant starts generating revenues instead of expenses, the utility's balance sheet improves — and the price of its bonds goes up. Some good-quality utility bonds in mid-1983 were yielding about 12%.

If you are in the 35% tax bracket or higher, you are a candidate for municipal bonds. You don't pay any federal income tax on the interest you collect on them. Some have been paying almost as much as taxable corporate bonds. (For more, see "Bonds: Municipal Bonds.")

Bonds

BOND FUNDS AND UNIT TRUSTS

BECAUSE gyrating interest rates have made prices of individual bonds so unsteady, investors are looking for less risky ways to get into the bond market. You can spread the risk of default by buying bond mutual funds and unit trusts, which give you a small share in a large number of bonds.

A bond mutual fund will always redeem your shares at the present worth of the underlying bonds. If the prices of bonds in the mutual fund's portfolio go up, then your shares immediately go up. Of course, it works the other way around, too. Brokers sell bond funds and collect commissions of up to 8½% from you, but you easily can buy commission-free, no-load bond funds by mail.

As an alternative, of course, you can buy individual bonds. And you can sell them back in the market at any time. But whether you are buying or selling, you will usually take a beating on the price because commissions are high unless you are dealing with very large amounts. So you stand to get a better deal on commissions with bond funds than with individual bonds.

Individual bonds do have some advantage over funds. If interest rates rise and a bond's price drops, you know that your bond eventually will be paid off at its face value — when it matures, or comes due. But bond funds never mature. So, if interest rates skyrocket and stay high, your bond fund shares may never again be worth what you paid for them.

Unit trusts are huge bond portfolios assembled and sold by brokerage houses in small slices of $1,000. They give you the combined benefits of diversification and good prices — you don't overpay for your bonds. After you have paid commissions, you generally get about $950 to $975 worth of securities for each $1,000 you invest. But the yields are slightly bigger than those of bond funds because the portfolios are usually riskier.

The trust's sponsor almost always will buy units back from you at a price equal to their net asset value. The advantage of liquidity and diversification, however, comes at some cost; you run a risk that interest rates will rise, and the price of your units will decline. Also, the sponsors usually buy long-term bonds maturing in 30 years and don't sell any of them unless the issuer is in imminent danger of default. By then, of course, it's usually too late. True, you won't be too badly clobbered because the trust owns many different bonds, and it's highly unlikely that more than a few bond issuers would default at any one time. Still, the way to safeguard yourself against turkeys in your trust — before you send in your money — is to read the trust's prospectus. It lists each bond in the portfolio along with its credit rating and tells you about any provisions that the bonds may be called in early by the issuer if interest rates fall.

You also can buy *tax-exempt* unit trusts. In mid-1983, they were paying interest of about 9½% — tax-free. Investors who are especially safety-minded can put some money into an *insured* tax-exempt trust. The bonds are backed by an insurance company guarantee that interest and principal will be paid on schedule, but the cost of the insurance reduces the yield to a shade less than you would get on an unsecured trust. (See "Bonds: Insured Municipal Bonds.")

Taking all these factors together, the easiest and safest way for most persons of moderate means to buy a diversity of bonds is to invest in a no-load bond fund. The interest income is reasonably steady, there are no commissions when you buy or sell and the annual fees are modest. Unlike unit trusts, bond fund portfolios are actively managed. The issues are traded, and presumably the managers know enough to escape from a troubled situation and sell out well before a bond encounters the danger of default.

Bonds

MUNICIPAL BONDS

ONE of your best tax-exempt investments is municipal bonds. The federal government does not tax the interest you collect on them, and if the bonds are from your home state, you probably will escape state and local taxes, too.

The interest rates on tax-free municipal bonds were unusually high in mid-1983. They were around 10½%, which is more than double the expected rate of inflation. In fact, in mid-1983 the municipals were yielding 80% to 90% as much as U.S. Treasury bonds, which are subject to federal income taxes, but not state or local taxes. The municipals were paying a lot because there was an oversupply of these bonds on the market. So, to induce you to buy them, they offered high yields.

Municipals have the usual risk: if interest rates rise, the prices of the bonds fall. Then, if you had to sell off your investment for any reason, you would get less than you paid for it. Another risk is that the state or city agency that issued the bond could go broke and default.

For that reason, small investors should stick with the highest-quality bonds — those rated AAA or AA by Moody's or Standard & Poor's. You should approach municipal bonds with more than the usual caution because the ability of many state and municipal borrowers to pay their debts is deteriorating. In 1982, Standard & Poor's downgraded the ratings of 105 municipal borrowers, while upgrading only 46. As discussed earlier, you can spread your risks by buying bond funds or unit trusts.

Despite the risks, the tax-free yield of municipal bonds is so high, and there are so many high-rated ones available, that they are a sensible investment for anyone in the 35% tax bracket or above. That's a taxable income of about $32,000 for a single person or about $42,000 for a married couple filing jointly.

Bonds

ADJUSTABLE-RATE OPTION MUNICIPALS

A NEW investment that allows you to earn tax-free income without tying up your money for more than a year is the adjustable-rate option bond. It is a long-term municipal bond, but the interest rates it pays are adjusted annually — up or down — to whatever the current market rate is. And once a year you will have the option to cash in the bond and collect what you paid for it.

Adjustable-rate option bonds sold by Kidder Peabody were paying one percentage point more than tax-exempt money-market funds in mid-1983. True, the adjustable-rate yield was almost four points below the rate available on conventional long-term municipal bonds. But investors in those regular bonds have no assurance of getting back the full amount they have invested if they sell out early.

If you plan to hold onto your tax-free bond for many years, you are probably best off buying a regular municipal bond. But if you think you will need your money back in a year, you might be well advised to consider adjustable-rate option bonds.

Bonds

INSURED MUNICIPAL BONDS

IF you are thinking about investing in municipal bonds, you may be worried that many states and localities are severely troubled by federal budget cutbacks and shrinking tax revenues. But there is a new way that you can invest in municipals and insure yourself against any losses from defaults.

You can profit from the high yields and be able to sleep at night by investing in an insured municipal bond fund or trust. A trust is a closed-end fund whose underwriter sells units in a portfolio of bonds that are held until they mature or are called. The units typically cost $1,000 each.

The portfolios of insured bond funds and trusts are all rated Triple-A by the authoritative Standard & Poor's rating service. The insurer is American Municipal Bond Assurance Corporation. It guarantees investors full payment of interest and principal when due. The insurance costs $2.50 a year for every $1,000 you invest. This has the effect of reducing your annual yield from a fund or trust by only one-quarter of 1%.

Insured trusts are sponsored by two firms, both with headquarters in Chicago: Van Kampen Merritt and Clayton Brown & Associates. You can buy units through your broker; he will deduct a sales commission of roughly 5%. That means that if you put up $1,000, you get about $950 worth of bonds.

Bonds

U.S. SAVINGS BONDS

THE Treasury Department has overhauled good old U.S. savings bonds to make them more enticing. Are the bonds better investments than before? Well, yes — marginally.

Until recently, series EE bonds, which come in denominations of $50 to $10,000, weren't paying much interest. To get the maximum annual yield of 9%, you had to keep a bond for eight years. You would earn less if you cashed it in earlier.

From now on, however, the return on EE bonds held five years or longer will fluctuate with market interest rates. The bonds' return will be 85% of the average yield of Treasury notes and bonds during the preceding five years. As of mid-1983, that would have been about 8.6%. To protect investors against sharp interest-rate drops, EE bonds held longer than five years will pay a guaranteed yield of at least 7.5%.

Books

HOW TO GET YOURS PUBLISHED

It seems that almost everyone wants to write a book. People read about an unknown author who sits down at the typewriter and then cashes in big with a best-seller — and they, too, want to get in on the money, and the fame.

Plotting to get your book published is frustrating, but talent and tenacity can lead to happy endings. Publishers receive more than 30,000 unsolicited manuscripts annually. They send nearly all of them back with the swiftness and compassion of Jimmy Connors returning a cream-puff serve. It's by no means impossible to get your first work of fiction or nonfiction published. To do it, though, you need to persuade a publisher or an agent at least to read your manuscript.

Most publishers urge that you do get an agent. You can find lists of well-known agents in two books at your public library. They are *Fiction Writer's Market* and *Literary Market Place*. Agents often act as informal editors and they can direct your book to a likely publisher. What's more, the fact that your book is being submitted by an agent known to the editor is a guarantee that the work will be considered.

If the publisher is interested, an agent probably will be able to get you a bigger advance. Don't expect anything more than $5,000. For their services, agents customarily charge 10% of whatever the writer receives.

Some agents also have a fee just for reading manuscripts. Before you agree to pay anything, find out what services you will be getting for your money. That's always a sound idea on any deal, of course. If an agent insists on a written contract, be sure you hire a lawyer to approve it before you sign.

It's perfectly legitimate for an unknown author who gets a nibble from a publisher to recruit an agent *before* proceeding further. The proper approach to an agent or to a publisher is to write a letter explaining the kind of book you have in mind. Enclose a chapter or at least a sample of your writing. Outline briefly what you have already published, if anything. Above all, include a self-addressed, stamped envelope if you want your chapter returned.

The easiest way to break into print is by writing what is known as popular fiction — that is, mystery stories, spy thrillers and adventure tales. Romances alone account for 30% of all the fiction published between hard and soft covers. Advances on romances are relatively low. Harlequin Enterprises, which started the boom in romantic fiction, pays about $2,500 plus royalties of 6% to 8% of the book's wholesale price. But a highly successful writer who catches on and learns the formula can count on earning $50,000 a book.

In nonfiction, a fresh and sharply focused idea is more important than writing style. But the novice author had better be an expert in his subject. Readers want specific information on specific topics. Books on cooking and dieting do well, as does anything connected with ways to make money. And sex is definitely here to stay.

Beginning writers should take time to learn how books get published. Two monthly magazines often carry solid information for aspiring authors. They are called *Writer's Digest* and *The Writer*. Among the many books of advice, a good one is *How to Get Happily Published* by Judith Appelbaum and Nancy Evans ($6.95, New American Library).

Literary Market Place also lists all the publishers. Check to see which houses are putting out books in your field. And be persistent. Many a best-seller was rejected by a score of publishers before finally being accepted.

If you can't find a publisher who is captivated by your manuscript, don't despair. For a fee of $3,000 to $15,000, a so-called vanity publisher will design, print, bind and promote your book. Vanity books, however, are seldom taken seriously by other publishers. Or, you can do what Virginia Woolf, Walt Whitman and Mark Twain did, and publish your own book. A spectacular do-it-yourself story is that of Mary Ellen Pinkham. She began publishing her collection of helpful household hints in 1976 and so far she has earned more than $2,500,000.

Borrowing

QUICK WAYS TO RAISE CASH

O NE of the cheapest ways to raise extra money fast is to borrow against your whole life insurance policy. Most life insurance policies written before 1976 carry a temptingly low 5% to 6% interest rate on loans. Another advantage of borrowing against insurance is the opportunity to repay at your own pace.

You also can raise cash by taking out a second mortgage. Unless your situation is desperate, it is better to do that than to sell your home. Second mortgages are available from banks, thrift institutions, finance companies and credit unions. The credit unions are likely to have more loan funds available and charge lower interest than thrift institutions. Some credit unions also offer free financial counseling.

Often you can join a credit union by depositing a nominal sum — sometimes as little as $5. Of course, to qualify you generally must belong to the group whose members formed the credit union — a church, labor union, residential community or professional association. For more information about credit unions in your area, write the Credit Union National Association, Box 431, Madison, Wisconsin 53701.

If you own stocks, you can borrow up to 50% of their market value at broker loan rates.

Most credit advisers steer clients clear of finance companies. That's because the companies' loan charges are very high. But when a debtor can't get credit elsewhere, raising cash from a finance company may be his only way of avoiding bankruptcy.

Brokers

HOW TO CHOOSE ONE

B<small>ACK</small> in the bullish 1960s, it almost did not matter whether your stockbroker was a genius, a guru or simply somebody's smiling son-in-law. The momentum of the market was so strong that you were fairly well assured of making money.

That's no longer true in today's volatile market. So, choosing a brokerage firm for the first time, or switching to a new one, becomes a key decision. It isn't easy, particularly if you are a small investor. Some firms don't want to bother with accounts of less than $15,000. Not many will turn you down flat, but your account is likely to get serious attention only if it can generate sizable commissions.

If you are a small investor, you will find that big, national brokerage houses are generally more hospitable than lesser outfits. These large companies stand to make a bit of profit from the sheer volume of their small accounts. Look for the major firms that offer special services, such as cut-rate commissions.

But if you want to concentrate on investing in companies located in your own area, you might do better with well-established regional brokerages. They often have the best research on the stocks of local companies. True, they also have a disadvantage: they are often less familiar with companies located far away, and with complex stock strategies, than are the bigger, national houses.

If you follow the market very closely yourself and feel you do not need regular, professional advice, then consider using discount brokers. They generally offer no frills and no handholding, but they often charge commissions of 1% or less.

Once you have picked the brokerage house that you like, how do you select the salesperson in that firm just right for you? Choosing the right broker is not quite as important as selecting the right spouse or the best boss, but considering that your broker will do much to determine whether you are affluent or financially uncomfortable in the future, it is a decision to be taken quite seriously.

The first thing to do is to get recommendations. Ask friends who are themselves successful investors. Ask accountants and tax preparers. They have inside knowledge of how well their clients are doing in the market, and legally and ethically they can tell you who the best brokers are.

You are generally better off with a veteran, well-experienced broker, one who has been through a few market reverses, a person who knows that stocks can go down as well as up, than with an eager newcomer who will learn his lessons with your money.

Before doing business with a broker, don't be shy to ask him or her for the names of people whose accounts he handles. Then call up two or three of them. You might uncover some unexpected blemishes, such as a tendency to overtrade. Too much trading may produce high commissions for your broker but very small returns for you.

Be sure to evaluate your market performance coldly after you have been with the broker for six months. And then do it yearly. Compare your gains and losses with the Standard & Poor's index of 500 stocks. If your portfolio's performance, before commissions, falls below the S&P, don't hesitate to take your money and run — to another broker.

Brokers

REGIONAL BROKERS

J UST about everyone is familiar with Merrill Lynch's thundering herd and knows that when E. F. Hutton talks, you're likely to get the soup in your lap because your waiter is listening. But a growing number of investors are turning their ears to lesser-known regional brokerage houses. They can get you into the stocks of small local companies that are among the fastest growing in the country.

Regional firms often specialize in fairly small companies with strong managements. Some firms limit their bailiwick to a single city; others specialize in regions — for example, growth companies of the Midwest or Southwest. Analysts read the local papers, understand the local economy and continue to follow local companies even if they temporarily fall out of favor with investors.

These brokers tend to have strong and deep ties to their region. Many began as municipal bond houses handling underwritings for towns and small cities too insignificant to be noticed by national firms. Gradually, the regionals branched out into selling common stocks as well.

If you think the economic prospects are bright for companies in a specific part of the country, a long-distance call to a regional broker will get you a sampling of current research reports. If you like what you see, you can open an account, also by phone, and start receiving monthly market letters with regional economic forecasts and lists of recommended stocks.

Many regional brokerage houses have notable records of performance. In the East, for example, are Advest, Inc. in Hartford, Connecticut; A. E. Masten in Pittsburgh; and Baker Watts and Company in Baltimore. In the South are Interstate Securities in Charlotte and Robinson Humphrey/American Express, Inc. in Atlanta. In the Midwest are Cleveland's Prescott, Ball and Turben and Milwaukee's Robert W. Baird Company. In the West and Southwest, there are Rauscher Pierce Refsnes, Inc. of Dallas, Boettcher and Company of Denver and Crowell, Weedon and Company in Los Angeles.

To find other regional firms, one good source is a Standard & Poor's guide called Security Dealers of North America. It lists securities firms and their addresses and phone numbers, by city and state.

When these firms venture out of their regions, it usually is to cover the competitors of local companies. Their analysts keep turning up small companies that have fast-expanding markets and earnings. Gradually the glitter of these little stars will attract attention by national firms. That is the regional analyst's dream: Finding stocks, getting clients into them early, then waiting until a big national firm discovers them, recommends them — and sends the price up.

Brokers

THE DISCOUNTERS

A DISCOUNT broker will execute stock trades for even the smallest investor at rock-bottom rates. But usually you will get no advice from him, and no handholding.

Are these firms safe and are the discounts real? The answer on both counts is yes.

Fees vary more sharply among discounters than among the full-service firms that provide research on stocks and a lot of personal attention. To buy 100 shares of a stock selling at $25, a typical full-service firm might charge a commission of about $63. For the same trade, discounters would charge between $25 and $45. For 300 shares, a full-service broker might charge a commission of $155. Discount brokers would execute the same transaction for $50 to $100 or in some cases less.

A discounter who is ultra-cheap for small trades may be less advantageous for large ones, which might require a great deal of research. And there may be hidden charges. So look over the rate schedules carefully.

Before you decide what is best for you, ponder the following points:

First, discount brokers *are* safe. All brokerage houses are subject to the same regulations and all stocks and bonds in an investor's account are insured by the federally chartered, nonprofit Securities Investor Protection Corporation for up to $500,000.

Second, when they buy or sell stock, discount brokers get just as good a price for their customers as full-service firms do.

Third, some discounters will not handle certain complex types of trading, particularly commodities or index options. But discounters are satisfactory for buying listed stocks or bonds for investment. Before you engage a discount broker, find out what kind of trading he is prepared to do for you.

Remember, discounters are inexpensive for a reason. To get a break on rates, you really do give up service. And one winning stock recommendation from a full-service broker's research staff could more than make up for his higher commission. But if you know exactly what you want to buy and sell, there is no question that discount brokers will save you a lot.

Brokers

HOW SAFE IS YOUR BROKERAGE ACCOUNT?

AFTER several stock brokerage firms failed during the bear markets of the early 1980s, many investors started wondering, "What happens if *my* broker goes broke?"

It is very unlikely that your brokerage firm will go belly-up. But if it does, your stocks, bonds and money fund shares are insured by the Securities Investor Protection Corporation against losses up to $500,000. This government-chartered private corporation — nicknamed "Sipic" — oversees liquidations of brokerages and restores securities to clients. To do this, SIPC has a $220 million fund raised by assessing the brokerage firms. It also can tap a $1 billion line of credit at the U.S. Treasury.

But commodity futures contracts are not covered by SIPC, nor is cash left with a broker specifically to earn interest. Options are covered, but they are usually too short-lived to survive the freeze put on customer accounts when a firm fails.

The process of liquidating a brokerage firm can take from four months to a year in extreme cases. Customers first receive any securities held in their own names. If their stocks or bonds are in the firm's name — that is, the so-called street name — clients will be given a prorated share of any street-name securities that the firm can produce. SIPC then will make up the difference between what the clients got and what they are owed.

If you are worried about your broker's financial health, there are signs of trouble to watch for. Does it take a long time for your broker to execute your orders to buy and sell? Do confirmation slips fail to square with transactions? Problems like these suggest the firm could be having back-office snarls, and it might be time to move your account.

Even if you are confident of your broker's stability, you should take steps to protect yourself. Certainly, don't hold more than $500,000 worth of securities in any single account. If you are really skittish, you can hold securities in your name instead of the firm's name or even keep the certificates at home or in a safe-deposit box. In a liquidation, you will get the shares in your name back faster than shares in a street name. And you will have them back in no time if they never leave your possession.

Brokers

SELLING WITHOUT A BROKER

Did you know that you can sell stock that you own without using a broker? That way, you can save the money that you would normally spend for the sales commission.

The procedure for transferring ownership of stock is not all that hard. First, sign the back of your stock certificate and have your bank guarantee your signature. That's to protect you against forgeries. Then, fill in the new owner's full name, as well as his or her Social Security number and address. Next, get the name and address of the company's transfer agent. That's easy. Simply write to the corporate secretary of the company in which you own stock. Finally, send the stock certificate by registered mail to the transfer agent. Attach a letter explaining that you are selling the shares. The transfer agent then will issue a new certificate in the new owner's name.

And what is the charge for this? Nothing at all.

Burglary

PROTECTING YOURSELF WITH LOCKS AND ALARMS

BURGLARIES are surging everywhere — in the suburbs and small towns as well as the big cities. But you can help make your home safe by installing the right locks and alarms, and it needn't cost you a fortune or create a fortress.

To stop a thief, first call the police — not for a squad car but for a free security checkup. Police departments often will send patrolmen to inspect your property and show you where it is vulnerable. Most homes can be adequately protected by strong locks and an alarm system for as little as $300.

It is important to have reliable locks on all windows, since most burglars find it easier to break in through windows than to pick a lock on a door. Of course, don't forget to have strong locks also on all doors, not just the front door. Crime prevention experts recommend replacing ordinary key-cylinder locks with pick-resistant ones. But ultra-sophisticated locks that replace keys with magnetic cards, voice recognition or coded pushbuttons are expensive overkill for most residences.

Most good locks are secured by a rigid dead bolt that extends at least one inch into the jamb. This kind of lock has to be locked or unlocked every time someone uses the door. The Kentucky Department of Justice's Office of Crime Prevention has tested residential locks commonly available in the state. Among the lockmakers whose products were rated superior were Ideal, National Lock Hardware, MAG, Schlage, Emhart and Medeco.

Homeowners who want more protection than locks give can choose one of several alarm systems. Among the companies that install and monitor alarm systems are American District Telegraph, Honeywell, Rollins and Wells Fargo. Wired alarm systems generally cost $800 to $2,500 — plus a monthly charge of $10 to $45, if the system is monitored. You often can get discounts on your property insurance if you put in an alarm system.

It pays to check out the craftsman who puts in the system, since alarms are only as reliable as the people who install them. Be sure to get competitive bids, to ask for and check references and call your local Better Business Bureau to see if there have been any complaints about installers whom you are considering. You should shop as warily for an alarm system as for a used car.

Burglary

BUYING VAULTS FOR YOUR VALUABLES

SINCE there are long waiting lists for small safe-deposit boxes in banks, more and more people are looking for a secure place to store their valuables right in their own homes.

The biggest weakness of a home safe is its accessibility. If you take a weekend away from home, professional burglars have plenty of time to find and defeat your safe. So a safe-deposit box in a bank or a vault at a private safe-deposit company is the most secure place for jewelry, securities, coins and other valuables, but a home safe can be useful for documents and records.

If you buy a safe, be sure it has been rated by the Underwriters Laboratories for fire resistance. Say it is rated a class 150 two-hour safe. That means that temperatures inside will go no higher than 150 degrees Fahrenheit during a two-hour fire. A class 150 two-hour safe is a good one for protecting stamps and other expensive collectibles.

If you insist on keeping not only your documents but also tiaras and gold bullion in your home, then forget about a wall safe. A burglar can drill around the metal box and pull it free. What you will need is a so-called burglar safe. It should be anchored with bolts or embedded in a concrete floor and concealed by a rug. A floor safe the size of a file-drawer cabinet can cost up to $600.

Fancier, stronger safes can go for much more. You can easily pay $4,200 for a medium-size model with inch-thick steel walls, a special locking mechanism in the door and an Underwriters Laboratories label marked TL-30. The TL number is an index of resistance to burglars' tools.

If you do not have a safe, the best protection for your valuables is ingenuity. Avoid the more common hiding places, like the toe of a shoe or the bottom of a sugar cannister. Some people have foiled burglars by using false-bottom books, sewing jewelry into stuffed toys or pillows or even freezing diamonds in the ice tray. Just be careful of gulping them down with that one-too-many martini.

Burglary

KEEPING RECORDS TO REDUCE YOUR LOSS

No one wants to think about having one's home burglarized. But it happens. And if you confront the possibility beforehand, you can reduce your financial loss.

To prevent a burglary from leaving you broke, make an inventory of everything you have in your home. Your insurance company probably can give you a form to fill out.

Go through each room, opening drawers and cupboards and carefully list everything of value. Record all identifying information, such as serial numbers of appliances and account numbers of credit cards. For tableware, note the manufacturers, pattern and number of place settings. Describe jewelry as fully as possible.

It's also wise to photograph the contents of your house, item by item. Do this yourself with self-developing film that does not need to be processed by strangers. If your possessions are extensive and of particularly high quality, you might consider videotaping and recording your verbal descriptions of them.

Get receipts and appraisals for particularly valuable items. Without these documents, you will have to rely on what the insurance adjustor says your goods are worth. An appraisal must be precise and explicit to back up a claim. Don't accept any that give only highly generalized descriptions of your valuables.

Appraisers for your goods can be located through the American Society of Appraisers, P.O. Box 17265, Washington, D.C. 20041. It publishes a free directory of those members who are personal property appraisers, plus a free pamphlet, *Information on the Appraisal Profession*. For $5, you can get its *Directory of Professional Appraisal Services*, which includes appraisers in all fields.

With a typical homeowners policy, you get no more than $1,000 coverage of all your jewelry. Most insurance companies won't pay more than $1,000 for stolen furs or silverware either. If your possessions are worth more than those limits in your policy, you will have to buy individual policies called floaters for them. Premiums vary widely, but a floater for jewelry usually costs $15 to $20 a year per $1,000 of value.

If your home is burglarized, you will need accurate records for both the IRS and the police. Those records will help you reduce your losses.

After a burglary, the criminals often melt down the precious metals in their loot and break up the jewelry to prevent its being traced. But most other stolen merchandise winds up back on the market intact. Police sweeps of pawnshops and suspected fences and crooked retailers sometimes turn up stolen property.

To help locate the original owners, the International Association of Chiefs of Police runs Operation Identification. For $15 a year, subscribers are assigned a number and sent an etching tool to engrave the number on their belongings. Marking your property with a number makes it less attractive to thieves, since it's harder to sell. When numbered merchandise is confiscated, police departments check with the association's computer. For information, write to the International Association of Chiefs of Police, 510 King Street, Alexandria, Virginia 22314. Many local police departments run their own free identification programs as well.

It's getting tougher to deduct burglary losses from your income taxes, so you may need more insurance coverage. On your income tax form for 1982, you could deduct qualifying losses above $100. But on your forms for 1983 and later years, you will be allowed to deduct only those losses that exceed 10% of your adjusted gross income. And the loss must be figured as the lower of two amounts: the price paid for the item or its current value. So, if you lose something that is worth less today than when you bought it, you can deduct only its current market value. But if an item has grown in value since you bought it, you can deduct only its original, lower cost.

Careers

DEFYING THE COMMON MYTHS

Ask a career counselor for the hottest job prospects, and you will hear that the future belongs to those who can command the computer. That's great news for anyone who cottons to modems and megabytes. The computer does indeed stand to create more careers than any invention since the wheel. But if you follow the herd to high-tech when your heart lies elsewhere, you may be making an expensive mistake. The wisest counsel in looking for a job is to pursue your own desires.

A surprising number of determined men and women are finding excellent jobs in fields that the career prophets have written off. They are doing it by challenging some of the common myths of job hunting. If you are determined to get into even the most glutted occupation, you cannot allow yourself to be daunted by common career myths.

Do not, for example, let Labor Department job projections be your guide. They are full of occupations that no longer exist and fail to mention many new fields, such as robotics or hazardous waste management. National labor forecasts often obscure opportunities in your own community. For example, by tuning into local trends, job hunters might have spotted how Connecticut, in the slow-growing Northeast, was making an economic comeback. Spurred by the rise of high-tech and financial services businesses, the state now has one of the healthiest employment rates in the country. Job projections often underestimate the time it takes for new technologies to spread. For instance, genetic engineering is breeding considerably less employment than early enthusiasts had predicted.

Don't fret about getting caught in so-called female ghetto jobs. For example, social workers are finding terrific corporate jobs in employee counseling. And believe it or not, the world can use another writer — in fact, many of them. They will be needed to interpret and organize the computer data flood. Newsletters, TV cable services and trade journals all will require people who can convert raw data into readable English.

Don't accept the myth that a high-tech boom means a low-tech bust. Far from it. There is a surge in demand for personal services. As the population ages, one of the fastest-expanding careers will be geriatric nursing. But the real sleeper among service occupations may well be teaching. Millions of computer buyers will need instruction, and so will millions of semi-literate workers. More than 300 corporations already run remedial English and math classes.

[64]

Don't fall for the line that it is better to be a specialist than a generalist. Across the country, Ph.D.'s are broadening themselves by enrolling in intensive short-term introduction to business courses — and becoming everything from factory managers to security analysts. Among the best-paid generalists are the so-called issues managers. They scan the horizons for developments that could affect a corporation's business. Issues managers have diverse backgrounds in the social sciences, hard sciences, finance, law, journalism and public relations.

Don't think you have to have an M.B.A. — a master's degree in business — to get ahead. The degree may get you in the door, but after that you'll have to scramble like everybody else.

Don't assume that big corporations offer the most opportunities. During the 1970s, the 1,000 largest corporations created only 75,000 jobs. But small business generated 9.6 million jobs — most of them in enterprises with 20 or fewer employees.

Don't be afraid to start your own business. The hours are long and paupers outnumber princes, but working for yourself gives you the chance to do things your way.

Careers

WHERE THE OPPORTUNITIES ARE

W HETHER you are self-employed or work for a company owned by others, you will find that the greatest job growth in the immediate future will occur in financial and business services, health care, recreation and, of course, telecommunications, computers and other high-tech businesses.

Careers in financial services are expanding because of the new attitude people have toward money. More Americans are willing to invest the effort and expense to plan their savings and investments. So, brokerage houses and insurance companies are setting up financial planning departments. In addition, banks, brokerage houses, real estate companies and other financial concerns will be hiring waves of analysts, portfolio managers, marketing specialists and, above all, salesmen. Some financial jobs will require M.B.A. degrees, but would-be stockbrokers who have sales experience in any area will be eligible for training programs at the brokerage firms.

In fact, the job prospects for salesmen are exceptionally bright in most industries. By 1990, according to the Bureau of Labor Statistics, more than 1 million sales jobs will open up — that's an increase of 19%. For example, Century 21, the real estate company, plans to hire 100,000 people by 1987. The company's chiefs are looking for property managers and people to put together syndications and arrange mortgages. But most of those new jobs will be in real estate sales.

The increase in the number of two-career couples will provide more work for the relocation, personnel and headhunting firms that will have to solve the problems of moving an executive who also has a working spouse. And with the 65-and-over population rapidly expanding, there will be a need for business consultants who do retirement counseling and pension planning. To provide sufficient health care for the elderly, more and more doctors, nurses and social workers will be required. Only several hundred doctors now are expert in geriatric medicine, but we will need some 9,000 of them by 1990 to serve an aging nation.

The rising American concern with staying healthy will create jobs. Medical centers will need technicians to run diagnostic equipment and nurses to treat patients. They also will be hiring office managers, marketing executives and accountants to handle the books.

Computers will create new jobs — and not only where you expect them. More openings will come in businesses such as banks and utilities that use the mighty microchip than in those that manufacture it. Businesses will be looking for programmers and systems engineers. And anyone who can develop software for micro and personal computers won't have to hunt long for work.

The United States is in transition from an industrial society to an information society. In this new world, man and computer will have to work together as a team. Everybody who wants to get ahead in this new society will need not only a skill but several skills. Humanists had better be able to communicate with technicians. Engineers should know how to read a balance sheet. In a world of expanded trade, people in business would be wise to know one or more foreign languages.

The workplace is shifting from emphasis on the narrow specialist who is in danger of becoming obsolete to the multiskilled generalist who can adapt. For people who can stay flexible in their jobs, the career paths of the future are wide open.

Here are some other growth areas for careers in the mid-to-late 1980s:

— Career counselors. Because fewer young people will be coming along to enter the job market, there will be a labor shortage in some sectors. So companies will have to hire more young mothers and semi-retired people, and many of them will want career counseling.

— Water resource experts. The water shortage of the 1980s and 1990s could become as severe as the oil squeeze of the 1970s. We shall require more hydrologists, environmental engineers and others to preserve our most important of all resources.

— Toxicologists. Business and government will want them to detect harmful effects of natural and man-made substances that pollute the environment.

— Molecular biologists and biological engineers. In time, they will be hired by the biological engineering firms.

— Industrial relations specialists. With the new emphasis on enhancing industrial and office productivity, these experts will be called on to work out corporate agreements between management and labor.

— Development economists. People with college degrees in international economics and business will help to market American products abroad.

— Technicians, entertainers and writers. They will bring entertainment into the home by means of the new cable television, videotape and videodiscs.

— Entrepreneurs. The U.S. will need plenty of these daring risk-takers to start new businesses in the fast-changing mid-to-late 1980s. For anybody who has a marketable idea — from the highly technical world of electronics and computers to the everyday realm of retailing — entrepreneurship can offer one of the best careers of the era. (See "Entrepreneurship.")

[67]

Careers

FIRST JOBS FOR GRADUATES

Every year thousands of graduates stumble out of college without having lined up jobs. But they have more choices than they may assume — if they know how and where to look, and if they are willing to rethink some of their assumptions about first jobs.

For example, if you are about to graduate, you will probably find it a waste of time to apply to the prestigious company that dominates a field. You may well find a job easier and get ahead faster at number two ... or three. You will also stand a better chance of being hired if you volunteer to work at a company's outposts in an unglamorous city. And you can score points with prospective employers when you are willing to travel, work odd hours or accept less than top salary.

The federal government continues to be a steady employer. The armed services need college graduates for civilian management jobs at military bases. Opportunities are principally in finance, personnel, logistics and printing. Pay begins at $13,369, and promotions can boost that quickly to $16,000 or more. Also, the Central Intelligence Agency regularly hires.

All professional and paraprofessional government job openings are listed in a biweekly publication available in many libraries. Called *Federal Career Opportunities,* it tells how to apply for jobs that interest you. You can get more leads on federal jobs from the government's Office of Personnel Management. Either visit one of its local branches or write to the Job Information Center, Office of Personnel Management, 1900 East Street, NW, Washington, D.C. 20415.

Careers

DOES AN M.B.A. STILL PAY?

To earn one of those cherished master's degrees in business administration typically costs $15,000 in tuition and expenses for a full-time student. That's besides salary lost by studying rather than working for two school years. But does it still pay to get an M.B.A?

The number of M.B.A.'s granted each year has doubled in the past decade to more than 61,000. Some 200,000 students, including part-timers, are enrolled in graduate business and management programs. Consequently, an M.B.A. no longer guarantees you an advantage in the race to top management positions. Entry-level jobs open to graduates of even the most prestigious business schools are somewhat harder to get than they were in the late '70s and early '80s. Starting salaries are still high, but many no longer seem as startling as they did in the past. The average M.B.A. with no work experience and a nontechnical undergraduate degree took a job paying about $24,000 in 1981. That was slightly less than many engineers with only bachelor's degrees got.

One way to gain the most benefit from an investment in an M.B.A. is to attend a first-rate graduate business school. The top ones include the schools at Stanford, Harvard, Chicago, Pennsylvania, Northwestern, Illinois, Texas, MIT, Berkeley, Michigan, Dartmouth, Columbia, Virginia and Carnegie-Mellon.

The payoff of attending one of those schools can be impressive: more than 18% of Harvard's graduates in 1982 took jobs with management consulting firms at a remarkably high median salary of $50,000.

It is also wise to earn a degree in science or technology *before* going to business school. The M.B.A.'s with undergraduate majors in engineering or hard sciences not only get jobs more easily than those without such backgrounds, but their starting salaries are typically 10% higher. Another smart move is to work for a few years before going to graduate business school.

The most successful combination for a new M.B.A. is to have a technical or scientific undergraduate degree *and* work experience. In 1983, such graduates typically started at more than $29,000. That was nearly 20% more than M.B.A.'s who majored in liberal arts as undergraduates and had never held full-time jobs.

[69]

Careers

OPPORTUNITIES WITHOUT COLLEGE DEGREES

THE Sunday papers are thick with openings for bank tellers, commercial artists, data processors, electronics technicians, medical technologists, nurses and secretaries. What's more, fewer and fewer of these classified ads stipulate a college degree as a requirement.

Graduates of four-year colleges still have a financial edge over workers without sheepskins, but that advantage is small and narrowing. Twenty years ago, beginning salaries for college men were 24% higher than for the work force as a whole. Today they are only 5% higher.

Most job openings call for skills that you are more likely to acquire in a technical school or on the job than on some ivied campus. Technical school graduates are routinely landing jobs with higher starting pay than newly minted bachelors of arts can command. A computer programmer fresh from a six-month course can earn up to $14,000 a year while an English major is still home rewriting his résumé.

Technical training is expensive, but because it is condensed it costs far less than a $40,000 university degree. At one technical school, for example, a two-year program in electronics engineering is $8,577.

Many two-year community colleges and private junior colleges offer vocational training at considerably lower cost than do private technical schools. Tuition averages $500 a year for such job-oriented studies as data processing, police science, real estate sales and auto mechanics.

What is most valuable in vocational education — whether at a community college or a technical school — is hands-on training. When choosing a program, first visit the school and ask a lot of questions. Inquire about the school's resources as well as about the time devoted to learning by doing. Also check to see which companies hire the most graduates. Then query those companies' personnel managers on how they rate the school's courses.

High-tech companies that need a competent work force often educate people in specialized skills. The list of such corporations includes AT&T, IBM, Xerox, Wang Laboratories and Control Data. A graduate of a 30-month course at Bell & Howell's DeVry Institute of Technology in Chicago can get a job starting at $16,500 a year on average. That's a big return on an investment of $12,800 in tuition and registration fees.

The best deal, of course, is getting paid to learn a skill. Competition for on-the-job apprenticeships has always been stiff, but as business expands, so will the need for trainees. Along with the standard apprenticeships for plumbers, pipefitters and carpenters, there are programs in hundreds of occupations, including biomedical equipment technician, meteorologist and chef.

The Labor Department's Bureau of Apprenticeship and Training supervises programs in some 500 trades. State agencies with information about apprenticeships are listed in the phone directory, usually under State Government, Employment Security Administration.

The most respected apprenticeships are employer-sponsored programs such as those run by Kodak, General Electric and Westinghouse. You can find out what is available in your locality by asking major employers in the area.

Even without training, high school graduates can land worthwhile jobs in marketing, retailing and a few other fields. And in some government-regulated sales fields — particularly real estate, securities and insurance — a beginning file clerk can impress a boss by studying hard and passing a licensing exam.

Careers

SECOND CAREERS FOR WOMEN

For many wives and mothers, work resumes at 40. But any woman who wants to re-enter the job market will find that she needs some shrewd strategies to do it.

The most serious problem confronting re-entry women is a lack of confidence and focus: they tend to undervalue their previous experience. If you are one of them, though, you should know that many of the skills needed to manage a household or organize a charity bazaar can be transferred to business. Are ill-defined ambitions a problem? The solution may be career-planning workshops offered by countless nonprofit agencies, individual counselors and almost every university and community college. Courses vary from six weeks to six months and cost about $150 to $200.

After determining your career objective, you may discover that you need to refurbish your skills before you try them out again. That's fine, but beware: some older women are tempted to dock in the safe harbor of academe. They go to college for year after year, stacking degree upon degree, never braving the rougher waters of the marketplace.

Although men tend to think that they would not want a job if they already know how to do it, women often think that they have to be able to do a job before they can take it. Thus women tend to "overcredentialize" themselves and hold back from the day of reckoning.

As a first step back into the market, draft a résumé. You will want to present yourself in it in a way that is meant to fit your specific goal. Unless your educational credentials are recent or sterling, you probably will want to downplay them and play up your volunteer and other experience. Employers often are unimpressed with degrees or other credentials older than your teenage son.

Omit the personal details. Nobody is going to say her health is *terrible*. By law, an employer cannot ask your age, marital status or whether you have children. These same statistics are best left out of a résumé. When many an employer sees "children" written on a résumé, he thinks of "sick days."

Your instinct may be to run off 200 copies of your résumé and wallpaper the town. But, instead, you should treat this master copy as a draft and customize your résumé to correspond to the specific opening you're trying to fill.

To get a job interview, begin by telephoning friends and informing them that you are leaving the homestead for the wage-paying world. Use that grapevine of contacts you have developed — everyone from old school friends to members of clubs you have joined.

Even if you have had many years of significant but unpaid experience, your first re-entry job is likely to be on the lower rungs of the labor force. You should not be either insulted or excessively concerned if it is less glamorous, less responsible and lower paying than you expected. What is critical is that the job positions you for growth within the company or your chosen field.

One starting spot that rewards initiative handsomely is often overlooked — or looked down upon — by women. That position is sales. Insurance, brokerage and real estate firms will pay you at least a modest salary to learn the business. Commissions can quickly fatten the pay envelope once you master the skills. Most important, sales jobs provide avenues for advancement.

Careers

PART-TIME JOBS

A NEW class of high earners is working less and enjoying it more. The number of part-timers is fast expanding, and so is the list of employers welcoming them — and willing to pay them well.

To be a professional and a part-time worker was once a contradiction in terms. But no more. Today about 2,200,000 professionals, from surgeons to sales managers, choose to work part-time.

Inventive variations in part-time work are becoming more common. Some people put in a full 40 hours or more a week but for, say, only six months or less a year. For some married couples or for two women who want to partially re-enter the work place, job sharing makes a comfortable fit. What they do is divide one position's hours and responsibilities.

The part-time work that is easiest to get is in hard-to-find specialized skills. These include medicine, law, accounting, engineering and, especially, data processing. Professionals who have experience in these areas can find many jobs in federal agencies. The Federal Employees Part-Time Career Employment Act of 1978 opened 30,000 part-time positions, not only for scarce professionals but for middle managers as well. And at least 36 states now have policies permitting part-time positions in government.

Such jobs are harder to find in private industry because most corporations employ only a handful of part-time professionals. Yet some exceptional firms have large numbers of part-time posts, from engineer to loan officer. Among those employers are the Aerospace Corporation in El Segundo, California; the Equitable Life Assurance Society in New York City; and the First National Bank of Boston.

Of course, the fewer hours you put in on the job, the less money you take out. At least half of all part-timers get some fringe benefits, and a small but increasing number of companies offer full health insurance coverage. Typically, however, businesses prorate benefits or just don't provide any at all.

Since managers offer part-time work chiefly to hold onto valued employees, you have more chances to reduce your hours on an existing job than to find a new part-time position. The most persuasive way to convince your boss to cut your hours is to keep a record for two or three months of exactly what tasks you do and how much time you need to do them. That will help you estimate how much you could get done with fewer hours and what responsibilities could be shifted to others.

You also should be able to show how you would keep up with responsibilities that normally require full-time hours, such as travel and staff meetings. Always stress the *quality* of your work above the money the company would save on your salary.

Tracking down a part-time job at another company will take considerably more time and effort. Such positions above the clerical level are rarely advertised, while ads that promise high earnings for part-time work at home are primarily misleading come-ons for such travails as pushing hard-to-sell goods.

No employment agencies specialize in part-time placement of professionals. So you probably will have to carve a part-time place out of an available full-time position. The wisest way to find a part-time job is to send a résumé with a brief covering letter stating your qualifications and what services you can provide — part-time. If you get an interview, be prepared to explain how you would handle specific problems that a job might present for someone working part-time. Also, volunteer to go full-time when emergencies arise. And offer to work a scaled-down schedule on a trial basis for a few months.

For more information on how and where to get part-time jobs, you can write to the Association of Part-Time Professionals, Inc., Flow General Building, 7655 Old Springhouse Road, McLean, Virginia 22102; or New Ways to Work, 149 Ninth Street, San Francisco, California 94103.

Careers

PART-TIME JOBS IN ADULT EDUCATION

THE boom in adult education has brought a roaring demand for part-time teachers of subjects as diverse as programming a computer or finding a mate. If you have a skill, you might be able to earn some extra money by teaching it.

Men and women are going back to school by the millions to study an enormous range of subjects. They are interested in courses from the practical, such as How to Live Well Without Going Broke, to the whimsical, such as The Art of Social Climbing. The teachers whom most adults prefer are not ivory-tower academics but those who have earned their knowledge on the job and have direct experience to share.

As a part-time teacher of an adult education course, you can expect to earn perhaps $18 to $20 an hour. But if your course is extremely popular, you can make as much as $400 an hour. And all expenses connected with teaching are tax deductible. There are nonmonetary rewards, too, such as learning more about your field and gaining potential clients and business contacts.

The most popular subjects are: starting a small business, making money in stocks and bonds, and how to buy, use and program computers. Demand is also brisk for courses in physical fitness, assertiveness training, practical topics such as plumbing and bicycle repair, and affairs of the heart, from divorce to middle-age dating.

The best places to get part-time jobs in adult education are at community colleges, municipal recreation agencies or the fast-spreading, noncredit independent learning centers, such as Houston's Class Factory or New York City's Network for Learning. If you teach through a learning center, you usually will function as an independent contractor, taking 30% to 50% of the fees. Tuition generally ranges from $20 to $75 per student a course.

For its cut of your fees, the center will promote your course in its catalogues, handle student registration and give both you and your curriculum a sense of legitimacy.

Careers

COMPUTER JOBS

U NEMPLOYMENT has been painfully high, but computer jobs are going begging. Not enough people have the necessary skills. Demand for those with the right training is expected to increase not just by 10% or 20% by 1990 — but by 50%. We shall need well over 1,000,000 specialists in computer fields.

Already there is call for whole new armies of trained workers to run computers: for systems analysts, who devise ways for computers to handle information; for programmers, who tell the machines what to do; for technicians, who maintain and repair the complex equipment. The need is also great for people who can teach others to use the machines. Thus, out-of-work schoolteachers are profiting from the new technology. After some retooling, many teachers are finding jobs training employees at companies that use computers. Small wonder that John Kemeny, former president of Dartmouth College, says, "It is as unforgivable to let a student graduate without knowing how to use a computer as it was in the past to let him graduate without knowing how to use a library."

People throughout the work force can improve their job status if they learn to adapt to computers. Word processors may put some typists out of work, but secretaries can use the machines to do the dull part of their jobs while they take on more responsibility. Similarly, the fastest-moving business managers will be those who are the most creative in employing computers to streamline operations and save money.

If you do not know much about them, you can plug into the world of computers by taking night courses at community colleges that give you some experience with the machines. You also can learn to program computers by enrolling full-time at one of the schools that specialize in retraining. The price can be steep, $3,000 or $4,000. Often, however, your employer will pay for much or all of your retraining course.

The cheapest way to start learning about computers is by reading specialized magazines, such as *Popular Computing*. That will set you back only $2.50. Or for a bit more you can buy a book on the subject. One thorough text that is easy to read is *Introduction to Computers and Data Processing* by Gary Shelly and Thomas J. Cashman. It is put out by Anaheim Publishing Company and costs $20.95 — money well spent.

[77]

Careers

COMPUTER SYSTEMS ANALYSTS

SOME people believe that computers may be wiping out countless traditional jobs, but rich career opportunities are opening up for computer systems analysts. They are the troubleshooters of the electronic age, working for most large companies as well as schools, hospitals and government agencies. The number of jobs in the field is expected to grow by about one-third in the 1980s. A shortage of analysts is expected, and that would kick up their pay. It is already high, about $25,000 to $38,000 — or more in some large cities.

Systems analysts seldom work directly on computers — some do not even know how to — but they have to understand what the machines can do. Their job is to figure out ways computers can solve problems. In brief, systems analysts are the human masters behind the electronic brains. They determine how to save a company time, effort and money. The analyst can streamline billing, keep track of inventory moving around the warehouse and devise ways to pull together a company's financial records.

Suppose a company wants to computerize its payroll department. Call for the systems analyst! He or she has to spend a few weeks in the department poring over records and interviewing people who work there. Next, the analyst makes up a list of all the pieces of raw data that go into calculating the payroll. For example, if the company has employees in more than one state, the details of each state's tax code have to be on the list. Finally, the analyst turns the list over to the computer programmer and gives him or her step-by-step instructions on how the computer is to put all that data together to produce the correct paycheck for each employee.

The instructions sound like gibberish. An opening sentence might read: "Build a table in working storage to accommodate 1,000 batch numbers." But that is as good as plain English to the programmer, who translates the instructions into terms the computer understands and does the physical work on the machine. Systems analysts can spend a whole year computerizing a payroll — and then come back if a major change is needed.

Suppose you or someone you know would like to become a computer analyst. To qualify, you usually need a few years' experience in the industry where you want to work. It helps considerably if you have had exposure to the company's financial dealings.

Many analysts have never been to college. They simply learned computer programming in night school, got jobs in a company's data-processing department and then moved up to the higher-paid post of systems analyst. True, companies are looking for people with a bachelor's or even master's degree in business from a school with a well-regarded computer science curriculum. But given a choice, employers still prefer an analyst who knows the company's business to one whose computer training is strong.

The basic skill required by systems analysts is the ability to communicate well. That is because they have to find out from a company's employees what jobs they want done. Nonanalysts often have an exaggerated notion of the wonders that computers can perform. A good analyst has to mesh these expectations with the realities of what computers actually can accomplish.

Are there any drawbacks to this career? The one serious complaint is that there are no well-traveled paths to top management. Usually the best an analyst can hope for is to become chief of computer operations. But analysts' jobs do take them around the company, from department to department. So a fortunate analyst may catch the eye of an executive who might offer him jobs that would move him into the company's mainstream.

Careers

ENGINEERS

IN Help Wanted ads around the country, one message is loud and clear: engineers are needed — badly. The computer revolution and other high-tech developments will fuel a huge demand for them throughout the decade. The Labor Department estimates that the U.S. will need at least 250,000 more engineers in 1990 than in 1980. Colleges will be hard pressed to educate enough people to fill all the jobs. There is one exception. Because of the recent construction slump, demand is low for civil engineers who design buildings, roads, refineries and power plants. But this could change fast if the economy starts to grow rapidly.

Spurred by equal opportunity laws, companies are bidding up salaries for women and blacks and other minorities in engineering. In fact, women often start out at higher pay than men. In the early 1970s, only 3% of all engineering students were women; at some schools now they make up 20% of the freshman class. Highly regarded engineering schools are at the University of California, Illinois, Michigan, MIT and Stanford. Of course, quality teaching is available in lesser-known schools, too.

Generally, oil, chemical and drug companies pay the most; government agencies and colleges the least. In many companies, engineering is a route to the top. Chief executives at Exxon, Westinghouse and AT&T started as engineers.

The higher the climb, the less engineering is practiced. Some engineers who prefer the drawing board to administrative chores choose not to advance. So a number of companies promote pure technicians to some sort of consulting or distinguished fellow status. These jobs carry salaries of $70,000 to $80,000 — roughly equivalent to upper middle management.

With the rapid pace of technological change, engineers constantly have to re-educate themselves. They say that their usable knowledge has a half-life of eight years. That is, half of what an engineer knows when he starts out is obsolete in that time.

Careers

HEALTH ADMINISTRATORS

Health care administration is a flourishing profession that gives you the chance to do well by doing good. Managing a hospital or nursing home is much like managing any enterprise — except that the decisions can determine whether someone lives or dies.

What a health care administrator does depends largely on the size of the institution he works for. A director of a 1,100-bed New York hospital spends his days and about a third of his evenings in meetings — on how to contain costs, raise funds, recruit specialists and whether to invest in the latest equipment. His salary is around $100,000 a year.

The administrator of a 70-bed hospital and nursing home in a small town in Idaho has plenty of meetings, too, but typically they are with surgeons about improving the light in the operating room or with the dietitian about how to contain the costs of meals. She also squeezes in visits to patients. Her salary is $30,000 — but, like her big-city counterpart, she also comes away with a sense of accomplishment.

As running medical institutions has become more complex, the administrative ranks have swelled to include not only the director or administrator, but also many middle managers who are skilled in accounting and market research. Some 200,000 people work in the field. In the next ten years, another 100,000 jobs will open up.

Many will be outside the medical institution — for example, in government agencies, where administrators may analyze regional needs for health care. Some experts also are hired by insurance companies, where they may design new types of coverage. Quite a few of the best opportunities are in the fast-expanding health maintenance organizations, which sell prepaid medical plans entitling subscribers to the services of a staff of salaried physicians.

Jobs in health administration can be both exciting and frustrating. At any moment, a hospital administrator is apt to get a call: a child needs a blood transfusion but her parents forbid it on religious grounds. On the spot, the administrator must decide whether to get a court order or go ahead with treatment.

These jobs call for stamina and patience. Administrators must wrestle with aggrieved patients and their relatives, feisty community groups, unions, demanding doctors and trustees. Administrators share chronic problems: too little money, too few nurses, constant turnover among low-paid aides, and strict, ever-changing government regulations. But the psychic rewards can be rich.

To get a job in the field, you usually have to have a bachelor of science degree or, for high-level positions, a master of business administration or a master of health administration. Some 20 schools offer undergraduate degrees in health administration; the two best regarded are the University of New Hampshire and Penn State. Among the outstanding graduate programs, all two-year courses, are those at the universities of Chicago, Michigan, Minnesota and Washington.

The average starting salary for an administrative assistant with a graduate degree is $24,000, except in nursing homes where it is $18,000. After 10 years' experience, the figure jumps to anywhere from $30,000 for a nursing home manager to $70,000 for the administrator of a hospital. Directors of hospital chains earn $100,000 or more.

People who want hospital careers can improve their prospects by joining chains such as the Hospital Corporation of America. And nursing home administrators are in such short supply that a number of states allow them to head more than one nursing home.

Careers

MANAGEMENT CONSULTANTS

As corporate profits become harder to achieve, demand will rise for those corporate doctors, the management consultants. So business school graduates are rushing into the field. During the mid-1980s, consulting should flourish as clients seek help with lagging productivity, inflation and new product development.

Most of the best beginning positions are with consulting firms or with public accounting firms that offer consulting services. To land a job with a top outfit, you usually need an M.B.A. from a first-rate school. A few years' work experience also will get you in the door. People seeking a second career in management consulting can bring it off only if they offer solid grounding in a specialty. A product manager at a major consumer goods company, for example, could turn into a consumer marketing consultant.

It is not uncommon for high-ranking graduates of the best business schools to start in management consulting firms at $30,000 or more — sometimes much more. Since their services are so expensive, successful consultants must be able to get to the root of a problem and produce solutions quickly. A consultant must be articulate, assertive and versatile enough to sell his or her solution to the assistant plant managers, as well as the company president, without offending either.

One drawback, even for those who like consulting, is travel. Executives of big firms say their staff members spend 30% of their time on the road. Another complaint is that consulting gives you influence but no real power to enforce decisions. But for bright young comers who are not sure where they want to work, consulting provides exposure within a corporation and a stepping-stone to a top-line job.

Careers

PARALEGALS

For a good career in the law without spending the time and money to get a law degree, think about becoming a paralegal. The Bureau of Labor Statistics estimates that the number of paralegal jobs will more than double, to almost 66,000, from 1980 to 1990. The median starting salary is $17,000.

Paralegals work for lawyers, researching cases and drafting documents. There is no standard licensing exam for them. Some law firms train their own paralegals, but many others prefer to hire a graduate of a certificate program. These are usually two semesters long, and they are offered by colleges and vocational schools. For a list of such programs, contact your state bar association. Or write to the American Bar Association's Standing Committee on Legal Assistants, 1155 East 60th Street, Chicago, Illinois 60637.

Careers

SECRETARIES

Tens of thousands of secretarial jobs are going begging as women turn their backs on traditional career roles.

Not long ago, the Bank of America declared that on any given day it was advertising openings for 30 secretaries. Of those who responded, many were overqualified college graduates who could not find jobs in their chosen fields, so they were unhappy from the start. Quite a few of the rest were inadequately trained high school graduates. The shortage of competent secretaries remains severe, and it is likely to grow worse. The Department of Labor estimates that 300,000 secretarial jobs will open up every year during the 1980s. Employers probably will court secretaries by boosting pay and by making it easier to advance to better jobs.

A record 3.8 million secretaries are now employed, yet one out of five jobs that open up goes unfilled. Firms seeking women who will stay in secretarial positions often hire back-to-work housewives who got their training 20 years ago. Their skills, employers report, tend to be superb and their work ethic excellent.

The complaint is common that today's high school graduates do not have the basic skills. As the women's movement has dimmed the desire for secretarial work, the number of students who want to learn shorthand has diminished. Many schools offer only a beginning course, though it usually takes three semesters to become proficient. High schools do not emphasize spelling and grammar the way they used to, so that many grads have trouble writing business letters.

Today, beginners start at $10,000 to $14,000 a year. Pay tends to be lowest in the South and Midwest and highest on the East and West coasts. The range for experienced secretaries is from $15,000 to $18,700, though many earn more than $20,000 and a few top $30,000. Those who take shorthand can make $1,500 to $2,000 more than those who do not, and a bachelor of arts degree can command up to $3,000 more than a high school diploma.

Job aspirants who can afford $4,900 may take an 8-month course at Katharine Gibbs, the country's best-known secretarial school. The curriculum includes the usual skills plus electronic word processing and accounting. There is also a course in poise — called professional development — which requires students to observe themselves on video-

[85]

tape as they perform their duties. A dress code prevails too: no jeans, sneakers or clogs.

Only 1% of secretaries are men, and that is not expected to increase because most think it's a woman's job. One man who disagrees is Herbert Nelson, secretary to the Chairman of the *Bergen Record,* a New Jersey newspaper. After 21 years, he still spends most of his time taking dictation and typing, and draws an imposing salary of $60,000.

The payoff for top skills in many companies is that a secretary's career path follows her boss's. When he gets a promotion he takes her with him, a practice sometimes called "fate-sharing." Militant women complain that this reduces secretaries to appendages of their bosses. They urge management to post job openings scrupulously and to encourage women to apply for higher-ranking jobs. Indeed, many of them do move into management. With demand for competent secretaries at an all-time high, opportunities to advance should become greater than ever.

Secretaries who stay in their jobs say they enjoy them for two reasons. They get to know a lot about what is going on in a company without having to take the heavy responsibility for it, and they enjoy helping their bosses be more productive. They make it easier for him — or her — to succeed, and when he — or she — does, they share the satisfaction.

Careers

TEACHERS

MANY teachers are finding lucrative jobs outside the schools and colleges. They are switching from the schoolroom to the corporate-run training room.

During the 1980s, millions of computer buyers will need instruction. So will millions of office and factory workers. More than 300 corporations run remedial classes in English and math. Large banks and insurance companies provide the most remedial education. The person likely to do the hiring of teachers is the director of training and development. The median salary is $31,700.

If you are a teacher, an essential strategy for making the switch is to develop — and use — acquaintances in business. Serve on school committees that have ties to local industry or participate in community organizations where you are likely to meet people in business.

Once you are in the corporate door, you can pick up other industrial training specialties. And from there you might be able to move to a job in management.

Careers

SUCCESSFUL TECHNIQUES OF HUNTING FOR A JOB

Job hunting is a skill, and it is fairly easy to learn how to do it right. Once you master a few techniques, you will greatly increase your chances of getting a job — whether you are entering the employment market for the first time or looking for a new position.

Take a case of how *not* to do it:

He seemed to have everything a job hunter could want: intelligence, charm and one of corporate America's prized credentials — a Harvard M.B.A. To distinguish himself, however, he wore a baseball cap as well as his three-piece suit to job interviews. He did indeed stick out — but he also struck out. Despite dozens of interviews, he got no offers.

The problem, of course, was the cap. Instead of marking him as a go-getting individualist, the hat told recruiters that he lacked self-confidence and was overly concerned with image. He had tried but misapplied the first rule of job hunting: stand out from the pack. The way to do that is to do your own research into the company and its business, ask probing questions, and project certainty about yourself and your career goals without appearing smug.

The first hurdle in job hunting is to get an interview with prospective employers. Perhaps friends, business acquaintances or alumni of your high school or college can recommend you to employers whom they — or *their* friends — know personally. If all else fails, you might get an interview by writing directly to the employer. Send a forceful letter outlining your achievements and likely contributions to the company. But don't use such ruses as implying that you are something other than a job applicant.

Résumés are important, but they are not worth the incredibly long hours many job seekers invest in them. You probably can spend your time better in researching the company and thinking about how you specifically can be useful to it. The ideal résumé is no longer than one page. It should concentrate not on descriptions of your previous jobs but on your accomplishments: for example, "I increased sales 50% in six months." Don't exaggerate. An applicant who stretches the truth even about something innocuous will be branded as dishonest.

In preparing for your job interview, you have to look on yourself as a product for sale — cold-blooded as that may seem. First, you have to decide what the product is going to be — that is, what skills and qualities you have to offer an employer. The next step is to package your product well and to devise a strategy for selling it.

Like any salesman, you might practice your pitch on friends. But be prepared for the interviewer to throw some tough stock questions. One favorite is, "Tell me a little about yourself." A poor response to that begins, "Well, I was born on . . ." You would do much better to say something like: "Lately I've discovered that I can combine my abilities to . . ." and then go on to state specifically what you can do.

What you wear to the interview matters less than you may think. Of course, a serious applicant for a job at a traditional firm shouldn't wear a scarlet jacket and white bucks or a diaphanous dress with a plunging neckline, not to mention a baseball cap. When in doubt, the best advice is to go conservative.

Since interviewers are impressed by applicants who ask sharp questions, it is wise to study the firm and its industry. You can read the company's annual report, ask a stockbroker for any written analyses of the firm and learn more about it in business reference books at a library.

Your sales presentation begins the moment you show up for the interview. Some personnel managers base their judgment partly on the office receptionist's reaction. If the applicant is rude to the receptionist, he will not get the job, no matter how smart he looks in the interview. It shows he is a two-class person.

Corporate recruiters recommend some techniques to help you stand out during an interview:

— Carry a folder marked with the company name — and take notes. That shows you are well organized.

— Convey enthusiasm. Try to turn your weaknesses into advantages. If an interviewer suggests that you lack qualifications, you can say that you are a fast learner who welcomes challenges — and then give an example.

— Prepare what vaudevillians used to call a "get-off line" — a parting comment that moves the recruiter closer to an offer. You might ask, for example, whether he sees any obstacles to hiring you.

Careers

WHAT TO DO IF YOU GET FIRED

Getting fired does not have to be the end of the world. Hard as it is to maintain your composure while the blade is descending, it's imperative not to lose your head as you are getting the ax. Losing your job should lead you to reappraise your whole career, and that could open new vistas.

The chances of becoming re-employed improve significantly if you proceed in a businesslike way. Keep your emotions in check and your wits sharp. Remember, there is considerable truth in those counselors' platitudes that you should devote at least six hours a day to the search, write 15 to 20 letters each week and consider job hunting to be a job in itself.

One practical reason for keeping your cool is that the person firing you might give you good leads to other jobs. And he is sometimes in a position to sweeten the terms of separation.

Although most firms have well-defined termination benefits, there is often surprising latitude in practice. For example, if you are a manager of any kind, it is reasonable to ask for up to six months' salary. Also ask for extension of group life and health benefits for at least as many weeks as you are collecting severance pay.

As quickly as possible, you should try to have letters of recommendation written by the person of your choice in the company. In addition, request a desk, telephone and secretarial help somewhere in the company. But to save face, it is wise to leave your old desk quickly.

Prepare for a long job search, particularly if your salary needs are high. Figure on one month of hunting for each $10,000 of salary.

Most people are paralyzed by anxiety for the first week or two. After that, they should force themselves to start looking. Counselors warn that this isn't the time for a vacation or other costly indulgence.

You should examine every option — such as moving to another city or changing careers. The biggest mistake some people make in their lives is to act as if they were born with a tag on their big toe that reads "I'm a middle manager" or "I'm an auto worker" or whatever.

But don't lurch into rash career decisions under pressure of finding another job. Don't switch careers out of anger at what has just happened to you. And don't go back to school simply to get away from the competitiveness of the job market.

You might browse through two books that career counselors recommend: *The Termination Handbook* by Robert Coulson, and *The Executive's Guide to Finding a Superior Job* by William A. Cohen. At the same time, update your résumé. List your objectives only in broad terms so as not to limit the kinds of openings interviewers might consider you for. A useful book is *The Perfect Résumé* by Tom Jackson.

A natural impulse is to call friends in other companies in hopes of immediately finding a new job. But that's simply trying to prove to your ex-boss and yourself that he had poor judgment in letting you go. The right time to begin calling around for leads is after you have a résumé and know where you would like to work.

Wangling job interviews is easier if you can use your friends for entrée. But if you have to start cold, one of the best devices is to write an enticing letter to the person who is in a position to hire. In four crisp paragraphs, outline why you are writing, who you are in terms of your previous titles and responsibilities, what you can do for the corporation you are writing to, and why you deserve a hearing.

Follow up your letter in a week or so with a phone call, but try not to sound too eager for the interview. If a potential employer senses that you are desperate, you've had it.

What do you say when a job interviewer asks whether you were fired from your last position? Don't hide it, lie about it or even dance around it. Being fired just does not carry the same stigma that it did 10 years ago. With so many mergers and corporate consolidations, it can mean simply that you were in the wrong place at the wrong time.

When you are looking for a new job, remember that personnel managers are impressed by someone who talks openly and honestly about himself. You can battle nervousness by rehearsing the job interview with a friend, preferably someone who personally has done some hiring. And although you want to cast yourself in a radiant light, managers really do appreciate a balanced self-appraisal. They like to hear a job applicant volunteer not just what he is good at, but where he is weak, too. Indeed, no one ever fits an employer's requirements perfectly.

It is equally important to have done your homework about the company and its field. Someone who has analyzed the firm's record and can speculate about its future impresses personnel executives much more than a job seeker who comes in asking, "What do you have open?"

Even if an interview goes splendidly, you probably will have to wait for a job to open. Without being overly pushy, the dedicated hunter finds reasons to keep in touch with potential employers. It is always wise to mail a thank-you note. You might even send along some news clippings or other information that might intrigue your interviewer.

But in the interview, don't be afraid to come right out and ask for a promising job. Like a salesman who is reticent about closing a sale, a job hunter who is squeamish can wreck his or her own carefully constructed campaign.

Careers

THE PERILS OF JOB HOPPING

For those people who wonder whether the surest way to the top is to hop from job to job within a given field, or to stay with one company, here's a good word for fidelity. Job hopping may have its short-term attractions for ambitious people, but those at the top know it pays to stay with one employer. Eugene Jennings, a Michigan State University professor, tracked the careers of corporate presidents since 1953. He found that more than half of them remained loyal to one company.

True enough, job hopping can help you gain valuable training and experience in the early stages of your career. After that, the best reason to switch jobs is to overcome obstacles in your career path, such as a hostile boss or a demotion. Yes, job hopping is the accepted way to move up the ladder in a few volatile lines of work, such as advertising, television, fashion design, marketing, publishing and retailing. In recent years, the demand for hoppers has risen especially in high technology and information processing.

But elsewhere, restless job switchers sometimes are suspected of being merely opportunistic, perhaps unable to get along with co-workers or unable to complete a job. And the rewards of job hopping can be fleeting. Professor Jennings found that though managers increased their salaries by 35% on average when they changed companies, those of equal ability who stayed on did *even better.*

Some job hoppers may sacrifice substantial benefits. For example, a sound reason to stay with one company is that your pension increases with your years of service.

Jennings calls job hopping a "high-risk maneuver" that "fails as often as it works." New jobs sometimes do not turn out to be as alluring as first perceived, or new bosses as charming. Even if the hopper succeeds at fulfilling a specific new assignment, he risks being stereotyped as fit only for that role. Job hoppers sometimes deceive themselves into thinking they have improved their position. In one survey, 85% of those who changed their jobs thought that their moves had helped them, but their new bosses reported that only 46% had actually advanced. So executive recruiters warn that job hopping within a field often should be a last resort.

Careers

HOW TO CHANGE YOUR CAREER

AMERICA is still a land where opportunities abound to improve your economic situation — in fact, to change your life by starting a new career or moving to a new community. We remain a nation of Daniel Boones looking for elbow room: Americans move an average of thirteen times during their lives and switch jobs about ten times. Each year, 2.5 million people enroll in courses designed to help them enter new professions.

Turnabouts in mid-career have been fairly common since colonial times. George Washington abandoned a long career as a surveyor to become a farmer. Jimmy Carter was 38 when he left peanut farming for the Georgia Senate. And Ronald Reagan was 55 when he gave up his movie career to enter full-time politics.

But today the reasons for veering off established career paths to explore whole new fields are often quite different from what they were just a few years ago. Career counselors say that mid-life job changers no longer complain about too little advancement or too little pay. Their reason for switching now is more likely to be a desire for personal satisfaction even though that often means lower pay and relocation to a job in another city.

People who have tired of commuter schedules and corporate politics often look for more autonomy. Teachers, social workers and doctors often say they reach a burnout point of physical or mental exhaustion; they tend to seek out less demanding professions. One teacher of emotionally disturbed children contends she felt guilty when she first took a job as a tour consultant for a motel chain. Now she wonders why she did not make the change several years ago.

Above all, the successful career changers are adaptable. Even though the switches do not always prove perfect, most people say the experience is worth the strain because it lets them regain control of their workaday destiny.

You can lessen your chances of making a big mistake in career switching if you turn to the right sources of information and counseling. For a good start, read a book called *Burnout*, which is published by The Free Press and costs $24.95. *Burnout* provides a thoughtful description of this increasingly common problem and ways to deal with it.

The most popular book that coaches people in career switching is Richard Bolles's *What Color Is Your Parachute?*, published by Ten Speed Press. This $7.95 paperback emphasizes self-evaluation and defining your goals.

[93]

The General Electric Company has developed useful workbooks to help you figure out what you want from life and to determine how well you're doing in your job. The titles are *Career Dimensions I* and *Career Dimensions II*. Volume I costs $6 and Volume II is $20. Write to General Electric, P.O. Box 368, Croton-on-Hudson, New York 10520.

For information about specific jobs, you can start in the reference section of the public library. Look for the Department of Labor's *Occupational Outlook Handbook* or *The Encyclopedia of Careers and Vocational Guidance*. Both tell you how to break into a field, and they explain the kind of work done in a variety of occupations. Then head again for a bookstore. For $9.95 you can buy the *American Almanac of Jobs and Salaries;* published by Avon, it lists pay scales in various fields. The *National Job-Finding Guide*, published by Dolphin at $12.95, can help you determine if the career you are considering is thriving in the places where you might want to live.

If the change you are thinking about requires you to earn a college degree, shop for a school that will give you academic credit for your achievements in life. Regional directories called *Wherever You Learned It* list the degree-granting policies of some 530 schools. You can order directories at $10 each from the nonprofit Council for the Advancement of Experiential Learning, Lakefront North, Columbia, Maryland 21044.

An excellent source for women wanting to re-enter or advance in the job market is the nonprofit Catalyst organization's network of 200 resource centers throughout the country. These offer career and educational counseling. Catalyst also has an impressive career library in its headquarters at 14 East 60th Street, New York City 10022.

You can't learn everything from books, of course, so speak with people in the fields you are considering. Professional and trade associations and college alumni groups will give you names. Use your free hours to work part-time in your new job before you plunge in. Even a pot-scrubber learns about such frustrations of running a restaurant as no-show reservations, late deliveries and long hours. And if you do better with a team than a tome, consider taking one of the courses or workshops in career change offered by community colleges and universities. The National Center for Educational Brokering (325 9th Street, San Francisco, California 94103) is working on a directory of these programs, due out in 1984.

If you are thinking of making a change, some public libraries offer free courses in self-assessment and job evaluation. Universities, community colleges, YM and YWCAs often have courses in career guidance for $200 or less. Private career counselors charge from $300 to $1,000 for several sessions.

Most of us also have undiscovered talents—artistic skills or money-making aptitudes—that we might not be aware of. If you want to make a career change and need help discovering a slumbering skill, consider having your abilities professionally tested. One of the oldest and best-known testers in the U.S. is the Johnson O'Connor Research Foundation. It charges $350 for 11½ hours of testing and evaluation of your aptitudes for logical analysis, artistic or musical talents and even executive ability. The foundation has 15 testing centers around the country. To get a list of them, write to Johnson O'Connor at 11 East 62nd Street, New York, New York 10021. Or call 212–838–0550.

Caterers

SAVING ON ENTERTAINING

Entertaining can be draining, but if you are thinking of having a party, you can save time and trouble by holding a catered affair. How do you keep the price within bounds?

It pays to bear in mind that small parties usually cost even more per person than large ones with the same menu. A catered meal at home for fewer than 25 people approaches restaurant prices. In New York City, a trendy dinner at home for 12 can run $600, plus an additional $150 for three people to help serve; liquor and wine will be extra. The total could easily be well over $750. So if your group is smaller than a couple dozen, a restaurant might be cheaper.

Still, it's possible to treat yourself to the luxury of a catered affair without paying luxury prices. Avoid large caterers and those that emphasize exotic foods. They can charge $50 a person for food alone. Instead, seek out small caterers or those new to the business. They often give far better service at lower prices. And look for catering firms that will prepare dishes *you* can heat and serve yourself.

Don't rent china, silver or linen. You could pay about $6 a setting. You are better off borrowing, or even buying, your own.

Another way to pare costs is to get by with less help, particularly those bartenders and waiters who collect $25 to $50 for an evening's work. Instead of the caterer's workers, waitresses or bartenders, enlist some college students or neighborhood teenagers who serve for half as much.

Don't let caterers provide drinks or setups. The mark-ups on them are intoxicating, so buy your own.

And if you want music or live entertainment, you can save a lot when you hire talented students from a local college or music conservatory to do the playing.

Cocktail parties, of course, are cheaper than fancy dinners. You also can lower food costs by scheduling your cocktail party for a time when people tend to be less ravenous. Guests may only nibble at the hors d'oeuvres at an open house scheduled from 3 p.m. to 5 p.m., but a reception from 6 p.m. to 8 p.m. substitutes for dinner for many party-goers. Caterers estimate that most guests will down three or four drinks at a two-hour party.

Wedding receptions introduce special expenses. For 100 guests, a wedding cake might add $100 to $200. Champagne for a toast could mean at least 20 bottles—or $150 for an inexpensive kind.

The Yellow Pages list columns of "caterers"; still, the best way to find one is to ask people who have used caterers in the past. If you work for a company, check with the person there who arranges corporate entertainment. Sometimes officers of churches, temples and fraternal organizations also know the reputations of local firms that cater parties in their halls.

Once you have gathered a few recommendations, call and get a price estimate from each firm. Before you telephone, figure out what you can spend—and what kind of people will be at your party. If you have invited many big drinkers, for example, you can cut back on food. They tend to eat less than those who drink only a little.

Ask any caterer you are considering if you may observe—at a discreet distance—a party he has arranged. Most caterers will agree and also let you sample the food. Once you have chosen a firm, be prepared to sign a contract that protects both sides from surprises. For instance, taxes and tips are sometimes included in the quoted price, but not always. Usually you will be required to pay a deposit of up to 50% with the balance due immediately before or after the party.

Book at least a month in advance for a cocktail party, and at least several months for a large wedding. You would be wise to call even earlier for a date in May, June, November or December—they are the peak seasons.

If you must cancel, call the caterer immediately. Each firm has its own refund policy but, with several days' notice, most will return all of your deposit in the hopes that you will re-schedule and call the caterer again.

Certificates of Deposit

BROKERAGE HOUSE CDS

You can get as much as one full percentage point more interest on your savings by putting your money into a certificate of deposit at a brokerage house instead of a bank. Many stockbrokers now buy small-denomination CDs in bulk from banks. The brokers then offer the certificates to the public in $5,000 units. The CDs are federally insured up to $100,000.

In mid-1983 some brokerage houses were offering 2½-year CDs at 10% and 10-year certificates at close to 11%.

When you buy CDs through a broker, you can take your money out before maturity without the early withdrawal penalty you would pay if you cashed it at the bank. And you will not be charged a commission.

Brokers trade CDs the way they trade bonds. So, if interest rates rise after you buy a CD, your certificate's value falls. But if rates drop, you can sell out early at a profit.

Charities

HOW TO RAISE MONEY FOR YOUR FAVORITE CAUSE

Raising money for your favorite charity takes the persuasiveness of a politician and the tough hide of a door-to-door salesman. Particularly in this time of tight budgets and federal cutbacks, any volunteer fund-raiser needs one other attribute as well: the ingenuity of an inventor to concoct clever ways to get donations.

If you are a volunteer fund-raiser, it will pay you to stage events that go beyond the standard charity ball. People around the country are raising money by sponsoring book fairs, art shows, auctions and much more. Whatever device you choose, it has to be something quite special. You have to have a gimmick.

A very successful one is the "no-dinner dinner." Rather than ask donors to pay hundreds of dollars to dress up and spend yet another Saturday night in a dull hotel ballroom, some charities let their supporters off the hook by telling them: "Just send the check and you can stay home."

When people support a nonprofit group, they usually get a warm feeling and a tax deduction. But it won't hurt your charity's bottom line to offer them something more. One such lure is the chance to purchase what money can't buy. With a little digging you can discover priceless opportunities that can be sold for a price. For example, at a St. Louis Arts Council auction, several music lovers bid for a chance to conduct the St. Louis Symphony in one of its regular evening performances.

If your charity sells donated goods or services, anything from crocheted potholders to dinner with the mayor, the money that's raised generally is not taxed. But before your charity sells anything to the public, it's smart to check with an accountant or a lawyer. You may have to pay taxes on your profits if your enterprise is not *directly* related to the purpose for which your group was granted tax-exempt status.

One other tip: most charities follow the 50% rule: if you don't earn at least a 50% profit on your fund-raising event, you haven't done your job efficiently.

A favorite means of achieving that profit is to hold an auction. The charity gets all the proceeds from the sale of donated items. And there are enticing tax deductions for both the donors and the buyers as well.

For example, if a contributor gives your charity six bottles of valuable wine from his private cellar, he can deduct their fair market value — say, $200. That price is printed in the auction catalogue. Then, if the winning bidder pays *more* than that for the wine, say $300, the bidder can deduct the extra amount — in this case $100 — as his donation to your charity.

When gathering goods and services to be auctioned off, ask for donations from as many individuals and businesses as possible — and nothing is too wild. Some auctions have included enough cement to repave a driveway (that was given by a construction firm) and even a gallbladder operation, which was contributed by a civic-minded surgeon.

Entertainment and vacation offerings are popular. A couple might contribute the use of their faraway vacation home for a week or two. You might persuade a travel agency to donate air fare to the destination.

Some staples at charity auctions include dinners given by restaurants. But even dinners need not be routine. Volunteers in several charities have persuaded their city mayors or other local celebrities to cook and serve a meal in the home of the highest bidder. It's amazing how often celebrities will help out a worthy charity. Yes, you will have to spend something to stage your fund-raising event, but those headlinable outsiders can help reduce your expenses. Ideally, you should keep costs to about one-third of the amount of the total receipts — by begging and borrowing as much as you can.

Charities

GUIDES TO SENSIBLE GIVING

AMERICANS give some $40 billion a year to thousands of charities. The average donor contributes 2% of pre-tax income. That's much less than the biblical tithe of 10%, but much more than people in other countries contribute. If you want your donations to do the most good, you should make a careful analysis before you give. Charity begins with homework.

Commonly, donors give small amounts to many charities. Yet it would make more sense for you to give fewer but bigger contributions. That's because the smaller your gift, the larger the share that will be spent on fund raising and overhead.

One local charity that you might wisely include on your list is the United Way — the well-known coalition of many health and welfare groups in your community. Some critics argue that the United Way supports only established charities such as the Red Cross and the YMCA and excludes newer groups such as minority and women's organizations. If such complaints bother you, just ask your United Way solicitor for a list of the charities that the organization distributed money to last year. If you don't endorse some of those groups, you may be able to make a "negative designation" on your donation card. Groups you mark off won't get any of your contribution. But you are likely to endorse most United Way recipients. So unless you are planning to send separate checks to most of them, donating to the United Way is an efficient method of helping a wide variety of local groups.

Make sure that your contributions to individual charities are tax-deductible. The IRS will allow you to claim gifts to most religious, educational, social welfare and health groups. But several that solicit widely for funds — such as Handgun Control, Incorporated, and the Moral Majority — are classified as lobbying groups. They are tax-exempt themselves, but your donations to them are not tax-deductible. If you are in doubt about any group, just ask the IRS for a copy of a so-called determination letter, which will state whether or not your donations will be taxed.

You can write to any charity and request both an independently audited financial statement and an annual report of the programs that the charity sponsors. If any group fails to respond, you probably will not want to give money to it.

Once you get the data from a charity, a couple of independent watchdog groups can help you interpret it. One is the National Information Bureau, which has thorough reports on hundreds of charities that solicit nationwide.

The reports include analyses of balance sheets, income statements and activities.

By mailing a postcard to the National Information Bureau, you can get a copy of its *Wise Giving Guide*, which lists the groups that either meet its standards, fail to meet them or have not responded to its requests for information. In a recent guide, for example, 145 groups — as disparate as the Sierra Club and the Puerto Rican Legal Defense and Education Fund — met the bureau's standards. But 45 charities did not meet them and another 65 groups did not provide adequate information to the bureau. If you request them, the bureau also will send you, free, up to three extensive reports on separate charities. The address is National Information Bureau, 419 Park Avenue South, New York, New York 10016.

Another watchdog group is the Council of Better Business Bureaus' Philanthropic Advisory Service, or PAS. It scores hundreds of national charities on reliability and responsiveness. For $1 and a self-addressed, stamped envelope, the PAS will send you its bimonthly guide to organizations that do or don't meet its standards. Its address is Philanthropic Advisory Service, 1515 Wilson Boulevard, Arlington, Virginia 22209. In addition, the Better Business Bureau in your own city often can give you similar information on local charities.

Children

THE COST OF KIDS

F OR many married people in the baby-boom generation, having children is not a fact of life but a matter of choice. Often they are postponing children because they worry that kids cost too much. But what is the real cost of raising children?

Bringing up baby is more expensive today than at any time in history. That's partly because the luxuries of a generation ago are considered middle-class birthrights today. The U.S. Department of Agriculture concludes that raising a child to age 18 costs anywhere from $81,000 to $117,000. But SAGE Associates, an economic consulting firm in Washington, is more generous than your kid's Uncle Sam. It estimates that a high-income couple will spend $278,399 by the time their son, born this year, turns 18. A daughter costs $17,000 more.

If Mom stays home until Junior toddles off to kindergarten, her lost income from a job could amount to another $116,000. And that dollar cost may be compounded by atrophying skills and evaporating seniority.

Knowing when the expenses of childhood rise and fall can help you prepare for them. Newborns come into the world at considerable cost. Routine hospital and delivery fees run about $2,300, and an untroubled caesarean birth adds some $1,150. But from age one to five or six, the costs of child-rearing are relatively low. This is the time parents should stash away cash in money-market funds, deep-discount bonds and other investments to pay for the expenses that start moving up as soon as the child goes off to school and really climb with the teenage years.

Puberty is pricey, due in part to dating and all its accoutrements. The annual insurance premium on your car can more than double with a 16-year-old son at the wheel. At 17, child-rearing costs are three times higher than the costs in the birth year. Welcome to the groves of academe and the most expensive years in a child's life. If you have — or plan to have — children, you can prepare now for those predictable costs ahead. Start by checking what your health insurance covers. A good maternity package in a group policy will pay two-thirds of the typical $2,300 in hospital and physician's fees for the birth of a child. Later on, most policies do not cover the routine examinations of a healthy baby. So, unless you belong to a health maintenance organization, you will have to budget at least $400 for those monthly visits to the pediatrician during a baby's first year.

While your child is still a preschooler and expenses are relatively low, the money you wisely start putting away for the future will grow along with the kid. You can save or invest some of your own income in your child's name. The interest, dividends and capital gains on that money will be taxed at the child's lower rate — usually nothing at all. Consult a lawyer, tax accountant or financial adviser to figure out the best way to do this. But there are three strategies.

First, *each* parent can give a child up to $10,000 a year without having to pay any federal gift tax on it. A gift, however, is irrevocable, and when your child legally becomes an adult, he will be able to spend it as he wishes, whether on college or cocaine.

Second, you may establish a so-called Clifford Trust, with the child as beneficiary. A Clifford Trust reverts to its owner 10 years and one day after the last deposit. In the meantime, any income earned on the money is taxed at the child's rate.

Finally, you can lend money to your child without charging interest. If the funds are invested, any dividends or interest are taxed at the child's rate. This is called a Crown loan. A Crown loan can be for any amount, but the money must clearly be intended for the child's use.

When making investments, look for conservative securities that do not require a lot of money initially or a lot of time to manage. Both time and money are short in the early stages of child-rearing. These considerations make government-backed bonds, Treasury bills or bank certificates of deposit also attractive. (For more, see "College Costs.")

Children

FINDING GOOD DAY CARE

Nearly half of all mothers with children under the age of six are working outside their homes. Many have trouble finding decent care for their kids. Full-time nannies are too expensive; they cost $150 to $300 a week. Baby-sitters are cheaper but not always reliable. Increasingly, parents conclude that the best solution is to put their children in a day-care center, which costs $55 to $70 a week.

Many new day-care centers have opened in recent years, but the number still has not kept up with demand. Shortages are especially critical in metropolitan areas such as Boston, Denver, Los Angeles, Minneapolis and New York, particularly for children under age two. Day-care centers just can't find and hire enough capable staff members at fees that are within most parents' reach.

It is hard to evaluate the quality of the care. Many state and local governments regulate the day-care business very loosely. Regardless of whether a center is operated by a family, a corporation or a church, the quality can vary from terrible to terrific. Investigators in some cities have revealed isolated cases of abuse, neglect, unsafe and unsanitary conditions at all kinds of centers.

About 60% of the 20,000 day-care centers in the U.S. are run by churches and other nonprofit organizations. Private operators make up the rest. They range from small independent centers to larger chains. Many parents assume that all branches of a chain meet uniform standards of quality. But this is not always the case. The difference between sound and sloppy centers is determined mainly by the quality of the local director and staff.

Sometimes parents overstress the importance of teaching academic skills in a day-care center. In fact, teaching everyday living skills to children may be more important than drilling them in the alphabet and numbers. But the main point is this: before placing a child in any center, parents must check it out thoroughly, by visiting it and by speaking both with staff members and with parents of other children who attend. Choosing the right day-care center isn't child's play. Parents have no choice but to trust their own judgment because government regulations are usually more permissive than Dr. Spock. The national antiregulatory mood has led some states further to weaken day-care standards, for example by cutting down on the frequency of inspections. Because state regulations usually provide no assurance of a center's quality, parents should shop carefully.

To keep fees down, many centers pay the minimum wage — and few well-trained people will work for that. Beware of centers charging suspiciously low fees. They can provide little more than custodial care for children.

Working parents should plan on spending as much as 10% of their gross income on day care. But they can reduce costs in a couple of ways. Many centers give discounts for the second and the third child enrolled. In addition, the federal government helps by giving you income tax credits amounting to 20% to 30% of your day-care expenses. The credits vary with your income.

You can find good day-care centers by consulting state or city department of social services, nonprofit referral agencies, the Yellow Pages or friends. Pick out three or four suitable centers. Then visit each one, not once but twice — first in the morning, when activities are in full swing, and then in the late afternoon, when children may be fussy and staff members tired.

The best indicator of quality is the size of the child's group and the extent of the staff's formal training in early childhood development. Be sure to interview the center's director and ask about the qualifications of the staff. Then observe them in action. The ratio of children to staff may be as high as ten to one in quality centers. Still, you should aim for the lowest possible ratio you can afford.

Surely every day-care center should be a clean, safe place that is well equipped with toys and games. If you are checking out a center, see that electrical outlets are protected and sharp tools and cleaning fluids are out of a child's reach. You should also expect sensible sanitary practices. But some clutter is normal. After all, kids will be kids — that is, messy.

Children

HOW TO CHOOSE A LEGAL GUARDIAN

CHANCES are your minor children will never need a guardian, but you should make provisions for their future in case anything happens to you and your spouse. Most people put off the grim chore of selecting someone to look after their children if they become orphans. Yet if you should die and there is no one ready to assume responsibility for them, the surrogate's court or the probate court will appoint a guardian. Often it is a relative. The judge won't be able to consult your wishes since you won't be around to express them.

The way to avoid this is to name a guardian in your will. There are two kinds of guardianships: first, guardianship of the person; and second, guardianship of the property or the estate.

A guardian of the person handles the children's day-to-day upbringing, while a guardian of the property manages whatever money you have left for the kids. A guardian of the property must submit an annual accounting to the court of how he is managing the assets and often must request permission to make various expenditures on behalf of the kids.

Although this system protects the children's interests, the guardian gets tangled in red tape. He also must post a bond to protect the estate in case he absconds with the money. A bond on a $250,000 estate would run about $860 a year, and the estate foots the bill, somewhat diminishing what you leave for your children.

To avoid these complications and expenses, lawyers recommend that, unless your estate is unusually large, you nominate only a guardian of the person and pass any assets along to your kids in a trust. The trust document, which should be drawn by a lawyer, should spell out how you want the money spent — on schooling, clothes, music lessons and so forth. A trustee then can write checks up to limits set by the trust without having to ask the court for approval. Ideally, the guardian should be a trustee, perhaps along with a bank officer.

The hard part about selecting a guardian is picking the right person. Choose someone who is about your age and, preferably, related to you. If you are not close to your relatives, pick a person who would bring up your children the way you would. Make sure you ask the people you have in mind whether they would be willing to take on the responsibility of guardianship. Discuss with the guardians the financial arrangements you have made for the children and how you want them brought up.

A guardian named in the will is under no legal obligation to accept the responsibility and can refuse it. If he does, the court will have to find another person, who may not be someone you would choose. For that reason, attorneys recommend that you also name a back-up guardian in your will.

Children, too, have the right to know who their guardian is going to be. So consult at least your older children before you make a decision.

Every few years, or whenever personal or financial circumstances change, review the guardianship provisions in your will. The brother you have named may have been divorced or your best friend may now run a head shop in Malibu. If you think you should name a new guardian, tell the current one and draft a new will.

If someone asks *you* to be a guardian, think hard about whether you should accept. Find out what the parents expect of you and whether the children are to live with you.

Ask how the parents want the children educated and if there are any restrictive conditions, such as a statement in the will that the children cannot be moved out of the country.

Inquire about money. You should be told what funds are available for the kids' day-to-day upkeep and to carry out any special wishes, such as sending Junior to Harvard.

Ask the lawyer who drew up the will to explain your obligations and rights. And, if you have children of your own, find out how they would feel about having other children in the household.

Children

SETTING YOUR CHILD'S ALLOWANCE

W ITH ice cream cones often costing 50 cents and more, children are being pinched by inflation, just like Mom and Pop. So they are getting jobs a lot younger, doing their own comparison shopping for toys and clothes, and turning to an inflation-fighting tactic as time-honored as the tooth fairy. Kids are clamoring for increases in their allowances.

What principles should parents follow when giving allowances?

Experts in child-rearing suggest that children should start getting allowances early, along with some basic lessons in cash management. Even pre-schoolers can figure out that a quarter is worth more than a dime.

The amount of the allowance should grow along with the child and his spending needs. According to a survey of 600 young people by *Money* magazine, children seven and under typically get 25¢ to 75¢ a week, eight- and nine-year-olds collect $1 to $2.50; 10- to 13-year-olds, $1.50 to $5. Those figures have more than doubled since 1972, and they have been rising much faster than the parents' income.

A youngster's spending money should be large enough to cover fixed expenses—school lunches and bus fares, for example — and still leave something to save or spend as he chooses. If he blows it all, parents only hurt the child by giving him more, except in very special cases. A child must be taught to manage well and live within his income.

Child psychologists also warn parents to beware of inadvertently causing children to confuse money with less tangible family gifts, such as love and attention. Sometimes divorced parents pay their kids hefty allowances to compensate for their absence — and that does the youngster no good at all.

But children can profit from a special clothing allowance as soon as they are old enough to spend large sums wisely, usually by age 12 or 13. How much to give? One guideline is what the government figures a middle-income family spends to clothe a child — $40 a month for a 14-year-old, $50 for a 17-year-old.

The recent inflation-age psychology of many adults — buy now, save later — seems to have permeated children's minds, too. By many measures, teenagers are saving less than they ever did. So, to encourage thrift, many parents open bank accounts for their kids. Wise parents also believe that just as kids must be taught to save, they must learn to give to charity. As a small child, David Rockefeller, retired chairman of Chase Manhattan Bank, was required by his father to save 10% of his $1 a month allowance for charity. His childhood financial training served him well.

College Costs

HOW TO SAVE FOR COLLEGE

If you are struggling to save money for your children's college expenses, you should set up some tax-sheltered accounts to allow savings and investments to grow faster. As discussed earlier, you can do this in three ways: first, by making gifts of money to your children; second, by setting up trusts in their names, which are known as Clifford Trusts; and third, by making interest-free loans to them, called Crown loans.

All of these transfer money to your child's name. The growth and interest and dividends on that money will not be taxed at your tax rate, but at your child's rate, which is often nothing at all. (For more, see "Children: The Cost of Kids.")

After you have transferred the money, invest it in a way that combines safety and growth. For example, you can take advantage of today's rather high real interest rates by investing in so-called zero-coupon certificates of deposit that are issued by banks and savings and loans. They are federally insured against loss. Or buy so-called zero-coupon bonds. You can get all of these so that they mature when your children are ready to start college.

These investments make no yearly interest payments, but they are sold at huge discounts from face value. They pay you that full face value at some time you pick in the future. In mid-1983, both the bonds and certificates of deposit were yielding about 11%. In practical terms, what that meant was that you could buy one for $560 that would pay you $1,000 in five years, or you could purchase one for $172 that would pay you $1,000 in 17 years. (For more, see "Bonds: Your Choices.")

Another alternative is to buy securities issued by the Government National Mortgage Association ("Ginnie Maes"). You will receive monthly payments of both principal and interest. You can get them in mutual funds or in unit trusts. These are fixed portfolios of Ginnie Mae securities. In mid-1983, they were paying 11½% to 12½% annually.

College Loans

STRETCHING OUT REPAYMENTS

ARE you a former college student saddled with high monthly payments on your education loans? Now you can stretch out repayments at bargain rates in a program offered by the quasi-governmental Student Loan Marketing Association, better known as Sallie Mae. Three kinds of federally subsidized financing qualify. They are: guaranteed and federally insured student loans — both of which are made by financial institutions — and national direct student loans, which are offered by colleges.

Normally you must repay government-backed student loans in 10 years. Sallie Mae's plan lets you cut your monthly payments by as much as 50% by extending the term of your loan to as long as 20 years — at 7% interest in mid-1983. You may pay more interest in the end, but it is all tax-deductible. For more information, you can call Sallie Mae toll-free at 800–821–7700.

Commodities Futures

BUYER BEWARE

You have read all those stories about big-time speculators who have made fortunes by investing in commodities. But before you plunge in, just remember: for every speculator who makes money in the commodities markets, four others lose it.

Commodities trading can offer impressive gains for that tiny portion of your investable funds that you are willing to put completely at risk — your mad money. The reason such gains are possible is leverage. When you buy a commodities contract, you do so on margin. You put up only 7% to 12% of the value of the contract. For example, in mid-1983 you could have put up only $2,250 to buy a contract for $30,288 worth of soybeans. If the price of soybeans rose a bit, you might have doubled your investment. But if the price declined just a bit, which often happens, your investment could have been wiped out.

In the early 1980s, some commodity prices suffered their longest decline in 15 years. Blame Mother Nature. She gave us bountiful harvests, which lowered prices for many farm commodities. Also blame the sluggish economy, which curbed demand for metals, and high interest rates, which lured investors out of commodities and into money-market funds. Commodity prices did start to revive when the economy pepped up and interest rates returned from their trip to the moon. Also, the tax law of 1981 helped commodities traders, since it lowered the maximum tax on their profits from 70% to 32%. But it cannot be stressed too much that commodities are risky.

A reasonable way for small investors to get into the market is to buy one of the publicly traded commodity funds. The advantage is that the funds are diversified among many types of commodities; losses are limited to the amount that you put up and you are never subject to a margin call. The average annual return of 25 publicly traded funds, after stiff management fees, was about 17% in the period from January 1978 to December 1980. But in 1980 alone, two funds took such heavy losses that they had to be dissolved. Buyer Beware!

Computers

SELECTING A PERSONAL COMPUTER

THE personal computer, for better or for worse, is here. In 1980, not quite half a million personal computers were sold in the United States. In 1983, after Santa has sprinkled his share of chips, sales are expected to be five or six million.

The decision to buy a computer should be made extremely cautiously. Despite all the talk about computerizing your stamp collection or your Christmas-card list, you probably don't need a computer — *unless* you need it for at least one of four or five very specific applications. Those basic uses include word processing, programming, personal financial or other record-keeping and bookkeeping for a small business. Of course, you might want to buy an inexpensive little computer to play games or just join the revolution.

When you give them simple jobs to do, computers look silly. Many a potential computer buyer has sat patiently with a neighbor while he spent 15 minutes loading and reloading programs and trying to remember keyboard commands that would enable him to call up — wonder of wonders — his wife's birthday.

But when computers get really complex tasks to handle, they shine. And those complicated jobs just happen to be the ones that could lead to a handsome tax deduction for what you paid for your computer. If you are an investor or an accountant, you could justifiably claim that the machine helps you to keep track of your investments — or your clients' finances.

If you decide to invest in a computer, you will need a well-planned strategy. As writer Augustin Hedberg has observed, the best shopping rule is summed up in a newspeak aphorism: software dictates hardware. What that means is that first you should find the program you want. The program usually comes in the form of a 5¼-inch plastic diskette, often called a floppy disk because it is thin and flexible. The diskettes contain the instructions that will enable your computer to do the tasks you assign to it. Then — only after you determine what program you want — find the machine to run the program.

It may seem backward to buy the program before you buy the computer. After all, you don't buy the phonograph records before you buy the stereo to play them on. But most stereos play all kinds of records. By contrast, personal computers are rigged to accept only certain kinds of software, and you could well discover that the marvelous application you read about in the newspaper is not available on the machine you just bought. For instance, that great electronic worksheet on which you can keep track of your family budget might not work on your computer — and neither might that terrific space game or educational program.

If the *ideal* program for your needs runs only on an 8-bit computer instead of the more powerful 16-bit, don't worry. Like those belchfire cars of the '50s and '60s with their rocket-blasting V-8 engines, the 16-bit machines have more computing power than most of us will need or could use.

Don't allow yourself to be lured away from your primary use for a computer. For example, if you have decided that what you really want it to do is keep business inventories, don't be distracted by a machine that plays games. Get the computer — and the program to run on it — that do what you need to be done. It's better by far to buy a separate game machine for a few hundred dollars and keep your serious hardware for serious uses.

When looking for software, don't buy anything until you see it work. Programs can sound better in conversation than they turn out in practice. Every system has its peculiarities. Take nothing for granted. And don't settle for a dealer demonstration. Would you allow a car salesman to give your new sedan its road test? Step right up and put your program through its paces. If you don't know how, have the dealer show you.

Unfortunately, once you have bought and opened a program you usually can't return it. But a few of the software manufacturers include smaller demonstration diskettes in their packages of programs so you can try them at home before opening the main diskette.

Before you buy any computer, find out how much ongoing help and support you can count on from your retail dealer. Visit a few dealers in your area and ask some questions to see if you can understand them. Many specialists know computers inside and out — but they don't know how to explain them to you.

Find out whether the dealer will help you learn how to use your computer. Does he hold classes for new users? Will he give you help over the phone? Be sure your prospective dealer understands software. Make certain he sells a variety of both hardware and software programs. Find out how well equipped he is to repair any breakdowns. Don't forget: in deciding where to buy a personal computer, dealer support is key.

The how-to manuals that come with home computers are often written quickly and under great pressure. Many are nests of bafflegab and glib misinformation. That is another reason why you may want to think twice before grabbing one of the tempting bargains that mail-order houses advertise in computer magazines. When you have bought a computer from an authorized dealer, you will have someone you can turn to for help.

The fact that new computers, new software and new ways of joining the two are coming out virtually every week may make you decide to wait awhile before springing for a machine. Admittedly, in nine months the world of small computers will have evolved considerably — but nine months after that, it will still be changing. If you decide to wait for the ultimate computer, you may wait forever.

Computers

HOW TO LEARN

Iꜰ you are a computer illiterate, take heart. There is help out there in the form of books, magazines, courses and other computer users.

Books are probably not the easiest way to learn about computers. After a few elementary chapters, you are likely to be struggling in a post-doctoral spider's web of circuitry, machine architecture and computer languages. But there are a few good reads available. Among them are *Why Do You Need a Personal Computer?*, published by John Wiley & Sons for $9.95, and *An Introduction to Microcomputers: Volume O, the Beginner's Book*, published by Osborne/McGraw-Hill for $14.95. For the truly committed computer fan, McGraw-Hill publishes a *Microcomputer Literacy Program*, which is a two-volume minicourse with nine cassette tapes. Be prepared to lay out $195.

Beginners also can find reliable information in such computer magazines as *Popular Computing, Personal Computing, Byte* and *InfoWorld.* Or, you can try to learn from the machine itself by means of a learner's program, which flashes step-by-step instructions on the video screen. Two of the best learners' programs are FriendlyWare, a three-diskette package for the IBM personal computer user, and How to Program in the BASIC Language, a 12-lesson package with two diskettes that work on most major machines.

If a course is what you want, be sure to find out if it is aimed at the personal computer user or at students wanting careers in data processing. Courses are given at junior, community and technical colleges across the country. You will want to find out how big the class is — smaller is better, of course. Look into user groups as well. These are clubs of computer owners and they offer members a chance to get together and discuss problems and programs.

If you are a rugged individualist about computers, consider buying an inexpensive machine for about $200 or less and spending an hour a day for a month just playing with it. You could learn more than you would in a $200 or $300 course.

Computers

SOURCES OF SECONDHAND SAVINGS

IF you want a personal computer and are willing to settle for less than the latest technology, you can save hundreds of dollars in the fast-growing secondhand market.

Experienced users can find attractively priced equipment through either local newspapers or special-interest publications. The monthly *Computer Bargain Guide* (455 Moody Street, Waltham, Massachusetts 02154; $15 a year) recently advertised a used Osborne I for $1,200, or about $600 less than a new model. The monthly *Computer Shopper* (P.O. Box F, Titusville, Florida 32780; $10 a year) devotes half its space to used-computer listings. One recent ad offered a TRS-80 Model I for $350. That's about $550 below the original list price.

If you are a neophyte user, you probably will need assistance in learning how to operate your computer. So you should buy it from a dealer. Some retailers sell trade-ins from customers stepping up to newer equipment. Typically, retailers offer service contracts and one- to three-month guarantees. They also help you get acquainted with a secondhand machine.

It's best to buy locally so that you can try out a machine before paying for it. Most used computers are mechanically sound, since there are few movable parts that can easily break. But check on some common trouble spots: keyboards, power switches and disk drives. All are simple to test.

Consumer Problems

GAINING THROUGH COMPLAINING

For customers bedeviled by faulty products, snarled-up bills or late deliveries, a few well-chosen threats can succeed when all else fails. You can gain by complaining shrewdly.

Any good gripe to a store or a manufacturer, as writer Marlys Harris has observed, has five simple elements: a clear statement of the problem; facts that back up your story; a request for redress; a deadline by which the problem must be solved; and a threat that you are prepared to carry out if you do not get quick and complete satisfaction.

Many quite proper threats can produce results. For example, you can threaten to stop payment to the offending store or serviceman, to end your patronage or to tell other people how badly you have been treated. If all else fails, you can threaten a lawsuit. But use that as a last resort, for you often will have to be prepared to spend thousands of dollars on legal fees.

Face-to-face gripes frequently fail because you take out your anger on a clerk or bank teller who does not have the power to correct a problem. To get any results from an oral complaint, of course, you should ask to see the floorwalker, manager, or whoever else is in charge.

One successful face-to-face technique is called the broken record. It has been developed by specialists in assertiveness training. You drive your listener to distraction by tirelessly repeating your problem and your request for redress in a helpful and unctuous manner. Or you can take this technique another step by announcing, "I'm *not* moving until you straighten this out."

You may be tempted to make your gripe by telephone. That's less daunting than face-to-face complaining, but it often feels like punching a cloud. If you elect to fight that way, demand the name or employee number of the person with whom you speak. Write it down, along with any promises the complaint handler makes.

If the first person you speak with fails to solve your problem, ask to talk with a supervisor. Keep heading upward until you get some response. If you suspect a complaint handler is giving you the runaround by sending you to another department, threaten to get back to him. That's why you have asked for his name or number.

The telephone is particularly suited to solving delivery problems. You just threaten to call the dispatcher every 15 minutes until the truck arrives. After a few such pesky calls, he usually manages to work miracles.

If you have a gripe about snarled-up computers, immobile bureaucrats, snooty clerks or an unreliable product you have bought, the most effective way to complain is generally by writing a firm but effective letter. Launch your missive directly at the head of the company. Although he will probably pass it to a subordinate, the chief's interest is often enough to turn the laziest employee into a dynamo.

Since scores of employees must pore over letters that are usually boring, vague, abusive and lengthy, you have to make your letter stand out. One way to do that is simply to write plain, forceful English. The first paragraph should be brief — no more than two sentences of ten or twelve words each. And it should summarize the problem in a dramatic way — for example, "I'm very distressed by a billing problem that your company refuses to correct."

In the second paragraph pop a surprise: compliment the company. You might say that you have been delighted with the company's appliances over the years. In fact, those appliances have been joys to own. Then, in the next paragraph, go in for the kill. "So you can imagine my dismay," you might say, "when my latest purchase turned out to be a dud."

Move on to the facts, but omit unnecessary details. Since most people only scan letters, you should state your demand twice — in the second sentence of the first paragraph and at the end. Also, try to establish a relationship with your reader to gain empathy. A businessman might say that he's in business, too, and would be upset to learn that one of his customers had been treated as poorly as he has.

A "P.S." is especially important. Tests have shown that a P.S. is one of the first things people read, so you want to make a statement that will get someone to read the rest of the letter. To a bank president, you might say you will be compelled to move your account elsewhere, notify the banking commission or take up the matter with your lawyer if you don't hear from the executive by a certain date.

If your complaint does not bring immediate results, step up your demands. Not only do you want your toaster replaced, but since you have had to put up with delay after delay, you think the company should throw in an electric can opener as well. When you keep raising the ante, management tends to become more eager to settle.

Consumer Problems

A FREE GUIDE FOR COMPLAINERS

IF you have been stung by shoddy goods or services, the surest way to get a cash refund or an exchange is to complain to somebody in authority at the offending company. The U.S. Office of Consumer Affairs reports that consumers resolve 88% of their complaints by doing just that. To help you do it, the office has published a free, 91-page *Consumer's Resource Handbook*. It lists the names, addresses and phone numbers of consumer affairs directors at 600 corporations. If you do not get satisfaction from them, the booklet directs you to the addresses and phone numbers of other sources of help, such as local Better Business Bureaus and government consumer protection offices. To get the new handbook, write to the Consumer Information Center, Pueblo, Colorado 81009. (See also "Better Business Bureaus: How to Get Them to Help.")

Contests

TIPS TO HELP YOU WIN

ANYONE who has ever jotted his or her name on a contest entry blank knows full well the tremendous odds against winning. But you can shrink the odds by taking some tips from a driven band of competitors. These people have methodically refined the art of winning promotional games into a quasi-science. They call themselves "contesters."

The vast majority of contests are not games of skill but lotteries. All you have to do is beat the stratospheric odds — they typically run as high as a million to one — against a blindfolded employee of the contest firm plucking your entry from a revolving drum.

But as contest junkies have learned, not all entries go in the drum. Unless the sweepstakes is completely computerized, employees select a fixed number of letters. To attract attention to *their* entries, contest junkies package them in a dazzling array of envelopes—or even boxes if the rules permit.

The only undisputed formula for beating the sweepstakes, however, is to enter and enter again. Consistent winners use as many entry blanks as they can find — or make their own if the rules permit — to inundate each sweep. One Boston computer programmer and his fiancée submitted 600 entries to an Air Florida sweepstakes. It cost them $240 in postage. But they won 23 round-trip air tickets, plus 110 days of auto rentals, 110 one-day cruises and 300 free cocktails.

Such experts offer these tips: Look for contests with relatively few entrants — for example, those that run for just a short time, receive little publicity and are open to people in a limited geographical area. Enter the most contests in summer, when many of your potential opponents are vacationing. Follow the rules slavishly — and make sure your entries are in by the deadline date.

Alas, victory can bring its own problems. The Internal Revenue Service will share your take, minus postage and other expenses of winning. Contest sponsors must report to the IRS any prize with a fair market value of more than $600.

Cosmetics

ARE THEY WORTHWHILE?

Americans spend more than $1.5 billion a year on skin-care products, but few of the potions, lotions and salves on the market will do you much good. Research by dermatologists and cosmetic chemists shows that no amount of collagen, bilberry juice, wheat germ oil, asparagus extract, sperm whale oil or similarly esoteric substances can restore the skin you had as a teenager.

Cosmetics can keep skin clean, moist and soft. They also can temporarily close pores, plump up skin to make wrinkles less noticeable and give you an artificial glow. But these effects are fleeting.

Each cosmetic company markets a skin-care regimen that usually includes a soap or cream cleanser, an astringent, a day cream or moisturizer, a heavier night cream and perhaps a "miracle" product that supposedly performs some age-defying feat. You might have to pay close to $200 for the whole collection, but in all likelihood you don't actually need any of those products.

A case can be made for a moisturizer if you have very dry skin. Women under 40, however, rarely need one. In fact, moisturizers can cause acne or an allergic reaction.

Don't waste your money on skin cleansers, either. Most dermatologists agree with Mother: soap cleans more effectively than anything else. But expensive beauty soaps that claim to moisturize, protect or lubricate your skin are not worth the money. They simply are not on your face long enough, and their costly ingredients, such as vitamin E and wheat-germ oil, wash down the drain with the suds.

As for wrinkle creams, the only product that can help you prevent wrinkles is a sunscreen containing an ultraviolet-absorbing chemical. Dermatologists recommend that you wear a sunscreen when you are outdoors for any length of time. But if your primary encounter with nature is the daily walk from house to car, you don't need one. (For more, see "Shopping: Sun Potions.")

Debts

HOW TO PAY THEM OFF

ARE you borrowing to pay off old bills?

Are you spending more than 15% of your take-home pay on monthly installment debts, not counting home mortgage payments?

Are you constantly forced to dip into your checking overdraft and rarely able to bring it down?

Do you find it hard to save regularly even a small part of your income?

A "yes" to any of those questions could be a warning that you are living beyond your means. If so, there are sensible steps you can take. In fact, it is precisely when they feel they are overwhelmed by bills and responsibilities that many people decide to plan for the future as they never have before.

Once you have concluded that you are in trouble, your first order of business is to determine exactly how much income you receive and itemize your monthly expenses. List all your monthly bills in their order of importance. Set priorities for paying them off. Probably the first priority will be to pay your home mortgage, and then your monthly utility and installment payments.

What if you find that you are still in debt over your head? Then it's wise to seek out your creditors and negotiate to stretch out your debts, that is, to arrange a longer term of repayment in smaller amounts each month. Creditors have a great deal of latitude to extend the due date on bills by up to 30 days — or possibly to refinance a debt to allow lower, though longer, payments — even if you are overdue 90 days.

If you have trouble meeting your home mortgage payments, go to your mortgage lender for help. The last thing a lender wants is to foreclose on your property. He would much rather have your cash. So, in most cases a loan can be rescheduled and payments reduced if necessary.

You might be tempted to sign up for a consolidation loan to pay off all your debts. But that is not smart. The lure of a consolidation loan is that a bank or finance company will take over your many debts and that you, in turn, will make payments to that one institution. The catch is that the interest rate on such a loan is likely to be high. So you could be simply replacing a heap of moderate debts with one big one that costs more to carry.

Debts

CREDIT COUNSELORS

PEOPLE who have trouble composing a debt repayment schedule within a workable budget would do well to seek a credit counselor's guidance. Credit counselors will be sympathetic but firm. A counselor will ask you to provide intimate details about your total monthly income and expenses, a list of your outstanding bills and copies of any correspondence you have had with creditors about debts and loans. The counselor also will want to know whether you have been dunned by creditors or threatened with legal action, or whether a creditor has sought to have your pay garnisheed.

Creditors often prefer to deal with counselors, so they have more clout than you might. The counselors will intercede on your behalf to reduce and stretch out monthly payments on debts. And sometimes counselors can even knock down the total balance due. Once you have renegotiated the debt terms through your counselor, you make your monthly payments to him, and he manages the debt for you.

People who seek counseling for debt repayment may actually be rated better credit risks in the future. If a person completes a debt-repayment plan, lenders often consider him rehabilitated and will entertain other loan applications. Bankers don't believe that once a deadbeat, always a deadbeat.

Even while working off your debt, you should plan to save. Financial planners say that setting aside as little as 3% to 5% of monthly income after taxes helps families to start considering saving as an integral part of their budget.

Before you approach any credit counseling agency for help, find out whether it is a nonprofit clinic, a for-profit company or simply a bill collector subsidized by creditors. The National Foundation for Consumer Credit will mail you its free directory of nonprofit services in your state. NFCC affiliates often provide free budgeting advice, although they may request a small fee for specific debt-repayment services. They also ask creditors to return 10% to 15% of the monthly payments that counselors make on their clients' behalf. For a list of these affiliates send a self-addressed, stamped envelope to NFCC, 8701 Georgia Avenue, Silver Spring, Maryland 20910.

The American Association of Credit Counselors represents privately owned, for-profit companies. They generally charge the debtor more than an NFCC agency does. Furthermore, 25 states specifically prohibit such operations. Where profit-making counseling is legal, state laws usually limit fees. They average about 12.5% of the total debt that a company manages for you. For a list of these counselors send a self-addressed, stamped envelope to the American Association of Credit Counselors, 1733 Washington Street, Waukegan, Illinois 60085.

Debts

PERSONAL BANKRUPTCY

FOR people who have no hope of paying off their debts within five years, bankruptcy could be a necessary last resort. Filing for bankruptcy under Chapter Thirteen gives you a chance of personal financial recovery. You retain your property and repay your debts while the court protects you from creditors' harassment for three years. But to file under that chapter, you must have current income and you must disclose it as well as your living expenses. A court-appointed trustee parcels out your monthly payments to creditors, usually after taking a fee amounting to 10% of the funds he handles. Repayments are ordinarily less than the full dollar amounts of your debt. But, alimony, child support and the prior three years' taxes must be paid in full.

Then there is Chapter Seven. Even if you file for straight bankruptcy under that chapter, the state will not strip you of everything. You may well be forced to sell off your possessions, but in most states you will get to keep something — for example, up to $7,500 from your equity in a house, $1,200 from the sale of your car and $750 from the tools of your trade. These exemptions are doubled if both a husband and wife file.

In spite of the advantages of bankruptcy, credit counselors urge debtors to avoid it if they possibly can. Over the long haul, you may well lose more than you gain. Declaring bankruptcy usually entails legal fees that could amount to many hundreds of dollars. Often, too, bankruptcy carries a social stigma. A Chapter Thirteen filing remains on your credit record for six years, and a Chapter Seven for 10 years. That certainly could impair your ability to get credit.

Dividends

BEWARE OF BIG PAYOUTS

IF you are collecting dividends on your stocks now, you should review your investments to see if you are really getting a good deal. Big payouts may be a sign of a poor investment.

High dividend payments, of course, can provide some hedge against inflation. But even retired people aiming for immediate, dependable income should look beyond the dividend yield in choosing investments. All investment profits are not equal under the tax law. The tax is much heavier on dividends or interest than on a long-term capital gain, which you can get when a stock's price rises. So shares with the possibility of a hefty price gain could provide a bigger return after taxes than those with dazzling dividends. In fact, the shares of some large companies that pay no dividends at all have achieved a much greater total return than high-dividend companies of the same size.

Many experts contend that big payouts simply signify bad management. Smart managers should be reinvesting profits in new equipment, research or other productive activity. In an analysis of 1,000 companies over five years in the late 1970s and early 1980s, the financial advisory firm of Mitchell & Company found that corporations which reduced by 20% the portion of their earnings allotted to dividends enjoyed stock price gains averaging 38%. Meanwhile, companies that increased the portion of their earnings spent on dividends showed an average 39% decline in stock prices.

The tax law of 1981 further dulls the appeal of dividends. Capital gains are even more attractive than they once were. For investors in the highest bracket, the tax rate has dropped from 28% to 20%.

If you do not need a steady stream of income, you might be wise to look for growing companies in expanding industries — and let the dividends go hang. If, on the other hand, you want some price growth along with the security of dividends, choose stocks selling at a low price/earnings ratio. And if you don't want to pick your own stocks, you can aim for a high total return by investing in a mutual fund that combines dividend income with a chance at capital gains. For the ordinary investor concerned about steady income, a well-managed no-load mutual fund may well be the best opportunity to achieve that high total return.

Divorce

THE NEW ECONOMICS OF SPLITTING

A REVOLUTION is under way in the property settlements after couples divorce. Alimony is going out, a concept called "equitable distribution" is in, and court decrees are so unpredictable that couples should avoid trial at almost any cost.

Since 1970, more than 20 states have adopted new concepts of what marital property is and how it should be split. The new theory is that any property accumulated during a marriage should be divided fairly and *finally* so that each partner can move on to the next stage of life, unencumbered by leftover financial ties. This is based on the two modern realities that many marriages don't last and that women are increasingly able to support themselves.

The use of long-term alimony has shrunk; only those spouses who are either over 50 or in poor health are likely to get it. Nationally, 14% of divorced wives receive alimony. *Temporary* alimony is becoming more common. This is meant to support a dependent spouse only until she — or sometimes he — can complete an education or find a job.

What are really on the rise are lump-sum, one-shot settlements. They are based on an analysis of the couple's financial assets. Figuring out the size of those assets, and just which partner is entitled to what, can mean lengthy litigation and high legal fees. Property judgments by a court are unpredictable at best and sometimes downright unfair. In a few states — among them California, Louisiana and New Mexico — property is divided fifty-fifty. But in most other states, the operative legal term is not equal, but "equitable." That means that if the couple cannot decide for themselves who gets what, the judge will. But these decisions are only as equitable and intelligent as the judge himself.

It's not unusual for a judge to award two-thirds of a couple's assets to one spouse and one-third to the other. In one New Jersey divorce, the husband kept a half-million-dollar inheritance while the wife came away with only $10,000 in assets.

Divorce is becoming so prevalent that more and more couples lay the groundwork for a potential financial settlement even before they get married. They draw up a prenuptial agreement, which spells out their rights, obligations and any future division of property. In the event of divorce, such documents are not necessarily binding. But they can be helpful in personal negotiations, and most courts will take them into account. (See "Sexes: Prenuptial Contracts.")

Other husbands and wives make an inventory of their assets every couple of years, just in case. They evaluate what they own, from cars and carpets to a stock portfolio. Then each partner outlines his or her individual contributions to this joint balance sheet, including the value of the wife's services if she is at home caring for children. Such written tabulations can save hours of high-priced legal time and help insure a fair division of property if a couple ever separates.

Couples actually facing a divorce can reduce the cost and pain by using a professional mediator to help determine who gets what. Mediation is being offered by a growing number of specially trained lawyers, psychologists, social workers and marriage counselors. They have saved thousands of dollars in legal fees for many, many couples.

Private mediators charge $40 to $85 an hour — and uncomplicated divorce settlements can be worked out in 10 hours or less. Or, put another way, for $850 — or much less.

How to locate a trained divorce mediator? The Family Mediation Association (5530 Wisconsin Avenue, Suite 1250, Chevy Chase, Maryland 20815) certifies mediators and can provide names of those in your area. Or try the American Arbitration Association. It has offices in 25 cities and, for a $100 fee, will recommend a mediator who meets its professional standards. For a free pamphlet titled *The Family Dispute Services*, write to its headquarters at 140 West 51st Street, New York, New York 10020.

Just remember: a peaceful divorce settlement is almost always better than a trial, because it's much cheaper.

Education

COLLEGE CREDIT FOR LIFE EXPERIENCE

Y ou can earn college credits for learning you have acquired on your own — simply by taking a test. Quite a few accredited colleges administer such exams in what are generally called "external degree programs."

Two of the biggest and best known are at the University of the State of New York (Education Center, Albany, New York 12230) and Thomas A. Edison State College (101 West State Street, Trenton, New Jersey 08625). Neither school has a residency requirement; both take students from all over the world.

To earn academic credit for work experience, you can take standardized tests. Or the college will tailor an exam to your special circumstances and let you take it by mail or in person. To enroll in the State University of New York's Regent Program, you pay $175 plus an annual record-keeping fee of $150 and $25 to $50 for each three-credit exam.

For information on about 100 external degree programs, see the *Guide to External Degree Programs in the United States.* It's published by Macmillan for $17.50.

Education

CLASSES FOR THE ELDERLY

MANY colleges are opening their classrooms to knowledge-hungry people aged 60 and up.

You can choose from hundreds of quickie courses through a nonprofit organization called ElderHostel. An average of $180 a week pays for anywhere from one to three courses taught by regular faculty members at U.S. colleges. That fee includes room and board, extracurricular films and parties. You can also sign up at universities in Europe. Two- and three-week foreign seminars range from about $1,200 to $2,000 including air fare.

ElderHostel enrolled about 55,000 students last year at 598 U.S. institutions. For information, write ElderHostel, 100 Boylston Street, Boston, Massachusetts 02116.

The Elderly

HOW AND WHERE TO GET GOOD CARE FOR AGING PEOPLE

J ust about everyone has heard an aged parent or grandparent plead: "Whatever you do, don't send me to a nursing home." Take heart. You have newer and better choices than the old nursing home.

Health care at home can solve the financial and emotional problems that bedevil ailing elderly people and their families. Services available to the elderly in their own homes are expanding rapidly, and so is the number of government, charitable and for-profit agencies that provide such care.

Fees vary. Upjohn HealthCare Services, the largest nongovernment agency, charges $13 to $25 an hour for a registered nurse, $9 to $20 for a practical nurse, $7 to $12 for a less skilled home health aide, $6 to $10 for a homemaker and $6 to $8 for a companion.

Limited services by a registered nurse normally are 100% reimbursable by Medicare if related to a hospital stay. Medicare also pays for the services of a home health aide, though only in conjunction with skilled nursing care. But even if an old person doesn't require skilled nursing, many private health insurance policies will pay for personal care and homemaking services. One way to determine whether the agency providing home care is a good one is to find out whether it is approved by Medicare. About 3,800 agencies are.

To find one of these services, get in touch with either your state's local office for the aging or your community's family-service bureau or a religious organization. You might also call a neighborhood senior-citizen center; its employees can guide you to programs for old people.

For a nationwide listing of services that provide care for the elderly in their own homes, write to the National HomeCaring Council at 235 Park Avenue South, New York, New York 10003. Another source is the National League for Nursing, 10 Columbus Circle, New York, New York 10019.

In-home services for the aged are improving as they expand. Growing numbers of home health-care workers now help more old people to live on their own. Also, special geriatric day-care centers enable old people to spend many hours there but sleep in their own homes.

Through a New York State program called Nursing Homes Without Walls, old people eligible for placement in a skilled nursing facility now can live at home without having to fend for themselves. In Florida, one similar state-sponsored program, Community Care for the Elderly, has been so successful that it recently was helping over 18,000 old people stay out of institutions. These elderly could have meals delivered to their homes or get transportation to needed medical services.

Many localities have set up agencies that find and match elderly roommates, something like a computer dating service. Also, there are agencies that make intergenerational match-ups between, say, a pensioner and a young couple who like the idea of having an extended family. Some state and private agencies pay the younger family for their care.

If you want to avoid a nursing home, you also should check into apartment buildings designed specifically for the elderly. Some are in so-called continuous-care communities and look like college campuses. They offer a variety of living choices: apartment houses for people who are fit enough to live alone as well as an intermediate-care facility for those who need some medical attention and yet another facility that offers around-the-clock skilled care. Continuous care can be ideal for the elderly person who is independent but realizes that the day of infirmity inevitably will come.

Still, nursing homes may be the only choice for some families with elderly relatives. In general, those homes have improved significantly since the mid-1970s. The best tend to be nonprofit institutions sponsored by religious, union or fraternal organizations. At the finest homes, the byword is rehabilitation, regardless of the patient's age.

You can get names of such nursing homes in your area by asking your doctor or hospital social worker. Also, you can inquire at a senior-citizen center and your state chapter of both the American Health Care Association and the American Association of Homes for the Aging.

You should visit any homes you are considering at least twice — once on an official tour and once as a surprise, if possible. Supervisors of a well-run home will welcome you and your questions. Make sure the residents seem content, clean and neat. Taste the food. To get free fact sheets on choosing a nursing home and finding financial aid, send a stamped, self-addressed envelope to the National Council of Health Centers, 2600 Virginia Avenue, NW, Washington, D.C. 20037.

Inescapably, nursing homes are expensive: from $1,200 a month to as high as $2,500, depending on the locality and the kind of accommodations. Medicare covers only part of the costs, and then only for 100 days. Private health insurance rarely pays for nursing-home care. Medicaid can pay — but Medicaid patients usually must first use up all their own money. That means selling most of their assets to raise cash. Then they must sign over their Social Security benefits, plus all but a small monthly allowance.

Families pondering ways to care for aging relatives should take them into their deliberations from the start, and to bear in mind their emotional as well as physical needs. If they know they have choices, they will be happier. And preventing depression and loneliness in the elderly goes a long way toward preventing physical decline.

Entrepreneurship

HOW TO LEARN

T HE orthodox wisdom until recently was that the only school for entrepreneurs was the school of hard knocks. But to survive in today's economy, small business people — like the big — require management skills that are often best acquired through formal training.

No fewer than 160 four-year colleges offer courses in starting a new business. Some, including Babson, Baylor, the University of Southern California and Wharton, have introduced undergraduate majors in the field. If you have neither the time nor temperament to work toward a degree, you can choose from a variety of commercial and government-sponsored courses.

A good new-business course will cover such fundamentals as evaluating an idea for an enterprise, raising capital and dealing with suppliers and customers. Students are commonly asked to prepare a detailed business plan for their firm's first five years.

You can size up a course's content by studying the catalogue or talking to faculty and former students. You usually can get names and phone numbers from those sponsoring the course.

The best and most accessible of the cram courses are those sponsored jointly by the Small Business Administration, chambers of commerce and community colleges. These courses meet at more than 300 community and junior colleges. They may last 50 hours — typically, for two hours on two nights a week. Usually they cost no more than $100.

The SBA also offers a free day-long seminar about twice monthly at its 75 regional and district offices. With a form from the SBA showing that you have completed the one-day workshop, you can take a more advanced course at one of the privately operated Control Data Learning Centers. They are located in about 100 cities. And with the SBA form you will not have to pay the usual $255 tuition.

Other commercial courses tend to cost about that much. For example, the for-profit Center for Entrepreneurial Management, 83 Spring Street, New York, New York 10012, offers three-day courses on videotape at hotels around the U.S. Instruction costs $234 for members, who pay annual dues of $96. Tuition for nonmembers is $275.

Estates

BANK TRUST DEPARTMENTS

IF you have saved up some money and hope to pass it on to your children or other heirs some day, you would be wise to ask an attorney if your taxable assets are large enough for you to set up a trust. By putting your assets into a trust, you lower the taxes on your estate and delay the day when your heirs have to pay.

So-called "living trusts" are popular, too. For example, parents in high tax brackets often put securities or real estate into a 10-year trust. The trust pays the income from its assets to the children of the people who have set up the trust. That gets the income out of the parents' tax bracket and into the children's much lower tax bracket.

Any trust needs a trustee who will take responsibility for the money. The trustee is both a watchdog and a safekeeper. He protects the assets in the estate; he collects any debts or dividends that are coming to the estate, and he pays a regular stipend to the heirs.

Very often people who write wills and set up trusts designate banks to be the trustee. For honesty, impartiality and continuity, banks are hard to beat. Their fees as trustees are not high, usually ½% to 1% of the assets managed per year. But how well do bank trust departments really do in managing estates and in guiding assets to growth?

In an earlier era of money management, bank trust departments minded the wealth of millionaires' widows and the heirs to great fortunes. The trust departments placed caution above all else, and so they invested in top-grade bonds and conservative stocks in order to produce returns of 3% a year or so. That hardly seems acceptable today.

Bank trust departments often sell off the assets in an estate and pool them in a much larger portfolio of common stocks, which they manage like a mutual fund. But a survey of such pools shows that during the decade of the 1970s they increased in value by only an average 110%, compared with 127% for the Standard & Poor's index of 500 stocks.

So it is no surprise that, when choosing trustees, more and more people are turning away from bank trust departments and instead selecting lawyers, accountants and other private trustees.

Most trusts designed to minimize estate taxes are irrevocable. Unless the trust specifically permits beneficiaries to switch banks, they can do little to upgrade performance or dismiss incompetent trustees. State and federal bank regulators are powerless to help. The courts can oust a trustee, but only on proof of fraud or misappropriation of funds. So lawyers offer some advice to anyone putting a trust provision in his will:

First, give beneficiaries an escape hatch by specifying their right to replace trustees.

Second, appoint a co-trustee, preferably a friend or relative whom the bank would have to consult before changing investments and who would serve without fee.

Finally, spell out the trust manager's responsibilities; they can range from simple caretaking to complete control.

Above all, you might be wise to investigate now whether your spouse, your children or your other heirs would benefit by your setting up a trust and getting a trustworthy trustee. (See also "Wills: Drafting Your Most Important Document.")

Estates

BECOMING AN EXECUTOR

IT seems like such an honor. A relative or close friend asks you to be the executor of his estate. You are flattered to be so trusted. But be warned: estate administration is tough, time-consuming and sometimes even risky. You could wind up spending months, or even years, worrying about death, taxes — and greed.

The first rule of being the executor, as writer Evan Thomas has noted, is not to be one in the first place. Tell Aunt Sadie to get a lawyer or a seasoned bank officer who knows how to administer an estate. The only problem is that such a professional costs money, and Aunt Sadie didn't get to be rich by spending a cent she didn't have to. If you refuse the job, then the fees for a professional executor will reduce the estate by about 2% to 5%.

If you do accept the request to become a nonprofessional executor, you will find that the job, for all its drawbacks, can be interesting. It's like having a person's life suddenly open before you. Of course, you may also find out a lot you didn't want to know.

But don't try to do the job by yourself. Get an expert lawyer to help, unless Aunt Sadie lived in Texas or one of the other few states that have fairly simple probate procedures. If the estate includes land, an ongoing business, a trust, substantial charitable bequests or anything else that could cause a tax problem, then whatever state you live in, hiring a lawyer is a must.

Finding that lawyer is not always easy. Start with the attorney who drafted the will. If he is not available, ask at your local bar association. Also, for help in locating an expert, you could write to the American College of Probate Counsel at 10964 West Pico Boulevard, Los Angeles, California 90064. The members of this organization have had at least 10 years' experience and are recommended by their peers.

When you become the executor of an estate, face up to the fact that you are going to be busy for quite a while. The very first thing an executor must do is find the will and read it.

Next, have the lawyer whom you've hired get the will probated, that is, "proved" in the probate court as a valid will. The court will issue to you what's known as letters testamentary that give you authority as executor. You then have to notify all the heirs and any relatives who would have been entitled to inherit under state law if there had not been a will.

Your real chore will be finding and taking possession of the deceased person's property. Tangibles such as the house, car or jewelry should be locked up. An obituary is an advertisement for burglars. Buy or renew the insurance on all property. If you don't, you could be personally liable for any loss.

Put any cash into a separate checking or savings account for the estate. Pay all the bills out of the estate checking account. Fortunately, it's usually the lawyer's job to pay any taxes, but you will need to give him a precise inventory of the assets and their value. And you — the executor — are responsible for seeing that the taxes are paid on time.

When the will has been probated and all taxes and debts have been paid, the executor prepares an accounting for the probate court of all assets received and sold, all claims and expenses paid and all amounts due to those who are to get the remaining estate. Then he is finally ready to distribute what is left to the heirs.

Sometimes the court will allow an executor to make distributions to needy heirs before the final accounting. Otherwise you allow at least seven months for creditors to come forward before parceling out, say, the deceased person's pearls or the 300 shares of General Motors. If you do not wait and there is not enough money left in the estate to satisfy creditors, you could be held personally liable.

Probably the most trying aspect of your job as an executor is keeping meticulous records of the estate's expenses and receipts. That means more than just filling up a shoebox with check stubs and random bank statements. It might be worthwhile to pay the minimum annual fee of $500 to a bank trust department to act as custodian. The bankers will keep the records for you.

If the estate includes a large portfolio of securities, the executor will need astute investment advice to preserve and perhaps increase the assets before he or she hands them over to the heirs. Hiring a professional investment counselor means another fee, but may save the estate money in the long run.

Executors are held to a high standard of fiduciary responsibility. They run significant legal risks if they act in any way that could be considered contrary to the heirs' interests. So, there are a few things not to do. Don't deposit in your personal checking account any checks made out to you as executor, and never make yourself a temporary loan out of the assets of the estate. Also, you shouldn't buy anything from the estate without permission of all the other heirs and possibly the court.

Should the executor take a fee? In a few states, compensation is set by law — usually a one-time fee of 2% to 5% of the estate. In most states, though, an executor simply puts in for a "reasonable" fee and the court upholds it as long as no one objects.

For years it was traditional for executors who were family members to forgo a fee for their blood, sweat and tears. The fee might reduce the executor's own inheritance, and as ordinary income it would be taxed at higher rates than estate taxes. But now lawyers are urging executors to go ahead and take the money. Chances are, by the time you have made all the distributions and the court has discharged you from your responsibilities, you will have earned every cent.

Estates

THE NEW RULES

For people who have worked hard to build up an estate through their savings and investments, there are encouraging developments ahead. By 1987 almost all estates will go to the beneficiaries free of any federal estate or gift tax.

Under the tax law passed in 1981, you can leave your entire estate to your spouse free of federal estate taxes. That's because there is now no limit on the so-called marital deduction.

In addition, beginning in 1984 you can leave a total $325,000 tax-free to heirs other than a spouse. But hang in there. You will be able to leave even more tax-free in future years. The estate and gift exemptions will rise in steps until 1987 — so that in three years you will be able to leave $600,000 tax-free, over and above what you leave to your spouse. The result of these changes is that by 1987, the heirs to fully 99.6% of all estates will not have to pay any federal taxes on them.

The tax changes make it more important than ever before that you have a will — even if it is only a simple will. Almost everybody has something to leave behind, and a will not only guarantees that your estate goes where you want, when you want, but also very often eases taxes.

If you already have a will, be sure you review it with your lawyer right away. You may want to change some bequests, now that you can leave more money free of taxes.

If you drew up your will before September 13, 1981, when the old law was still in effect, and you used the conventional wording of that time, the bequest would be interpreted to mean that you wanted only 50% of your estate to go to your spouse. Unless you change the wording now, your estate could be taxed on the other 50%. But a simple rewriting can reduce that tax to zero. So don't wait to write — or rewrite — your will.

Another consequence is that you may now have more insurance than you need. Because few people will pay estate taxes in the future, the necessity for that insurance coverage will fall off. There is also less reason to have your insurance policy assigned to your spouse. Assigning insurance is usually done to keep the proceeds of the policy out of the estate. But since it will be less important than in earlier years to reduce the size of your estate, the chief reason for assigning insurance disappears. By holding onto the policy yourself, you retain the right to change the beneficiary if and when you wish. (For more, see "Wills: Drafting Your Most Important Document.")

[141]

Financial Futures

CHANCY "COMMODITIES"

EVEN for the experts, the commodities futures market has always been a gamble. But now there are futures contracts for people who don't know beans about soybeans. The so-called commodities in this case are good old stocks and bonds, and they are traded in the fast and furious financial futures market.

The financial futures include contracts in Treasury bills, bonds and notes, bank certificates of deposit and a variety of other interest-bearing securities. When you buy one of these contracts, you are betting that, for example, interest rates will go down in the future, and thus the prices of the bills, bonds or notes covered by the contract will go up.

You also can do trading in stock index futures. These contracts let you bet on the performance of stock market indexes, such as the Value Line Composite Stock Index and the Standard & Poor's 500.

You can buy financial futures through commodity firms or through brokers who specialize in commodities at large stock brokerage houses. But if you are a would-be buccaneer in the financial futures market, take a tip from the experts and do your trading on paper for a while, until you get your sea legs. If and when you are ready to start wheeling and dealing for real, then pick active markets, such as those trading in Treasury bill and Treasury bond futures. The more trading that is going on, the more likely you are to find a buyer or a seller for your contract at the price you want.

And don't forget to place stop orders with your broker. They instruct him to close out your position when the price reaches a certain level — and they can help you limit any losses.

The risks and rewards of futures trading are great because it is a highly leveraged business. If you put, say, $2,000 into the futures market, that entitles you to the gains — or losses — on Treasury bonds with a face value of $100,000, or Treasury bills worth $1 million. But if the value of your contract drops, you will have to ante up more cash to cover the losses. If you have guessed wrong, you can easily lose as much as $2,000 in a day's trading in most financial futures. Of course, you can make substantial gains, too, but this kind of trading — while increasingly popular — is not for those who aren't prepared to take substantial risks.

Financial Planners

WHAT THEY CAN DO FOR YOU

He is part investment adviser, part accountant, part lawyer and part psychologist. He is the financial planner, a Renaissance type who perhaps should be playing an important role in your life.

The financial planner promises to fit together the pieces of your own personal financial puzzle. Even if your income is modest, you can get specific help from a planner, usually for a fee of $50 to $150 an hour. If your annual income is higher — say, $35,000 or more — and quite a few two-income families *are* in that category, you may well find it worthwhile to locate a professional who can map out a comprehensive master plan for you. If it is done wisely, it can put you on the right path in budgeting your spending, making your investments, paying your taxes, setting up your estate and insuring yourself. For that you will pay anywhere from one thousand to several thousand dollars. The costs are steep, but planners' fees for tax and investment counseling at least are tax deductible.

Some planners earn their money not from fees but from commissions on the securities, mutual funds, insurance, tax shelters and other so-called financial products that they sell you. But you run the risk that this kind of planner may be more interested in selling than creating the best plan for you.

When picking a planner, you also have a choice between an independent or one affiliated with a big institution. Independents tend to offer more personalized service, but the institutional planners have advantages, too. The most active of the institutions in this field are stock brokerages. They often have financial planning subsidiaries, and their members try hard not to oversell stocks as solutions to all your investment needs. But the subsidiaries can tap the parent firm's research and provide the kind of stock-picking skill that independents often lack.

Some banks, insurance companies and mutual funds simply churn out a computer-generated boilerplate plan to attract new accounts. Although you might pay only $40 for such a plan, the mounds of preprinted information you will receive could be little more helpful than advice to update your will. And that is counsel you hardly have to pay for.

Financial Planners

WHAT THEY ARE ADVISING

W HAT do some of the country's best financial planners advise their clients?

One tip that planners often give to their clients is to spread their income among their own family members. For example, Mark McCormack of Cleveland recommends that parents should make interest-free loans to their children. The money is then saved or invested, and the kids pay low taxes or none at all on what the money earns. Two planners in San Antonio, David Bridgforth and Eugene Duff, think parents should consider giving each child as much as $10,000 a year — if they possibly can afford it — so that the money can accumulate income at low rax rates.

Financial planners also say you should take a hard look at your life insurance. Gary Pittsford of Indianapolis believes that many people who bought a policy just five years ago are spending too much on premiums. He notes that competition in the insurance industry has brought rates down. His strategy includes cashing in an old whole life policy, investing the proceeds and buying annual renewable term insurance.

Some people tend to put all their investment eggs in one basket. As Atlanta planner Harold Gourgues observes, "People tend to stick with whatever has worked for them once." Fortunately, it is easy for you to diversify. A number of planners are high on tax-sheltered limited partnerships, which you can buy for several thousand dollars from brokers and some planners themselves.

Taxes, of course, figure strongly in the advice that financial planners give to clients. Planner Donald Wright of Philadelphia notes that you can benefit from astute tax planning even in your charitable donations. Say that instead of giving cash, you donate $500 in stock on which you have a profit. In that case, you can get the same $500 tax deduction and you actually save money because you don't have to pay capital gains taxes on your profit.

Financial Planners

HOW TO FIND ONE

MANY people can benefit from consulting a financial planner. If you are one of them, make sure that any planner you get knows a lot about taxes, investments and estate planning.

You can start looking for the right financial planner close to home. Ask your friends, your co-workers, and perhaps an accountant, a lawyer or other advisers for their recommendations. Look for a planner who also has professional credentials such as a broker's license in securities or real estate. Then question him closely during an interview.

You might ask how he is going to supply expertise in complex tax or estate problems. Some large planning firms have in-house specialists or close ties with top outsiders. Also, find out what other clients say about the planner. Even though the planner-client relationship is confidential, it is not out of line to ask for a reference or two.

You should find out how many accounts your prospective planner handles. And how big are they? If he is juggling 25 or so clients who have more money than you do, you may get shortchanged on service.

Your planner should be able to spend his time devising solutions to your problems. That time should not be wasted on doing arithmetic. So there is another question well worth putting to the planner you are interviewing: in figuring out the tax and other consequences of his various proposals, does he have access to a computer? The days of working with a pencil and yellow pad are over.

Two professional organizations can give you the names of planners in your area. One is the Institute of Certified Financial Planners. Its headquarters are at 3443 South Galena, Suite 190, Denver, Colorado 80231. The other source is the International Association for Financial Planning. It's located at 5775 Peachtree Dunwoody Road, Suite 120C, Atlanta, Georgia 30342.

Financial Supermarkets

PICKING AMONG THEM

FINANCIAL institutions have been rapidly merging, acquiring each other, and expanding the lines of products and services they sell in one location. Thus has dawned the era of the financial supermarket.

Sears is fast becoming a place to buy common stocks as well as stockings, houses as well as housewares, auto insurance as well as auto parts. And along with the lettuce and pork chops, Kroger is marketing mutual funds, annuities and insurance. You also can get a vast array of financial services at J.C. Penney, not to mention Merrill Lynch and Fidelity, among many other companies.

But before you close your bank account, cancel your insurance policy and bid your broker adieu for the bliss of one-stop financial shopping, you ought to consider the trade-offs. By opting for convenience, you may have to narrow your choices. For example, if you use a Sears financial supermarket for all your needs, your insurance policy will have to be from Allstate — because Sears owns Allstate.

People who want the most for their money from financial supermarkets should do as they do at regular supermarkets. Shop for the best that each has to offer and take advantage of their loss leaders. For instance, you might have an asset-management account with one firm but buy your insurance from another.

At times, instead of working together to create a coordinated financial plan for clients, the salespeople at some of the new combines compete with one another. A stockbroker, for example, may recommend that you buy low-cost term insurance and put the money you save in the stock market, while his insurance agent colleague at the adjacent counter may urge you to buy instead a costlier whole life policy.

If you're thinking about shopping in a financial supermarket, you can pick from quite a variety. One of the largest is Merrill Lynch. At its 430 stockbrokerage outlets, the firm offers what has become standard fare at any big brokerage plus certificates of deposit issued by various banks. And Merrill Lynch Realty, with offices in 32 cities, provides first mortgages. What you can't get is auto, life and homeowners insurance.

The Sears Financial Network includes the Dean Witter brokerage firm, Allstate insurance and Coldwell Banker real estate. Their services are offered in over 100 stores in most regions. At 23 of the stores in California, a fourth component of the financial center is Allstate Savings & Loan. Since each financial division in the Sears Network is quite distinct, don't expect anyone to coordinate your insurance, investments and savings.

The granddaddy of financial supermarkets is Investors Diversified Services. It has been selling financial planning, insurance and mutual funds across the U.S. since the 1950s. The sales force of 4,000 persons also sells tax shelters, but you cannot as yet trade stocks or bonds through IDS.

The Invest brokerage chain has offices in 23 savings and loans and savings banks nationwide, and plans soon to be in as many as 300. Through Invest brokers you can trade stocks, bonds and options, and you can buy the mutual funds of eight fund families.

Then there is the Boston-based Fidelity mutual fund group. You can call Fidelity's toll-free number (800–225–6190) and buy and sell its 25 mutual funds. You also can move money in and out of an asset-management account, trade stocks, bonds and options and invest in an Individual Retirement Account. Fidelity's brokerage fees can be as little as 30% of full-service commissions.

Franchises

HOW TO GET THE RIGHT ONE

Y OU could have bought a fast-food franchise for peanuts a few years ago and sold it today for as much as half a million dollars. But it is not too late to be your own boss and perhaps take a ride to prosperity. You can do that by acquiring one of the many *new* franchises.

If you get into a strong franchising system, the odds of surviving and making good as a small-business man or woman multiply impressively. And some of the strongest new franchises are those that provide services to businesses that cannot themselves afford to hire the people and buy the expensive equipment to do the work.

For example, you could open a barter franchise that helps business clients swap, say, old typewriters or backlogged inventory for extra airline tickets or machinery. A company in Greenville, South Carolina, called Barter Systems, Inc. runs such an operation. Or, you could provide such services for businesses as typing, copying, telexing and mail pickup. A company that franchises these services is Mail Boxes Etc. USA; it is based in Carlsbad, California.

Other promising franchise opportunities include photocopying and printing, specialized employment agencies and business brokers. These brokers bring together people who want to sell their small businesses with people who want to buy them. By doing just that, one Atlanta grandmother earned roughly $240,000 in commissions in only her second year of operation. Another group of franchises performs household services for people who are too busy to do them themselves. These chores run from housecleaning to protecting empty houses.

Service businesses have added a new dimension to franchising, but you also can find opportunities in its traditional backbone — retail stores. There is strong potential in stores that sell home computers, TV equipment and inexpensive furnishings. Restaurants that serve ethnic specialties such as Greek or Mexican food are taking off as well.

According to the U.S. Department of Commerce, these should be excellent times to run a franchise. The department predicted that franchise revenues would rise an average 13% in 1983. The reasons for that impressive jump are an improving economy and greater public recognition of franchise trademarks. Revenues of some franchises are expected to grow much faster than the average in the immediate future. They include health spas, exercise studios, private safe-deposit-box companies and automobile repair chains.

The "sleeping giant" of franchising may well be the mobile-phone industry. That's because the Federal Communications Commission is taking steps that will expand the use of phones in cars. Franchises will sell those phones and service and install them for people on the move who want to keep in touch.

If you are considering buying any kind of franchise, it may be wise not to wait. Although the average down payment has not risen in more than a year, it is expected to go up 10% as the economy recovers. That can be a sizable amount, considering that the average down payment for, say, a physical fitness or an automotive maintenance franchise is now around $30,000.

The Commerce Department puts out an excellent 430-page guide. It lists names and addresses of more than 1,000 franchise businesses, how much money a buyer has to invest in each and what kind of financial and managerial help he will get from the franchising company. The book is called *Franchise Opportunities Handbook,* and it costs $10. You can get it from the Superintendent of Documents, U.S. Government Printing Office, Washington, D.C. 20402.

Another comprehensive list of the offerings is in *The 1983 Franchise Annual Handbook and Directory.* It costs $19.95, plus $2 postage, and you can get it from INFO Press, 736 Center Street, Lewiston, New York 14092.

There are professional franchise consultants, but be careful in choosing one. According to the International Franchise Association in Washington, D.C., some people with little experience have set themselves up as franchise consultants and promise much more than they can deliver. Your best bet is to deal with a lawyer who is familiar with drawing up franchise contracts and with Federal Trade Commission rules on franchising. For a recommendation, try a franchise operator in your area or the local bar association.

Before you sign a contract to buy a franchise, the parent company must give you a disclosure statement. From it you can get the names and phone numbers of several franchisees. You would be wise to phone them to find out how well they are doing.

When you buy a franchise, you pay the company an initial fee and later a continuing royalty that can vary from 3% to 12% of gross sales. In return, you can use the company's trademark and franchising services for a set period, usually 10 to 20 years. The basic service is to give operating instructions, often covering everything from sales tactics to the color of the office carpeting. Capable companies also help you pick a business location and buy equipment and inventory. Their representatives sit in with you when you hire your first employees. They also hold your hand through crises.

Instead of running franchises themselves, many investors hire managers to operate them. But franchisors usually feel that the owner's attention is crucial and therefore will not sell units to people who intend to be absentee owners. That's understandable: few salaried managers will put in the 60 to 80 hours of work each week that it takes to make a business succeed.

Getting Organized

TACTICS FOR WORKING SMARTER

W HETHER you work at home juggling carpools and piano lessons or toil in an office trying to get everything done, you have probably vowed that someday — at long last — you will *get yourself organized*. In fact, with the help of a calendar, a notebook, a few file folders — and willpower — you can work not harder, but smarter.

The principles of good organization are the tried and tested old clichés, and they really work: "First things first" and "One thing at a time" and, of course, "When in doubt, throw it out."

The tactics of sensible organization are just as obvious: make lists, plan ahead, avoid distractions, clear away clutter. But staying organized is a lifetime project. You must hew to it with the ardor of a 12th-century monastic as you avoid gossip sessions in the office, unnecessary phone calls and long, liquid lunches.

Where to begin? Most experts on organization believe you should start your program by tackling the most difficult problem — time management. There always seems to be too much to do and not enough time to do it.

First, you should unjam your schedule by taking on less. Have the nerve to say no to those requests to head the Chip-and-Dip Committee for the company picnic or write a memo on the Misuse of Company Stationery.

Then there are the tasks that you can delegate to others. That is just what a Los Angeles career couple did when they went to the extreme measure of hiring a 22-year-old person to do their shopping, pick up their cleaning and perform other household chores. The couple called him their "wife."

No matter how much or how little you want to accomplish, getting it all done usually requires following the standard practice of making a list. Writing the list just before you leave work at the end of the day helps get you off to a fast start the next day. You might even keep a second list that would detail all the foreseeable tasks you want to accomplish. Each day you pick 10 items from that list and put them on your daily sheet.

You might be wise to construct a personal time log. Write down everything you do for two weeks. That way, you can get a sense of the amount of time you typically need to perform certain jobs. Try to drop or delegate those tasks that take huge amounts of time but produce small rewards. Concentrate on the chores that produce large benefits for the time you put in.

Do you keep putting off little tasks because they are boring and have nothing to do with your real goals in life? If so, make an appointment with yourself once a week when your energy is running low to get through all the niggling but necessary paperwork that has to be dealt with.

Are you the victim of unwelcome interruptions such as drop-in visitors who plunk down in a chair and keep you from getting anything done? Maybe you are encouraging them — for instance, by making eye contact as a co-worker passes your desk. Some time-management specialists recommend turning your desk around so that you sit sideways to the door. That should keep you from making the first fateful eye contact without alienating co-workers.

Is your desk a mess? Just throw out the clutter, the memos, clippings, reports and monthly summaries you keep. Chances are you will never look at most of what you save. If you could readily replace a document, then why not chuck it?

As for the material you do decide to keep, try sorting it into four piles: first, items that require your action; second, papers that must be referred to other people; third, all reading material; and fourth, items that have to be kept in your files because it is part of your job to keep them.

Unfortunately, each mail delivery brings with it more paper, including a request that you do something at a future date. To organize all those new piles take an accordion-shaped file folder and number the compartments from one to 31, for each day in the month. Put the papers in them. Then, first thing each morning, run through the file for that date and act on all those notes that say what you must do that day.

If you are really in a mess, you may have to seek professional help. It is available from specialists called time managers, who stand ready to sort out your schedule and your clutter. They are listed in the Yellow Pages under "Management Consultants," and the best way to sort them out from corporate consultants is simply to call around. They charge from $100 a day to $150 an hour.

Ginnie Maes

SAFETY AND HIGH YIELDS

I F you like the safety of U.S. government securities, you might want to consider buying so-called Ginnie Maes. These securities are issued by the Government National Mortgage Association and in mid-1983 they were paying 12.7%. You receive monthly payments of both principal and interest.

Ginnie Maes come in minimums of $25,000, but you also can get them in mutual funds or in unit trusts. These are fixed portfolios of securities. A number of large brokerage houses in mid-1983 were offering such trusts with a 11½% to 12½% yield and a minimum investment of about $1,000. The sales charge is typically 3½%. If you wish, you can buy these units for your IRA or Keogh accounts.

Some unit trusts allow you to write an unlimited number of checks; the minimum check amount is usually $500. You can reinvest your monthly interest or principal, which allows your interest to compound and keeps your money continually working for you. And you can cash in your units at any time without fees or penalties.

Gold

YOUR CHOICES FOR INVESTING

THE price of gold fluctuates for reasons that are as much emotional as economic, and it always shines brightest when the world looks darkest. So when the metal loses some of its luster, as it has done several times since its high of $875 an ounce in January 1980, an investor in the stuff has mixed feelings. He is relieved that the armies of the night have decided not to camp in his backyard, but he bemoans his lost profits. If you believe that high inflation, oil-supply interruptions and world monetary crises will erupt yet again, you might be inclined to invest in precious metals. Then you have to decide which of the many forms of metal to buy.

Extreme pessimists who have no faith in any country's currency probably would prefer gold bars. But owning gold bullion can be a nuisance. You have to pay for storage and insurance, and you also may have to transport the metal to and from dealers, and perhaps pay assay costs when you sell.

A simpler way to invest in gold — or silver and platinum — is to buy certificates of ownership. They signify that you own a specified amount of the metal stored in bank vaults. When the time comes to sell, a phone call is all that is necessary. Your minimum initial purchase might be $1,000. After that, you can make subsequent investments for as little as $100. Commissions range from 2% to 5%, depending on the kind and quantity of the metal.

Many people prefer to buy one-ounce gold coins such as South African Krugerrands or Canadian Maple Leafs than to purchase certificates. In April 1983 banks, brokers and coin dealers also began trading in U.S. gold medallions; they come in one-ounce and half-ounce sizes. Although you pay 4% to 5% more than their gold content is worth, and sales tax on top of that, coins are easier to resell than gold certificates or bars. The easy portability and worldwide acceptance of coins appeal to the so-called refugee mentality.

Shares of high-quality South African mining companies offer high dividends and a chance at capital appreciation. In mid-1983, when gold was selling for about $425 an ounce, the dividends were 10%. But if and when the price of gold rises, the mines pass along almost all of their increased profits to stockholders. At $600 an ounce, dividends would leap to 12% to 14%. But buying gold stocks subjects your investment to political and economic risks, notably racial unrest in South Africa.

Another way to buy gold without acquiring the metal itself is to invest in one of the half-dozen gold mutual funds. They acquire the shares of gold-mining companies, and so they provide some diversification. These funds lately have done better than gold, in part because gold stocks pay dividends but gold alone does not.

Of the 350 mutual funds of all types that are analyzed for *Money* magazine, the one that rose fastest in the 12 months through June 1983 was United Services Gold Shares. It jumped 188.7%, and in the five years through mid-1983, it rose 645.9%. Number five on the mutual-fund list was another gold fund, Strategic Investments. It was up 157.4% in the 12 months through June 1983 and 575.8% over the past five years. But before you rush out to buy, remember that just as gold stocks generally rise faster than gold when the market is up, so too they usually plunge faster than the metal when its price falls.

Health Care

HOW TO CUT YOUR COSTS

THE price of a visit to the doctor has tripled since 1967, from an average of $11 to more than $33. In that period, the cost of a day in the hospital has more than quadrupled, leaping from $34 to $152. Although health insurance policies are more generous than ever, you will probably still face some sizable medical bills if you or a family member become ill or injured. But you can negotiate with your doctor, save on drugs and use other safe strategies to trim the bills that your insurance does not pay.

One way to cut your costs is simply to ask your doctor to lower his price — if you consider it out of line or if you think your steady patronage entitles you to a discount. Physicians' fees are surprisingly negotiable.

You also can save on drugs. Health insurance may pay up to 80% of your prescription drug bill. But you will pay 20% of a smaller amount if you buy generic drugs. They are virtually identical to brand-name drugs in all but a handful of instances. Ask your doctor to write out the generic name or indicate on his prescription that the pharmacist is at liberty to substitute a generic equivalent of a brand-name drug.

When you buy either kind of drug, remember that you will likely get a better price from a chain drugstore than from an independent druggist. That's because chains can buy in bulk. So can mail-order outlets, which are another good alternative.

Only six out of 10 Americans have dental insurance, so it's helpful to know that comparison shopping for a dentist can produce significant savings. In New York, for example, you can pay as little as $15 or as much as $50 for a routine cleaning.

A way to save on simple procedures is to let dental students practice their skills on your teeth at a clinic of any of the 60 U.S. dental schools. Clinics do work at fees that are roughly half what you would pay a regular dentist. Students are in the final two years of their four-year dental school education and you will be relieved to know that they are closely supervised. Trouble is, they may subject you to three times as much time in the chair as experienced dentists.

A less trying way to save may be to seek out a dental clinic run by a hospital. These clinics are staffed by new graduates. They are faster, less error-prone and command higher fees than students. But they charge as much as one-third less than private practitioners.

Medical insurance usually does not cover more than half the cost of psychotherapy, and psychiatrists in private practice charge $40 to $100 for a 50-minute hour. Fortunately, there are less costly — and equally beneficial — options.

Psychologists and specially trained social workers can treat people with emotional problems at a fraction of what psychiatrists charge. For anything other than private, individual treatment in the therapist's office, you usually can save money. The same therapist might charge you only half as much to treat you in a clinic as in his own private office.

Another way to save is group therapy, which costs $15 to $40 a session. Or if you suffer from a well-defined problem, such as anxiety about a new job, so-called brief psychotherapy might be your best course. The treatment aims to accomplish a specific goal in a limited number of sessions, typically 20.

Still another expense you can reduce is that for eyeglasses or contact lenses. Ophthalmologists provide the contact lenses that they prescribe, but usually you must take an ophthalmologist's prescription for eyeglasses to an optician. He grinds the lenses and sells frames but has no set training. Ophthalmologists charge $30 to $50 for a routine examination and up to $350 for a pair of soft lenses.

But, if you don't have complex vision problems, investing in an exam by an ophthalmologist is like retaining a Nobel Prize–winning economist to figure your taxes. For a routine eye exam, an optometrist is good enough. Optometrists prescribe *and* sell both eyeglasses and contacts. Including eye exam, a pair of glasses bought through an optometrist is roughly 10% lower than a pair prescribed by an ophthalmologist and bought from an optician.

Health Care

CHECKING UP ON YOUR HEALTH INSURANCE

MANY people who rely on their health insurance to pay their big medical bills are leaning on a rubber crutch. Some 7.5 million families a year spend at least 10% of their income for uninsured medical expenses. Even if you are among the 85% of Americans covered by health insurance, you will find that almost no policy will pay all your medical bills all the time. That is why you should give your health insurance policy a thorough examination, diagnose its weaknesses and take steps to remedy them.

Many of your policy's ills can be cured with additional coverage. If you are hospitalized, for example, most policies will pick up 100% of the cost of your stay in a semi-private room up to a certain length of time. After that some will pay for 80%. But if your plan will not do that, your best protection against bankroll-breaking bills is to buy an individual major medical policy from Blue Cross/Blue Shield or one of the big private insurance companies.

This picks up where basic hospital and doctor-bill plans leave off. Benefits usually range from $25,000 all the way to $1 million — and some policies provide unlimited coverage.

It is also wise to buy an individual major medical policy if your current plan has limits on how much it will pay for surgery. But don't waste your money on the so-called dread-disease policies, which insure you against specific illnesses such as cancer. That's like insuring only part of your car.

Most health plans have limits on the total benefits you can collect in your lifetime. The Health Insurance Association of America recommends $250,000 for each person covered. If you are ill at ease with your plan's maximum, you can supplement it at relatively low cost. For example, a family of four can buy a policy that pays all costs above $25,000 — up to a maximum $1 million. The price is $360 to $500 a year.

About the only thing you cannot buy additional insurance for is your deductible for such outpatient expenses as doctor's appointments, prescription drugs, lab tests and private nurses. The deductible is the bare minimum you absolutely have to pay. These deductibles vary from $50 to $500 a year.

When you give your health insurance policy its routine physical, you will discover that some expenses just are not covered. In addition, two-income couples with different employers have two policies to scrutinize. The strengths of one may make up for the weaknesses of the other.

Try to avoid so-called indemnity plans — which pay no more than the fixed and specified amount listed in the policy for particular operations or for a hospital bed. An indemnity policy that pays $100 a day for your room takes care of as little as a third of the cost.

In group health plans, the insurer cannot cut off anybody's coverage, no matter how many claims he collects. But at the end of many an individual policy's term — usually once a year — the company can cop out. To head off cancellation of an individual policy, buy a guaranteed-renewable policy. It specifies that the company can neither cancel the coverage, so long as you pay the premiums, nor raise your rates merely because you have filed several expensive claims.

You should keep your policy up to date, especially at major milestones in your life. Will you or a family member soon reach age 65? Watch out! It is *your* responsibility to apply for Medicare at your local Social Security office no later than three months after you turn 65. Most group plans stop regular coverage at 65 and offer only a supplement to Medicare. If you do not apply and then become ill, you may have to pay your own medical bills.

If you are retiring before 65, make sure you are still covered under your group plan. Otherwise, you will have to buy a high-priced policy on your own. And if you are laid off or fired, ask your employer to continue your coverage for at least 30 to 90 days. If you do not get that protection, shop around for an interim policy to insure you for a few months.

When your child turns 19 years old — or 23 if he is a student — he will have to fend for himself. Your policy does not cover him. And remember, divorce ends a nonworking spouse's coverage. But laws in some 38 states allow him or her to convert readily to an individual policy with the same carrier — at his or her own expense. Also, if a working spouse dies, find out how long an employer will continue the widow or widower's coverage.

One further tip on health insurance. Look for a policy with what is called stop-loss protection. That limits your maximum out-of-pocket medical expenses in any year, usually to $1,500 for a single person or $3,000 for a family. The policy pays for everything above that. If your group policy does not have a stop-loss clause, you can urge your employer to add it to the company policy. The cost is reasonable: $60 for an individual, $180 for a family of four.

Health Care

HOW TO FIND A GOOD DOCTOR

O NE of your most important investments, surely, is your investment in health care. So it is smart to spend at least as much time selecting a good doctor as it is, say, to pick a new car or a house. Not all doctors are created equal. You can measure them against certain yardsticks of quality, but you must be willing to do some research.

Start your search by assembling a list of candidates. Ask neighbors, friends and fellow workers for recommendations. If you are moving to a new town or neighborhood, get a few names of prospective physicians from the doctor you have been seeing in your old town and neighborhood. You also can request referrals from your company's medical department; that is the simplest way to get the names of professionals who have earned reputations among patients for reliability. In addition, you can ask local medical and dental societies for the names of practitioners who take new patients.

You can consult the American Medical Association directory, which is available in large public libraries. It lists the names, education and specialties of all U.S. doctors. Alternatively, you can telephone the internal-medicine or family-practice department of the nearest university-owned or university-affiliated teaching hospital and get the names of doctors who are on the staff. Finally, you might ask your pharmacist to suggest doctors who he feels are well qualified. He or she is in a good position to know which ones are up to date on the latest drugs.

Once you have found two or three candidates, call their offices and speak to the doctor if you can. Ask what he or she charges for some selected procedures such as a basic physical exam. If the physician won't say, move on to the next. You can even drop by for a get-acquainted interview. Doctors often do not charge for a few minutes' talk with a potential patient.

You will want to find out whether the doctor practices alone or as part of a group or in a health maintenance organization, a so-called HMO. This is a prepaid group health plan that provides physicians and hospitalization for its members as needed. There is little scientific evidence to suggest that your care will be any better or any worse in one type of practice or another. But many people feel that they get more individual attention — and hence better care — from a solo practitioner. On the other hand, in a group or an HMO the patient can receive free consultation from many specialists. (For more, see "Health Care: Health Maintenance Organizations.")

Studies indicate that the prestige of the doctor's medical school or its location — in the U.S. or abroad — makes little difference in the quality of care that he delivers. Two other criteria are far more important.

First, where did the doctor complete his residency? The best training programs generally are found at university-owned hospitals.

Second, has the doctor passed a certification exam given by the professional organization that oversees his specialty? Certification is no guarantee of excellence, but it is the best yardstick you have. You can check the doctor's credentials in the *Directory of Medical Specialists,* available at many public libraries.

When you judge a doctor, also consider the hospitals he uses. You can't check into a hospital, except in an emergency, unless your doctor can admit you there. To do that, he must have been screened by its credentials committees and granted admitting privileges. Good doctors use good hospitals, so selecting the right physician can solve two potential problems.

When you are traveling and need medical care, you should call the county medical or dental society or the Travelers Aid Society for names of available practitioners. Be sure to take along an ample supply of any medication you may need. Carry it with you — not in a suitcase that might get lost. If you run out, you probably will need to see a local doctor for a new prescription.

When you are overseas, an American embassy or consulate can provide the names of English-speaking doctors, although the U.S. government does not guarantee their expertise. Doctors' and hospital bills overseas usually must be paid in cash, but your health insurance program may reimburse you — after you return home.

At home or away, once you have found a doctor, if you think his bills are too high, tell him so. To repeat: It is remarkable how many doctors are willing to come down in price.

Health Care

HOW TO PICK A HOSPITAL

W HEN you need to go to the hospital for medical care, it is not necessarily the best idea to head for the nearest one.

In judging a hospital, the basic gauge is whether it has the approval of the nonprofit Joint Commission on the Accreditation of Hospitals. You can be sure that an accredited hospital has met certain standards of excellence in 24 categories.

For most medical problems, accredited community hospitals without teaching programs are good enough. Their staffs are competent, their costs tend to be about 15% lower than those of university hospitals and they have the reputation of being more hassle-free. For fairly routine treatment, it usually does not matter whether the hospital is municipally owned, or is privately owned and nonprofit, or is privately owned and for-profit.

However, for major surgery or serious illnesses, it just does not pay to be anywhere but in a university-owned hospital, or a hospital that conducts teaching programs for a university or a specialty center such as a children's hospital or an institute devoted to the treatment of a particular disease.

Teaching and specialty hospitals tend to have doctors who are the most up to date. Another advantage of those institutions is that they generally see hundreds of patients a month. And, in medicine as in most disciplines, practice makes nearly perfect. Especially in surgery, volume is key. If the surgeons at a hospital do not perform 40 to 50 operations each year, they are probably not maintaining their skills. For heart surgeons, it should be closer to 200 or 300 operations annually.

How do you find out about a surgeon's or a hospital's volume? You have no choice but to ask. If your doctor does not want to tell you, try to gather information from local consumer groups, from insurance companies or from your state hospital association.

When surgery seems called for, a second opinion also makes financial sense. It can save your insurer money and you an operation. Many of the nonprofit insurers in the Blue Cross network have recognized the importance of second opinions. And in some states, these organizations are encouraging them — and paying for them.

Health Care

HEALTH MAINTENANCE ORGANIZATIONS

IF you want to keep your medical bills down, consider joining a health maintenance organization. These HMOs are prepaid group health plans that provide physicians and hospitalization for all your needs. The HMO takes your family aboard for a flat yearly fee. Usually it is $1,800 for a family of any size, and often it is paid by employers. The HMO bets that it can keep you well. If it does, it comes out ahead.

HMOs do whatever they can on an outpatient basis. And they often reward their doctors in the form of year-end bonuses and profit sharing if they succeed in keeping their clients out of the hospital. A common criticism is that HMOs are too impersonal. At most of them, members cannot count on seeing the same doctor every time. But by and large, HMOs do provide good health care at reasonable prices — as their 11 million members can attest.

Health Care

THE COSTS OF PLASTIC SURGERY

PLASTIC surgery is performed on an astonishing 1 million patients a year. But what are the costs — and the real values — of those operations?

Depending on the procedure and the doctor, surgical fees range from $500 for common dermabrasion to $5,000 for a thigh and buttocks resculpturing. But a trend toward performing plastic surgery right in the doctor's office is eliminating steep hospital costs for many patients. A single overnight stay in a hospital for a face-lift might easily cost $2,000 to $3,500 for operating room fees and a private room; in a surgeon's office the same person would pay only $250 to $400 in fees for the room and various equipment — in addition to the doctor's bill, of course.

The operations now routinely done in doctors' offices include face-lifts, eyelid and nose surgery and hair transplants. An office nose job, for example, can take as little as 30 minutes. Then the patient spends a couple of hours resting in a recovery room and goes home with a lot of dos and don'ts and a telephone number where the doctor can be reached, if necessary.

At least 10% of cosmetic surgery patients are men, and the ratio is rising. Some of them hope to enhance their business careers by getting rid of a receding chin or an oversized nose; others simply want to smooth away the signs of aging. But, as one surgeon warns, "We can't make people into movie stars or mend broken marriages — the only way to get rid of every line and wrinkle is to embalm you."

What a doctor can do is help you look younger or more attractive, after explaining the surgical risks. They are slight — if you have a good surgeon. And what are the doctor's fees for these surgical procedures?

Hair transplants run $1,000 to $2,000 for a moderately bald man.

A face-lift can cost between $2,000 and $5,000. In the newest procedure, the surgeon not only tightens the skin but also resculptures the jawline and neck by removing excess fat. Then he cuts and resews a neck muscle to form a kind of sling to support the neck and chin. Pain should be minimal and discoloration is gone in ten days or so. It is still too soon to know how long the lift will last with this new procedure.

The news about nose jobs is that they are no longer the assembly line reshaping of a decade ago. At a cost of between $1,000 and $3,000 you should get a nose that is natural and fits your face. The operation is done mostly from the inside out, so there is no visible scarring.

Whatever the estimated cost, a plastic surgeon will not raise his scalpel until you have paid him in full. The doctors say that since the surgery is elective, high postponement and cancellation rates mess up their busy schedules. More likely, though, doctors fear that some patients would refuse to pay after seeing the results. If you are less than pleased with the results, your only recourse is to sue.

Even if you are satisfied with the surgery, medical insurance probably will not pay for it unless the work is considered rehabilitative, such as breast reconstruction. One uplifting note: plastic surgery often qualifies for a medical deduction on your income tax. But no matter how much you have to pay, don't expect the moon. While cosmetic surgery can help you turn back the clock, you can't stop it forever.

Health Care

SELECTING A PLASTIC SURGEON

IF you pick a plastic surgeon, you should do it as though your life depended on it. In rare cases of complication, it might. An alarming number of practitioners are charlatans. There is nothing to prevent an M.D. from hanging out a shingle, calling himself a plastic surgeon and making extravagant advertising claims. According to the head of a plastic surgeon's watchdog committee in San Francisco, misleading advertising has resulted in numerous catastrophes and three known deaths in California.

One way to measure a surgeon's skill is to check his certification. If he does all kinds of cosmetic surgery, he should be certified by the American Board of Plastic Surgery. You can get a list of board-certified surgeons from the American Society of Plastic and Reconstructive Surgeons in Chicago. A dermatologist doing hair transplants and skin peelings should be certified by the American Board of Dermatology.

Your surgeon should be affiliated with a reputable hospital or a medical school, even if he performs most of his operations in his office. Without the right qualifications, a hospital would not accept him. Moreover, doctors on hospital staffs are subject to review by their peers.

A plastic surgeon should be willing to spend plenty of time answering your questions. Some charge nothing for the first consultation, whether you decide to go ahead with surgery or not. Others ask for $35 to $50 as a consultation fee. If you don't think a surgeon is right for you, it is better to write off the consultation fee and find someone better.

The stakes in plastic surgery are always big. Your best protection is to put yourself in the hands of a responsible surgeon.

Hobbies

PROFIT FROM YOUR LEISURE

To enhance their incomes, more and more Americans are finding ways to get money for their fun. They are turning spare-time hobbies into ready cash. People are trading coins, playing the saxophone, performing magic, hybridizing plants — all for money.

Pastimes involving sports and entertainment seem most likely to turn into money-makers. One rewarding way for sports fans and aging athletes to stay close to the action is to become referees. A basketball ref can start out officiating at high schools for $15 to $40 a game. After a while he can graduate to college basketball for $60 to $200 a varsity match. Working just fifty nights a year, a college referee can earn as much as $10,000.

Some hobbies hardly ever work out well as profitable money-makers. Many indoor gardeners, for instance, try to convince themselves that cash can blossom on their blooms. In practice, the commercial growers offer such wide variety and low prices that you simply cannot compete with them from your home.

What is really blooming is the market for crafts. There are between 6,000 and 8,000 craft fairs a year, and most of them are markets for amateurs. A growing number of boutiques and even department stores also provide outlets, but their standards for handmade items are high.

A basic guideline for any hobbyist is that only quality sells. So whether you want to weave a rug or blow a trumpet for money, you have to do it well. Even the amateur has to be professional, businesslike and original. Countless talented people fail because they never grasp the importance of such basic business principles as sensible record-keeping or promotion.

If you decide to turn your hobby into a moneymaking activity, you may find that it produces some fascinating tax breaks. For example, a New York stockbroker earned $2,000 a year by catering parties that featured such concoctions as his pink macaroni salad. His entire earnings went to hospitals and charities in the form of contributions made to his own nonprofit foundation by the party-givers. Since it is a nonprofit foundation, both the party-givers and the broker benefit. They get a tax deduction on their contributions. And his catering fees, which he really does not need anyhow because he is an affluent stockbroker, don't become part of his taxable income.

Hobbies are treated under a special section of the tax code. Any expenses you incur can be deducted, but only from the income you derive from the hobby. Suppose you spend $1,000 to buy yak teeth. Later you find you have overestimated the market for yak teeth bracelets and you can sell only one of them for $8.75. Result: You can deduct from your taxable income just $8.75 of the $1,000 you spent.

This hobby loss limit is waived when your pastime becomes a business. Then you can take deductions larger than your hobby income; that is, you can create a shelter for other income.

If you can manage to make a profit in two out of five years, the IRS automatically assumes your hobby is a business. Even if you cannot pass the two years out of five test, you may still be able to convince the IRS that you are seriously trying to make a profit. You can help make a solid case by keeping accurate and up-to-date records, showing you work hard at your avocation, and by expending a serious effort to sell. If you are convincing, the tax court may let you claim losses for a decade or more, even if you cannot muster one profitable year.

In a cash business — most craft and part-time paid activities are strictly cash — the temptation to ignore the taxman is strong. Since there is no record of the transactions, the IRS probably will never hear of them. But your anonymity will not last long if you are determined to succeed in business. Then you will become profitable, maybe even rich and famous, and you can be sure that the taxman will not overlook you.

Home Improvements

COPING WITH CONTRACTORS

A MAJOR home improvement project is not likely to be a tranquil experience, but it should not be a calamity either. Your satisfaction with the job may depend more than anything else on how skillfully you choose and deal with the carpenters, plumbers, electricians and any other contractors you hire to work on your house.

To get the best deal from a contractor, first of all be careful whom you hire. You can get names of financially sound workmen from bankers and storekeepers who deal with them. Local chapters of such trade groups as the National Association of Home Builders and the National Association of the Remodeling Industry also can point you to reliable contractors. And the Better Business Bureau keeps files on tradesmen who have drawn complaints.

Once you have located several candidates for a substantial job, evaluate them carefully. One consideration is rapport. It's a mistake to hire a workman just because he is engaging; yet it's also wrong to dismiss personal chemistry. Pick someone you can communicate with. And visit one of his job sites. If the place is messy and disorganized, it's reasonable to wonder whether the tradesman takes meticulous care in his work.

When picking a contractor, ask yourself the following questions:

— Was he recommended by a trustworthy source?

— Has he supplied the names of previous customers whom you can check for references?

— How long has he been in business under the same name? More than 10 years is a definite plus.

— Will the contractor give you his home address and phone number?

— Has he agreed to include starting and completion dates in the contract?

— Does a check with his bank indicate that he is financially sound?

— Did he offer you a *written* guarantee?

Finally, if you answer yes to the next two questions, perhaps you should look for another contractor:

Has he made oral promises that he won't put in the contract? And, did he offer you a discount for signing up at once? If so, those are danger signals you cannot afford to ignore.

For your big home improvements, try to get at least three bids. When all have come in, discard any astronomical ones. But you may want to choose the contractor who comes highly recommended even if his bid is *not* the lowest.

No bid is set in concrete. So negotiate with the contractor you really want. Contractors expect their profit to be 10% to 25% of a project's total cost. But if they need work, they will accept less.

Whether you are renovating your whole house or simply adding kitchen cabinets, following some basic rules will help you get the most from your contractor.

First, before hiring any workmen, write a tight contract that cites the details of the job practically to the last nut and bolt. For example, in remodeling a bathroom, you would designate the brand name, model number and color of appliances and fixtures. You would also specify materials for cabinetry, countertops and hardware.

Start with a standard form, called an owners and contractors construction agreement, to spell out your expectations. The forms are available at many stationery stores. Be sure to put down the particulars of your job, including the following: a precise list of all work to be done and appliances and fixtures to be installed; the starting and approximate completion dates of the work; a stipulation that all work must be done to the highest standards and a guarantee to provide replacement materials and additional labor, if necessary; and, finally, a provision that the contractor is responsible for obtaining any required building permits.

If work goes awry, your most potent weapon is to withhold your payment. Homeowners customarily put down 10% when the contract is signed, then another 30% as each third of the job is completed. But in making payments, be sure you always keep enough money in reserve to hire someone else if the necessity arises.

Home Maintenance

GIVING YOUR HOUSE ITS SEMI-ANNUAL PHYSICAL

Every spring and autumn is the time to save some money, and protect what is probably your biggest investment, by giving your house its semi-annual top-to-bottom physical examination. No matter how invulnerable your home may look, hazards to its health lurk almost everywhere. So it pays to head off problems in the early stages by practicing preventive maintenance.

The most serious peril to your house is probably water. It's wise to get out and check that your gutters and shingles are well maintained. If your shingles are loose or cracked, leave any repairs to a professional. He should charge $20 to $25 per shingle for any that he replaces. But a $3 tube of latex caulking compound should be enough for you to fill any gaps in the seal around windows and doors and the junctures between the foundation and patios, porches and walks. Such steps can save you hundreds, even thousands, of dollars in emergency repairs later on.

You also can save both time and money by repairing your house in stages rather than all at once. The south side usually needs painting every three to six years. The other sides require it only every eight to ten years.

It's tempting to postpone brick, concrete and asphalt repair jobs. However, you shouldn't underestimate the damage that can be done by water freezing in masonry cracks. The repair work is often back-straining, but the consequences of not doing it promptly can be costly.

You don't need a plumber to fix your dripping faucets. Usually you can do that with just a wrench and a 10¢ washer. Your savings on water can be surprising.

The indoor preventive maintenance you should perform most often is to change or clean the filters in air conditioners and hot-air furnaces. Tend to furnaces about three times a year and central air-conditioning systems twice as often. Filthy filters can reduce their efficiency 10% to 25%. Yet you can get new ones for only about $1 each. That's a real money-saving investment. An oil-fired furnace should be professionally cleaned and serviced once a year. The charge should be about $40.

Not even the most well-meaning homeowners are always the best equipped to perform preventive maintenance without professional guidance. Fortunately, there is a wealth of books that can help you do many repairs yourself. One way to choose among the wide variety of books is to focus on a project you know something about. Say it's repairing a faucet;

then check that section in several volumes and get the one that describes it most clearly.

Among the best is *The New York Times Complete Manual of Home Repair* by Bernard Gladstone. It costs $14.95. An even better guide is the *Reader's Digest Complete Do-It-Yourself Manual*. That $19.99 tome contains almost everything a homeowner could possibly want to know.

The 36-volume home repair and improvement series published by Time-Life Books also gets high marks from do-it-yourself advisers. Each volume concentrates on a particular subject — for example, masonry, plumbing or wiring. For $9.95 you can buy the specific volume you need.

Two more narrowly focused books can help you forestall problems. One is *Homeowner's Handbook* by Michael McClintock, at $5.95. It's especially helpful in diagnosing difficulties. The second is *Principles of Home Inspection* by Joseph G. McNeill. If you skip the technical parts aimed at professionals, this $15.95 book will give you a lot of readily understandable advice.

Home Movers

HOW TO FIND ONE

T HE act of moving from one city to another is among life's most stressful events, yet you can avoid the three major hassles of moving: delay, damage and overcharging.

How do you find a good mover? First, ask friends and co-workers who have moved recently, or your real estate agent or the person who arranges transfers at your company. Then, call the local Better Business Bureau, or consumer protection agency or state licensing authority, which is usually the Public Utilities Commission. Ask if substantial numbers of complaints have been lodged against any of the companies' agents.

Next, pick at least three moving companies, and then invite the local agents of each one to inspect your belongings. The agents will give you written estimates of the cost and propose pickup and delivery dates. Some movers "lowball" their bids by underestimating the weight of a shipment just to land a job. You can protect yourself against lowballing by getting more than one estimate. And watch out for "weight bumping." That's the unethical practice of adding men to the truck or filling its huge fuel tank before going to a weighing station with your goods. To prevent that, you can arrange to be at the station when the empty truck is weighed, and check its fuel level. Then, return to the weighing station and check once more when the truck, now loaded with your belongings, is again on the scale.

It pays to read the Interstate Commerce Commission's booklet called *When You Move: Your Rights and Responsibilities.* For a free copy, write to the ICC, Office of Compliance and Consumer Assistance, Room 6328, 12th Street and Constitution Avenue, NW, Washington, D.C. 20423. And, if you ask, your mover is required by law to give you this booklet.

Housing

BUYING A HOUSE AT AUCTION

THE familiar auctioneer's chant of "going, going, gone!" these days can mean not that paintings or antiques have been sold — but a new house. To unload homes in a slow market, more and more builders and real estate developers have been auctioning them off to the highest bidders. California is the center of the auction action, and houses are also being auctioned in Florida, Georgia, Colorado and many other states.

If you are thinking of buying a house or a vacation condo, an auction could be your chance to pick up a bargain. That's because most houses are auctioned off in desperation only after they have languished on the market for a time. Usually they will go for less than the original asking price — often 20% to 40% below. More than that, developers frequently arrange favorable financing for such purchases.

But watch out. Savings can be illusory. Sellers sometimes jack up the asking price before the auction to encourage higher bidding. To be sure you are getting a bargain, you will need to find out whether the pre-auction price was in line with the asking prices of similar homes in the area. A local real estate broker should be able to tell you.

Fortunately, most developers advertise auctions in local newspapers at least a month in advance. *The Wall Street Journal* also carries ads for auctions of condos in popular resort regions. If you study the ads in advance, you have plenty of time to talk to agents and to comparison shop. Make sure you inspect any property you are thinking of buying and find out if there is any minimum bid.

Once your auction bid on a house is accepted, you will be asked to sign a standard sales agreement and fill out a mortgage application on the spot. Be prepared to leave 5% to 10% of the purchase price as a deposit. But if you change your mind, the seller is not obligated to return your money unless you fail to qualify for a mortgage. So look carefully before you leap into an auctioned house. And be sure you set a numerical limit on what you will bid, before you bid on anything.

Housing

INVESTING IN RENTAL HOUSING

THE real estate market seems poised for a comeback. So, investing in rental housing is looking good again as a tax shelter.

In mid-1983, you could buy many rental houses and apartments for less than they would have cost you a few years ago. At the same time, the government has made its real estate depreciation rules more generous. Landlords can deduct not only their taxes, mortgage interest and operating costs but also a fraction of the value of their property each year. Under the revised rules, that fraction has been increased. Some investors also will benefit from the new tax credit for rehabilitating a landmark house.

Buying a rental house is only a little different from buying a house to live in. Make sure that the neighborhood is economically stable. There is no quicker way to lose your money than to buy a house on a block that is about to be engulfed by crime. Look for solid construction and sturdy appliances before you worry about charm. As a landlord, be prepared for a lot of work and bother, unless you can find a reliable professional to manage the property. His services normally will cost you 6% to 10% of the rent and could go as high as 20% if you have a single-family house.

If you have older parents who need shelter, there is a great way for you to enjoy the tax benefits of being a landlord. The IRS used to outlaw most tax deductions when you rented your property to a close relative, but Congress eliminated that restriction starting in 1981. Now you can buy a condo or house, lease it to your elderly parents, and take deductions for maintenance, mortgage interest and depreciation, as well as for the cost of an occasional out-of-town visit to inspect the premises. The same applies when you buy a little bungalow in a college town to house your son or daughter, the student.

The IRS insists only that you charge your kin a fair market rent. You can easily document that by asking a local real estate broker for a written estimate of what rent the property should command.

Housing

INVESTING IN CONDOMINIUMS

THE best way to invest in the real estate market may well be by buying into condominiums. Investors are putting their money into condos despite predictions that from now on the rate of appreciation in housing prices will be not much higher than overall inflation. In fact, about one in five of all condos in the U.S. is held as an investment — that is, the owner rents it to others.

Real estate investments offer an attractive mix of rental income, tax benefits and capital gains. But ownership of a condo — that is, a dwelling unit in a group-owned building or on group-owned land — has additional advantages. Condos generally require less capital and have fewer maintenance problems than single-family houses do.

You can start out by buying a unit for personal use. All condo owners can deduct mortgage interest and real estate taxes from their taxable income. But people who rent out units also can deduct monthly maintenance and depreciation. These benefits, along with the rental income, often offset the costs of ownership.

Other investors convert whole apartment houses into condos. You can invest in one of these deals either directly, by buying a building and converting it, or indirectly, as a limited partner who supplies some of the capital but stays on the sidelines.

If you are a tenant in a converted building, you generally will have to pay twice as much per square foot for your apartment as the converter did. Even so, that price is almost invariably well below the market value of similar homes. Some tenants make a profit by immediately reselling. That's known as flipping.

Tenants who buy and stay on then generally have to pay more per month in maintenance fees and mortgage expenses than their previous rent, but much of that extra cost is offset by tax deductions.

Housing

SELLING YOUR OWN HOUSE

W HEN the housing market was in a severe slump in recent years, many desperate homeowners sold their houses all by themselves. *They* financed the buyer. But any homeowner who resorts to that so-called seller financing can lose plenty — if he is not careful.

Say that you decide to help provide the financing for the buyer of your house. Your first problem could be neglecting to do a thorough credit check on him. Although you might be planning to get tough the moment your buyer misses a payment, there is not much you can do.

You might figure you could threaten to foreclose — that is, take back your house. Just try it! Foreclosure can take months. All the time, your debtor can enjoy the comforts of your old home — and you can't exactly expect him to treat the house with tender loving care during the whole nasty affair.

After any foreclosure, your house probably will be sold at auction. Chances are the auction price will be a lot less than the house is really worth. And, you will have to pay around 5% of that winning bid to the foreclosure trustee.

Even the best-referenced creditor can go belly-up. Whatever you can do to make that option as unpleasant as possible for him will stand to your advantage. So demand a healthy down payment, at least 10%. For an insolvent buyer, it's a lot less painful to walk away from a mortgage contract with nothing to lose but a good credit rating than to lose both his credit rating and, say, $15,000.

If you want to finance the sale of your house yourself, you can enlist help from officers at your bank or savings and loan association. For a fee of 1% to 2% of the loan amount, they will service the mortgage you give to a buyer. The banker will do a credit check on the prospective buyer, collect his payments and handle a foreclosure — if one becomes necessary. In addition, the bank or savings and loan will sell you insurance against default. Typically, the cost is $300 for a $40,000 loan.

If you are considering financing the sale of your own house, make absolutely sure that you get professional help. That will help you avoid the perils of seller financing.

Once a mortgage contract is signed between seller and buyer, it's usually too late to make adjustments. So a mortgage contract always should be drafted by a professional — usually a lawyer — to meet the specific needs

[177]

of both home buyer and seller. Real estate agents, who are often involved in arranging owner financing, generally use blank forms that are filled in by the buyer and seller and later checked by the agency's lawyer. If the contract turns out not to be what you want, too bad.

In many states, for example, if a mortgage contract does not say that the loan you give to the buyer of your house is nonassumable, it is legally considered to be assumable. Thus, by simply promising in writing to make a loan in these states, you have agreed to make it assumable. If the buyer decides to sell the house, you will have to accept as your debtor whomever he chooses.

One common problem with giving the buyer a so-called balloon mortgage is that it ties up your money until the note matures and he has to pay you back. But an arrangement known by the dismaying name of hypothecation allows you to negotiate a way around that grim obstacle to liquidity. Essentially you use the money owed you as collateral for a new but smaller loan that you get from a bank or savings and loan association. Then you can use the loan money to add to the down payment on your new house. (For more on balloon mortgages, see "Mortgages: Seller Financing.")

With hypothecation, you might well work out the figures so that your home buyer's monthly payment to you will be exactly the same as what the bank asks you to pay on your own smaller loan. Your buyer could send his check directly to your bank and, in one stroke, he will be paying an installment on both your loan and his. In any case, ask your bank or savings and loan about the possibility of using hypothecation.

If you are thinking of financing the sale of your own house, here is what you should do:

— Get a lawyer to write *all* your contracts — even if you use a real estate broker.

— Cover in writing everything that could possibly happen.

— Do a proper credit check on the buyer.

— Make sure you get a big enough down payment to keep your buyer from hightailing it.

— And insure your loan.

[178]

Interest Rates

ANSWERS TO COMMON QUESTIONS

Everyone is asking just where and how he can save and invest his money in this era of volatile interest rates. Here are answers to some common questions.

Can you make profits on bonds when interest rates fall?

Yes, you can. When interest rates fall, bond prices rise. And when interest rates climb, bond prices decline. So a skillful trader can make money by buying bonds at the top of the interest-rate cycle — and then sell at the bottom. The trouble is those once-steady interest rates have been bouncing down and up quite quickly — and this new volatility makes bond trading riskier than ever.

When interest rates fall, does it make sense to buy stocks?

Yes, it often does. Lower interest rates reduce a company's costs and thus lift its profits — and often its stock price.

What stocks do best when rates fall?

Many stocks do well at those times. Among them are the shares of banks and savings and loan associations, because they can pay lower interest rates to depositors. Utilities are big borrowers, and so they stand to gain when their interest costs decline. Lower rates also help boost the housing market, so real estate investment trusts, lumber companies and appliance manufacturers also prosper.

Do any stocks perform well despite high interest rates?

High rates reflect expectations of steep inflation, and investors turn to natural resources as inflation hedges. So oil, gas and mining company stocks tend to rise.

Should you buy stock on margin when rates are high?

Not unless it's a very promising stock. When you borrow to buy stocks, you pay roughly one to two percentage points over the banks' prime rate. The interest is tax-deductible. But when rates are high, your stock still would have to rise quite a bit for you to break even after taxes.

If you want to play absolutely safe, where can you invest your money?

Four financial instruments offer a safe return at close to top interest rates: money-market funds; bank money-market deposit accounts; six-month money-market certificates; and U.S. Treasury bills with maturities of from 90 days to a year.

But do these four have any disadvantages?

Yes, they do. Since these investments are short-term, you can't lock in

[179]

high rates for very long. Also, the minimum investment for Treasury bills is $10,000.

Should you invest in foreign stocks when interest rates decline?

No. Often the best time to buy foreign stock is when rates are relatively high. That's because steep interest rates attract foreigners to invest in the U.S., and their demand strengthens the dollar. Then, if you invest in the stock of a foreign company when the dollar is strong, you get more shares for your money.

Should you borrow on your life insurance to invest when rates are high?

Yes, if you have a whole life policy that you bought before 1976. You often can borrow against the face value of such a policy at a rate between 5% and 6%, put the cash in a money-market fund and earn considerable profit with little risk. But since you decrease the value of the policy by the amount you borrow, you should be sure to make your beneficiary the heir to the investment.

Should you buy gold or silver when rates are steep?

When Treasury bills and other safe alternatives start paying around 14%, precious metals lose their luster for many investors, and prices tend to drop sharply.

Inventors

HOW TO GET YOUR PRODUCT TO MARKET

A<small>MERICAN</small> ingenuity still thrives — and countless tinkerers are working away in countless workshops and garages, hoping to become the Edisons of tomorrow. The lonely inventor who aims to make it big faces tremendous obstacles and risks. He also faces rousing rewards, if he plays it right.

Close to 59,000 new patents were granted in 1982, but only 5% of all patented inventions ever make it to the marketplace, and scarcely 1% of them earn money for their originators. Still, individuals have brought forth plenty of recent new products, from the Water Pik to the laser amplifier.

If you are an inventor, the first thing you need is a patent attorney. For a fee of $200 and up, he will conduct a search to see if your idea is already covered by one of the 4 million existing patents. If it isn't, you then apply for a patent. After waiting an average 26 months, and paying roughly another $1,000 to $3,000 in lawyer's fees, two out of three inventors get it. A patent protects your invention for 17 years. But you will also need to apply for patents in other countries, at a cost of several hundred dollars each, or else you may find your idea exploited abroad.

After you get one or more patents, you will have to build a prototype of your invention; that can cost anywhere from $5,000 to $20,000. Before making such an investment, you would be wise to have your invention evaluated for its market potential. If the invention is energy-related, you can have it evaluated free of charge by the National Bureau of Standards in Washington, D.C.

A few universities also provide evaluation services. The University of Utah does it free. Baylor and the University of Wisconsin at Whitewater charge $75. In addition, the Small Business Administration has institutes at 530 colleges that aid entrepreneurial inventors with such tasks as market research and feasibility analysis.

Once you have your invention patented and evaluated and build a prototype, you will face the really hard part: getting it produced and bringing it to market. You can accomplish that in many ways.

If your invention seems worthwhile, you can find backers who will shepherd it from the evaluation stage all the way through to production. For example, the Center for Innovation at P.O. Box 4050, Butte, Montana 59702, has an impressive record. It has helped bring many products to market. Take just one case: James Low, a Denver auto salesman, invented a freight trailer that is compatible with almost any commercial vehicle. He queried the Butte center, which then sent a specialist to refine the trailer's design and arranged financing. In return, Low agreed to hand over 20% of his profits to the Center for Innovation. His trailer went into production under license in Fremont, Nebraska.

Arthur D. Little Enterprises of Cambridge, Massachusetts also supports inventions, but only those in the high-technology field. Little typically pumps some $50,000 into research and development for each such product, though the amounts can range from $15,000 to $500,000. Then the company uses its considerable connections to bring the invention to market and shares equally in the revenues.

But beware of firms that want their money up front and often in alarming amounts. A number of so-called development companies promise to mount a marketing campaign that will turn the seed of a hopeless idea into a money tree. Such unscrupulous outfits prey on inventors' gullibility, vanity and pocketbooks. They extract $1,000 to $3,000 in exchange for little more than sending a form letter to prospective backers culled from the Yellow Pages.

Don't count on selling your invention to big corporations. They are seldom receptive to products that are N.I.H. — that is, "Not Invented Here." But small businesses are much more willing to buy a stake in outside innovations because that is cheaper than doing their own research. So, roughly half of all new products and services are brought out by small businesses.

Investment

WHERE TO PUT YOUR MONEY NOW

F ACING rapid change and a remarkable variety of choices, investors are asking an old question with a new plaintiveness: "Where do I put my money now?"

Forget what you learned in the 1970s about making money on investments. No longer can you park your money in just one place, then relax and wait confidently for it to grow. There are no totally safe and sure investments anymore. You have to *diversify* — and you face a bewildering array of investment alternatives. It spans far beyond the familiar stocks, bonds and even money-market funds into hard assets and all those bank certificates. To make your investment choices even harder, a major shift in the ground rules is taking place. Inflation has headed back to a single-digit territory, and that weakens the prospects of all those inflation havens of the past decade, such as gold, collectibles and real estate.

Just remember: your own investment decisions should be based on two factors. First, how you think the economy — and the country — will perform in the long run. Second, your own personal situation and your financial goals.

You work toward different financial goals at different times in your life. If you are young and have few responsibilities, you can invest, for instance, in the stocks of small but promising companies and hold onto some of them for the long term. But if you have a family — and you are worried about putting away enough money for your children's college, you need a safe investment that guarantees returns by a certain date. If you are older and your children are grown, you should point your investments toward building maximum retirement income and thus may want to lock in steep yields. You might split your investments evenly between bonds or other high-interest-yielding investments on the one side and, on the other side, high-dividend stocks such as electric utilities.

Regardless of whether stock prices rise or fall in the next few months, most investment advisers believe that the surging bull market that began in August 1982 still has a long way to run. So if you want future investment profits more than current income, many market professionals will advise you to keep as much as 60% to 65% of your investments in stocks or mutual funds that buy stocks. Put another 20% or so in bonds — tax-exempt municipal bonds if you are in the 35% federal tax bracket or above.

If you are still worried about a possible revival of hyper-inflation, you could keep 5% or 10% of your assets in gold or silver. The remaining 10% of your money should be tucked away in a money-market fund or some other easily accessible place, ready for you to deploy quickly as new investment opportunities arise.

These percentages are only rough guides. Naturally, someone who is retired or nearing retirement would have much more than 20% of his assets in municipal bonds in order to collect the tax-free income. And a younger professional with a fairly high salary might not want municipal bonds but a real estate or an oil and gas tax shelter. It's riskier, but it can offer big tax deductions now and income in the future. (For other formulas for allocating your investments, see "Personal Finance: How to Avoid Mistakes with Your Money.")

Investment

LAUNCHING A SUCCESSFUL PROGRAM

Almost anyone can be a successful investor — if he has a regular, systematic program of investing.

Your program should go through four stages.

First, before you invest in anything with the slightest risk, you have to build up a safe and secure savings account — something for a rainy day.

Second, after you have done that, you can get started in the stock market by buying into mutual funds.

Third, after you have built up some mutual funds, you can start picking your own stocks.

And fourth, once you have a balanced mixture of a few stocks, you can consider going into other investments, such as options or tax shelters.

Now, some more about Step Number One:

Before you buy any stocks, be sure that you have securely saved enough money for emergencies. How much is enough? Figure on three months' after-tax pay. Don't worry if it takes you two to three years to save it up.

You may well find that the best place to put your savings is in a money-market fund or bank money-market deposit account. Most funds require a minimum investment of $1,000 to $2,500, and the banks require $2,500. But then you add whatever you can afford each month, as little as $25. Even if interest rates drift down, money funds and bank money-market deposit accounts are likely to pay much more than the 5¼% to 5½% of ordinary passbook savings accounts.

Some money funds invest in tax-exempt securities. In mid-1983, they paid about 3% less interest than the regular funds. The tax-frees make sense if you are in at least the 35% tax bracket.

You also can put some of your savings into the 2½- or 3½-year wild-card certificates. In mid-1983, they paid fixed rates of about 9½% to 10% and variable rates of 7.3% to 9%, which was as much as 2% higher than money funds. But if you needed to withdraw your cash early, you would lose at least three months' interest. Or you can put your money in Treasury notes and bonds. You can buy them in $1,000 amounts, but they padlock your money for at least a year.

Once you've built up your savings, you're ready to get into the stock market. The best way to start is regularly and systematically to put money into a mutual fund.

Mutual funds offer just what beginning investors need: professional management and a diversified portfolio of stocks, bonds and other investments. To find out about funds, you can talk to a stockbroker. Or you can scan the ads of financial publications for the names, addresses and phone numbers of various funds. Many of them have toll-free 800 numbers.

If you find it hard to set aside money to invest each month, try having it deducted from your checking account and put automatically in a mutual fund. Also, many employers let you have a specific amount taken out of your paycheck and invested in a company-sponsored profit-sharing or thrift plan.

After you have been investing in mutual funds or company thrift plans for a while, you may start itching to buy some stocks on your own. You are best off leaving your emergency savings fund intact and continuing with your mutual-fund program or company thrift plan. You should buy stock only with additional investment funds.

As a novice, you probably will be able to afford only one or two stocks at first. Ultimately, you should aim to own about 10. That's a small enough number to be manageable and large enough for diversity.

A quarter of your portfolio should consist of small and promising companies that give you a chance for big gains, along with — let's face it — the possibility of big losses. Another quarter should be invested in the largest, most conservative companies; they can offer stable growth. You would be wise to put the remaining half into medium-size concerns that are growing faster than the economy as a whole. Among the current growth fields are telecommunications, computers and health care.

Investment

DOLLAR-COST AVERAGING

It never fails. Every time you get into the stock market, you find yourself buying in at the top. Then, prices tumble and you get so discouraged that you sell — precisely at the bottom. You can avoid these expensive errors by investing a set amount of money each month — regardless of whether the market is heading up or down. This is a canny and often profitable investment strategy called dollar-cost averaging.

Think of it as investing on the installment plan. You regularly invest, say, $50 or $100 each month. If stock prices then go up, you can congratulate yourself for having earned some profits. But what if prices go down? Well, you congratulate yourself on your new opportunity to pick up some bargains. Several months ago, your $50 monthly investment could buy, say, only two shares; now it can buy three!

Many people find that a sound way to practice dollar-cost averaging is to buy the shares of a mutual fund at regular monthly intervals, particularly a no-load mutual fund with a record of having done better than the broad market averages over the last several years. No-load mutual funds give you professional management of a diversified portfolio of securities for a small fee.

Dollar-cost averaging also can be used to buy shares of individual stocks, but brokerage fees on small transactions can be prohibitively high — as much as $30 to $35 a trade. And because mutual funds have diversified portfolios, they tend to bounce back from market disasters — when the market ultimately recovers. But an individual stock can fall through the floor and stay in the cellar for years.

True enough, if you sink all of your money into the stock market in a lump sum, and then the market proceeds to rise like a rocket and continue climbing for many years, you will do better than if you put in your money bit by bit, month after month. But think of dollar-cost averaging as a defensive strategy. It will keep you from getting crushed in the wild up-and-down market swings.

The discipline of investing fixed amounts in regular installments helps you to avoid two common errors: putting all your money into the stock market at a time when it might be getting ready for a sharp tumble, and selling out at big losses when stocks are deeply depressed.

Investment

THE ELECTION CONNECTION

A CLOSE connection exists between national elections and price movements in the stock market. In fact, politics and economics make such predictable bedfellows that you might well make some money if you follow an investment strategy based on the four-year election cycle. For several decades now, the stock market usually has dropped during those years when a new President was inaugurated. But then it has hit bottom in the years of midterm Congressional elections — and begun a strong and sustained rise.

Why has the market behaved this way? It's because a newly inaugurated President is highly inclined to call for tight budgetary and monetary policies in line with his campaign promises to reduce those famous budget deficits and fight inflation. So the market began sagging not long after the election or inauguration of *every* newly elected or re-elected President, from Dwight Eisenhower in 1953 through Ronald Reagan in 1981. The drops varied in length but usually averaged a year or more, and the declines averaged a walloping 22%.

Then a recovery began as the mid-term Congressional elections approached. That was largely because the incumbent Administration and Congress — regardless of whether they were Republican or Democrat — have tended to veer toward economic policies that would please or placate voters. The ensuing stock-market recoveries invariably have been long and substantial. They averaged slightly over three years in the period from 1948 through 1980, and the average advance in the Dow Jones Industrial Average has been 60%.

One simple stock-market strategy is to invest according to the presidential election cycle. For example, you could put your money into a growth-oriented mutual fund or a well-diversified portfolio of common stocks on November 30 of any mid-term *Congressional* election year. Keep it there for two years. But on November 30 of a *Presidential* election year, sell out. Park the proceeds in a money-market fund or Treasury bills. Then repeat the cycle all over. Between 1962 and 1980 such a strategy would have netted an investor in the Standard & Poor's 500 stock index a total return of 1,110%.

[188]

Investment

GETTING A PROFESSIONAL ADVISER

W ITH inflation to the right of them, taxes to the left of them, ordinary investors have never been more in need of advice about where to put their money. Fortunately, high-grade help for investors is more widely available than ever before. A fair number of savvy, substantial amateurs are quite capable of managing their investments for themselves — if they are prepared to spend several hours every week reading intensively about the markets. If they are not, then they might well need professional aid. And their basic choice is to hire an individual investment adviser or buy into a mutual fund.

Mutual funds offer the advantages of greater diversification than you can get with an independent adviser, and management fees that are usually only one-third as high. Funds are willing to handle small amounts of capital; they typically require a minimum investment of only $1,000.

Funds are flexible, too. They allow you to shift your investment strategy as market conditions change. If you deal with a company that manages a whole family of funds, you can switch your money from one fund to another within the family at a nominal cost—or none at all. You can move your money from an aggressive growth mutual fund to a more conservative one, or from a stock fund to a money-market fund and sometimes a bond fund in the same company. (For more, see "Mutual Funds.")

But most mutual funds fall short in personal contact with investors. There isn't much. So an unsophisticated investor might cash in at just the wrong time. On the other hand, if he had a personal investment adviser, that professional might help him wait out a bad period.

To find an investment adviser, start by asking for recommendations from your lawyer, accountant or stockbroker. You also can write to the Investment Counsel Association of America, 50 Broad Street, New York, New York 10004. That is a professional organization of advisory firms, and it will mail you a free list of its members.

To determine whether or not any adviser is up to managing your assets, check his record. Ask for figures going back at least 10 years, so that you can determine how the adviser performed during falling markets as well as rising markets. Then compare his record with Standard & Poor's 500 stock index.

It's crucial to find out what an adviser's investment philosophy is before you hire him. Advisers follow one of several different strategies. Some aim for high growth, others for safety. Still others are the so-called contrarians.

They look at which stocks are in fashion and then assume that they are overpriced. So the contrarians avoid those stocks and steer you into more neglected issues.

If you hire an adviser, you generally will have to sign a contract giving him discretion over your account. He then will be free to buy and sell securities without further authorization from you. If this makes you uncomfortable, perhaps you shouldn't have an adviser.

Professional advisers typically charge an annual fee — tax-deductible — of ½% to 2% of your invested assets. But they usually can arrange discounts of at least 30% on your stockbrokerage commissions.

Good advisers promise nothing more than hard work and honesty. They send you quarterly reports on how your investments are doing and, at the end of the year, a statement summing up your account. At that time, your evaluation of an adviser's performance should be unemotional — based purely on how well he has met your objectives.

Investment

INVESTMENT ADVISORY SERVICES

W HEN you read all those ads offering investment newsletters and other advisory services for anywhere from $50 to $500 a year, just remember: they vary enormously in quality. The best of the stock advisory services often beat the market averages. But many are worthless and potentially harmful.

Almost anyone can register with the Securities and Exchange Commission and put out a stock-market advisory letter. In fact, the publishers have included high school dropouts, an electrician and a hairdresser. Some of the investment services are addicted to self-congratulation, often making ambiguous forecasts and then boasting that they have been "right on target." Published performance records often overstate gains and understate losses because they don't take buying and selling commissions into account. For example, if a service advises buying a stock at $10 and then decides it should be sold at $11, the service credits itself with a 10% gain. In fact, after brokerage commissions on a trade of 100 shares, the investor's real gain might well be closer to 3%.

If you don't know much about the market and have a few hundred or few thousand dollars to invest, you might be better off letting mutual funds manage your money. But a good service might be helpful if you have, say, $15,000, to invest.

Before committing yourself, it's wise to sample as many services as you can. Most will offer a one- to six-month trial subscription for a low price, and some will send you a sample copy at no charge. The best way of getting to know a variety of services is to write for the free catalogue published by Select Information Exchange, 2095 Broadway, New York, New York 10023. It describes hundreds of services and offers a subscription to 20 of your choice for $11.95.

The major advisory services that focus mainly on fundamentals often are the most useful. They provide earnings estimates, industry and company analyses, investment strategies, stock recommendations and model portfolios — a package of investment materials that you cannot find assembled elsewhere in one place. A first-rate investment letter must be precise. It should give clear recommendations and be accurate.

The *Hulbert Financial Digest* (409 First Street, SE, Washington, D.C. 20003) is a monthly publication that rates and ranks 50 stock-market investment advisory newsletters according to how well — or poorly —

their advice has worked out. A first year's subscription is $67.50, and you can get a trial subscription of five issues for $33.75.

One of the largest advisory services is *The Value Line Investment Survey*, 711 Third Avenue, New York, New York 10017. This weekly service costs $365 a year, or you can try 10 issues for $37. For those who can afford it and who learn to use the vast amount of information and guidance it offers, *Value Line* can be very valuable. Every week its staff of 70 analysts, economists and statisticians evaluates 1,700 stocks. The service also offers one portfolio strategy a year that each investor can adapt to his particular needs, and each issue includes a comprehensive overview of the market.

Another major service is *The Outlook*, published weekly by Standard & Poor's Corporation, 25 Broadway, New York, New York 10004, for $175 a year; a 13-week trial subscription costs $29.95. *The Outlook* is cautiously bullish. It's easy to read and digest, does not encourage taking great risks and is backed by the large analytical staff of Standard & Poor's. It lists the best- and worst-acting stock groups and gives about 35 recommended issues graded on the basis of risk.

United Business and Investment Report, 210 Newbury Street, Boston, Massachusetts 02116, which costs $170 a year, is similar to the Standard & Poor's *Outlook* but gives more space to Washington news and business trends. *United Business*'s advice tends toward the conservative.

Other reliable newsletters include: the *Zweig Forecast*, 747 Third Avenue, New York, New York 10017, $245; Stan Weinstein's *Professional Tape Reader*, P.O. Box 2407, Hollywood, Florida 33022, $250; and Charles Allmon's *Growth Stock Outlook*, 4405 East West Highway, Bethesda, Maryland 20814, $95.

In choosing an investment service, remember this: the best of them don't claim to be right all the time but readily admit when they have been wrong. Beware of any service that promises you the moon. The most that you can expect from a service is that it provides a sound basis for your own decision-making.

Investment

INVESTMENT CLUBS

INVESTMENT clubs are becoming more popular than ever among the people who want to learn about the stock market — and make a little money while they are at it. New clubs are being formed in college classrooms, corporate offices, condominium living rooms and even church basements. The National Association of Investment Clubs, which helps the new ones get started, estimates that there are more than 20,000 of them across the country. They have well over 300,000 members and roughly $1 billion in investments.

Each club typically has about 16 members, and for them the monthly meetings are an opportunity to learn about investing and dabble in stocks at an affordable price. Clubs usually require members to ante up only $25 a month.

At some meetings the atmosphere is relaxed and informal; at others it's almost as intense as a session of a billion-dollar mutual fund's portfolio committee. In successful clubs, members usually do their own research rather than rely on brokers or investment analysts. The members spend long hours poring over annual reports and such resources as Standard & Poor's Corporation Records and *The Value Line Investment Survey*. Both of those are often available free in public libraries. Some clubs even send members to interview the chief executives of local firms that look like promising investments.

Only a few clubs determine by majority rule whether to buy or sell a stock. Most use a weighted voting system so that long-term members with the most money at stake have the biggest say. No one seriously expects to grow rich solely through a club. According to the National Association, the average club's portfolio contains 18 to 30 stocks with a total value of less than $52,000 — meaning about $3,250 a member. But some clubs have impressive growth rates on their investments.

Because most investment clubs are partnerships, individual members must pay capital gains taxes on their share of any profits. New investment clubs with only small amounts to invest may find brokerage costs running more than 10% of their trades. As a result, some of them use discount brokers, who charge considerably less but give you no advice on where to put your money.

Most investment clubs do not want new members, and a few have stiff entrance requirements: you usually have to put in as much money as the other members have. Therefore, if you want to become a member of an investment club, you are probably better off starting a new one than trying to join an existing group. The majority begin simply, with two friends deciding to start a club, and they each sign up two or three other friends, and the chain grows. If you want to create a club of your own, you can get valuable help from the National Association of Investment Clubs. It will send you a handbook with advice on organizing a club, and a primer on the fundamentals of stock analysis. Write to: The National Association of Investment Clubs, P.O. Box 220, Royal Oak, Michigan 48068. The NAIC's dues are a modest $25 per club, plus $6 for each member.

The NAIC recommends that all clubs, especially new ones, follow these conservative principles:

— Invest regularly, preferably monthly, no matter where you think the stock market is heading — because a club that tries to predict broad stock trends is often wrong.

— Reinvest all earnings so that your club's portfolio can grow faster through compounding.

— Invest in growth companies. The association defines them as firms with both earnings and dividends outperforming their industry average.

Clubs should aim for 15% annual growth in their investments. To start you toward your goal, the association will send you a model portfolio, which is updated quarterly by its professional stock selection committee. The organization also provides work-sheets to help members analyze stocks on their own.

Investment clubs tend to do well, but when they fail it's often because they allow a trading attitude to sweep away the more reliable accumulation attitude. When the market moves sideways or down, impatient members often urge the club to follow an in-and-out strategy. It is much wiser — and more profitable — to hold onto sound investments for long-term growth.

Investment

BUYING INTO SECOND MORTGAGES

ALMOST everybody complains about high mortgage rates, but those rates are a cause for rejoicing for one kind of person. He is the investor who puts his cash into second mortgages.

Second mortgages are loans made to homebuyers whose down payments and primary mortgages still don't add up to the purchase price. Anyone with $5,000 to $10,000 can grant such second mortgage loans and earn an annual return of 13% or more.

With most second mortgages, the borrower makes monthly payments only on the interest. The investor, that is, the lender, gets his principal back in a lump sum when the loan expires; typically, that is in three years. The interest rate is negotiated by the lender and borrower. As a rule, it's two percentage points above the rate local banks charge on first mortgages.

Recently there has been an alternative to the second-mortgage formula called a shared-equity deal. Here an investor puts up part of the down payment on the house. Technically, this is not a loan; the investor becomes a co-owner. Instead of collecting monthly interest payments, he typically pays a portion of the monthly carrying costs, including the property taxes and first-mortgage installments. However, the investor also gets to split the deductions for interest and taxes with the co-owner who occupies the house. Eventually they divide the value of the property, including any appreciation. Usually after a period of three to 10 years, the owner-occupant must buy out the investor.

Say that you want to invest in a second mortgage or a shared-equity deal. You can get leads to people who need such financing by asking builders, real estate agents or mortgage loan brokers. With either a second mortgage or a shared-equity investment, however, it's easier to get in than get out. If the investor in a second mortgage needs his money before the term of the loan is up, he can sell the note. But if interest rates are higher than at the time the loan was made, he will have to sell the note at a discount.

The investor who wants out of a shared-equity arrangement is really stuck. There is no secondary market at all for such investments — not yet, anyhow.

So if you are prospecting for high annual returns, you may want to consider the second-mortgage investment market. But be prepared to keep your money locked up for the length of the loan.

Investment

GEMS FOR INVESTMENT

Diamonds, rubies, emeralds — ah, what romance! But as investments, those luscious gems are quite risky. Before you try to profit from your jewelry box, remember that gems that have been bought to wear are seldom of investment quality. When you buy them, you rarely pay wholesale prices. The dealer takes a substantial markup — sometimes as much as a third. And if you try to sell the stone, dealers would usually offer you even *less* than wholesale prices.

Unlike stocks and bonds, there is no easily quoted market for gems because no two stones are identical in quality or value. Diamonds are evaluated by four measures: carat (or weight), color, clarity and cut. Even the color of white diamonds is graded from D for the whitest to Z for dingy yellow. The difference of just one letter grade can amount to thousands of dollars per carat in the price.

If you do invest in diamonds, insist on receiving a certificate from an independent laboratory that has graded the stone within the last 12 months. Even with that, you also should get a recertification by having your jeweler send the stone, insured, by registered mail, to the Gemological Institute of America. It has offices in New York City and Santa Monica, California.

In short, if you are acquiring jewelry for pleasure, fine. But don't deceive yourself into believing you are making a sure-thing investment. Unless you are an expert, gems are for buying, not for selling.

With occasional exceptions, colored stones are less costly than diamonds — but more risky. That's because a world diamond cartel usually keeps a floor under prices, but there are no cartels to hold the prices of rubies, emeralds or sapphires.

Among the colored stones, good rubies have risen the fastest lately. Supplies are short because few rubies are being exported by Burma, the source of the richest and reddest stones. The next most valuable rubies come from Thailand, while the lighter Ceylon rubies are less coveted. Sapphires are almost as rare as rubies, and some of the best and the bluest are from Kashmir. Emeralds may be a safer investment because they are easier to resell than sapphires.

The steep price of precious stones is stirring interest in much more speculative semiprecious stones, notably aquamarines and topaz stones, which come in shades of orange and yellow. The finest opals are too fragile to be a solid long-term investment; they can crack fairly easily.

There is no universally accepted grading system for colored stones, as there is for diamonds. But before buying, an investor should insist on independent written appraisal of the gem's quality, weight, color — and, of course, its dollar value. (See also "Jewelry: How to Get Good Value.")

IRAs

HOW THEY WORK

It's one terrific tax shelter. So, for almost every working American, it makes sense to have an Individual Retirement Account.

You have until April 15 to open your tax-saving Individual Retirement Account and put some of your previous year's earnings into it. Each year you can invest up to $2,000 of income you have earned from a job, even if you are covered by a company pension plan. A married couple who are both working can each put in $2,000, and families with one working spouse can invest $2,250.

All those contributions are tax-deductible. And that relief can be powerful. Just one example: If you contribute the full $2,000, you will cut your taxes by $640, if you are in the 32% federal tax bracket — that's a taxable income of $23,500 to $28,800 if you are single. You will still save — but proportionately less — if you are in a lower bracket. And you will enjoy higher savings, of course, if you are in a higher bracket.

What's more — *much* more — income from your contributions goes untaxed during your entire working life. You pay Uncle Sam only as you withdraw your money. You can take it out anytime, but it's best to hold off until you are at least aged 59½.

IRAs are more than tax shelters. Your account can help make your retirement years as financially comfortable as your working years. By the year 2000, Social Security benefits are likely to be less generous than they are today. So when you retire, you are going to need a hefty savings to take up the slack. That's where your IRA comes in.

The further you are from retirement, the more an IRA's tax-deferred compound earnings can do for you. If you are 35 and start depositing $2,000 a year for the next 30 years and your money earns 10% — which is a reasonable figure — you will be richer by $330,000 when you turn 65.

If you are earning money but don't have $2,000 readily available to put into an IRA, borrow it. Then, when you compute your taxes, you will get a double benefit: you can deduct both the IRA contribution and the interest you pay on your loan.

Your employer also can help you find the money. Some companies are offering payroll deduction plans for IRA contributions. These periodic deductions are a convenient method of forced savings. One disadvantage is they do not let you shelter the maximum amount possible on your IRA because your total allowable contribution is not working for you the entire year.

When you start to withdraw your IRA money, it will be taxed as ordinary income even though some of the profits may have come from long-term capital gains. But presumably, you will be retired by then and in a much lower tax bracket than you are now.

Unless you are disabled, you cannot withdraw the money before you turn 59½ without facing stiff consequences: the IRS will claim 10% of any funds you take out as a penalty, and you will also owe income tax on them at your regular rate.

You can start withdrawals when you turn 59½, but you *must* begin them by the time you are 70½, taking out at least the minimum amounts decreed by the IRS on the basis of life-expectancy tables. If you are dependent principally on the IRA income, it might be safest to transfer the entire sum when you retire into an insurance company annuity that provides lifetime payments for you and your spouse.

When you die, the money you have in an IRA goes to any beneficiary you have named. If it is not your spouse, the beneficiary must withdraw the money within five years and pay income tax on it. But if the beneficiary is your spouse, he or she has the option of rolling over your IRA into his or her own within 60 days. That way the money won't be taxed until he or she withdraws it.

As mentioned, if only one spouse is employed, the couple can contribute a total of $2,250 annually under the "spousal" IRA provision. But each partner must have a separate account. The $2,250 spousal IRA can be divided as the couple wishes, so long as no more than $2,000 goes into either account in a given year. In case of divorce, the ex-husband and wife keep individual control of the funds already in their separate accounts.

You don't have to contribute the maximum $2,000 to your Individual Retirement Account every year. The law lets you put in as little as you want, although banks, mutual funds and other IRA sponsors can set their own minimums. You can even skip a year, but you can't make up for it by putting in more than $2,000 the next time. You also can open as many IRA accounts as you want and divide deposits among them, but your total contribution in one year must not exceed $2,000.

In sum, anyone should think seriously about opening an IRA if he or she has earned some income from a job and can afford to put aside savings that he or she will not need at least until the age of 59½. Not only does an IRA reduce your taxes, but the earnings on your investment compound tax-free.

Some people, however, should not open IRAs. As a rule, children ought not to put earnings from summer or after-school jobs in an IRA because they are already in a very low tax bracket. And if you think you will need your savings in a few years to buy a house or put a child through school, then that money should not go into an IRA either. Unless you are in the highest tax brackets, the penalty for withdrawal probably will exceed what you have gained in tax deferrals on several years of IRA contributions.

[199]

IRAs

WHERE TO PUT YOUR IRA MONEY

Banks, insurance companies, brokerage firms and mutual funds are all clamoring for your IRA dollars. Before turning over your money, there are three questions you should ask about any IRA investment: Is it safe? Is it flexible? How much does it cost?

If safety is your primary concern, then banks or savings and loan associations give you both federal insurance on deposits and high interest — at least for now. Otherwise, the best IRA deals are probably offered by no-load mutual-fund families. (See "IRAs: Mutual-Fund Plans.")

There is no limit to how often you can switch your IRA funds from one place to another, provided the money is transferred directly between financial institutions and is not given to you in the meantime. But transfers can cost you some small fees. Once a year, you can even withdraw your money personally, as long as you reinvest it within 60 days in another IRA. But if you forget or delay past the 60-day limit, you will have to file additional tax forms and pay a stiff penalty as well as taxes on your IRA funds. Depending on where you invest your IRA money, you can pay practically nothing in start-up and annual maintenance fees — or quite a lot.

Generally, the IRA investments offered by banks or savings and loan associations have the lowest fees — from nothing to only a few dollars a month. The banks usually sell you an 18-month certificate of deposit for your IRA. If you decide to transfer your money to another kind of investment, there is only a modest charge, providing you don't switch out of your CD before it matures. By law, if you cash in your 18-month IRA certificate early, you will forfeit the last three months' interest.

No-load mutual funds also charge minimal fees, usually $5 to $15 a year. These funds are the kind that you buy directly from the mutual-fund company rather than from brokers. But if you choose a so-called load mutual fund, the kind that is sold through brokers and some financial planners, add a hefty 8½% sales commission.

You can set up your own self-directed IRA at a brokerage house. The fees range from nothing at some discount brokers to $30 or more a year at full-service firms. In addition, you will have to pay commissions on all your stock trades for the IRA.

Annuities that you buy from insurance companies tend to have the heaviest fees. If you put $2,000 into an annuity plan, and then withdraw it in less than a year, the experience could cost you as much as $179.

Most institutions subtract your fees from your account. But if you don't want to drain assets from your IRA — and if you want the maximum tax deductions it offers — you can arrange to make separate payments of your fees. And then on your income tax return you can itemize them under "miscellaneous" and have Uncle Sam split the cost with you.

IRAs

MUTUAL-FUND PLANS

Now that every working American can put $2,000 a year into an Individual Retirement Account, or IRA, the big question is where to stash the cash. The best place may well be in a large mutual-fund group — that is, a company that operates several different kinds of mutual funds. When you do that, your fees are low, your investment choices are numerous and at many fund families you can move your money around from one investment to another, usually by simply making a telephone call.

No fewer than 36 mutual-fund companies have funds that invest in stocks, bonds and the money market — plus an astonishing array of permutations and combinations of the three — and let you switch your money among them. A big mutual-fund company may offer as many as 25 different choices, ranging from a money-market fund that invests exclusively in federal government securities to a fund that buys stocks of fast-growing, high-tech companies. The primary advantage of such variety is that you are not locked into one type of investment. That's important when you are putting money aside for a retirement that is possibly decades away.

When you buy a so-called load mutual fund, you pay a commission of typically 8½% — most of which goes to the salesman or broker who sells the fund to you. But you can save a lot of money by investing instead in a "no-load" fund family. In that case you will generally pay only an annual charge of $5 to $15 and a management fee, normally one-half of 1% of the value of your account. You buy directly from the fund group instead of from a broker. There is no evidence that either load or no-load funds outperform each other.

You can use an IRA's tax advantage to the fullest if you invest the entire $2,000 at the beginning of each year. But you can also arrange to have your bank automatically deduct an agreed-upon amount — say, $25 a month or more — from your checking account and send it to the fund group. And if your employer offers an IRA program, you can have your IRA investment deducted from your paycheck.

What kind of fund you invest in depends on your age, income, temperament and your view of how the economy will fare in the future. A young person with many working years ahead can afford to think seriously about putting his or her IRA money into a maximum-capital-gains fund and taking some risks. But as you near retirement, you can't afford such gambles. So at some point in your fifties, you should move that nest egg into money-market funds or bank certificates of deposit.

How much you decide to invest in various kinds of funds depends partly on how large a portion of your retirement income your IRA will constitute. If you expect to rely only on Social Security in addition to your IRA fund, then be very conservative. On the other hand, if you have a generous pension and other investments, you can take some chances in your IRA.

As an IRA investor, give a lot of thought to the amount of stress you are willing to accept. It does you no good to be in a mutual fund that goes up 300% in a decade if it's so volatile that it scares the wits out of you and you sell after the market turns down. For this reason, the ordinary IRA investor might feel more comfortable with a fund that aims at long-term growth rather than maximum capital gains. (For more, see "Mutual Funds: Switching among the Funds.")

IRAs

SELF-DIRECTED PLANS

IF you are the kind of person who wants to make your own decisions, manage your own investments and be responsible for your own future, then consider opening a self-directed IRA. This will give you a nice variety of investment choices. Of course, you can buy stocks for your IRA, either shares that pay high, dependable dividends or growth stocks that offer the chance for fat profits — along with, alas, the risk of big losses. You also can fill your account with bonds, mutual funds, commodity funds, promissory notes, certain kinds of options, bond trusts and income-producing real estate limited partnerships. About the only things you cannot do through a self-directed IRA are buy stocks on margin or borrow to buy any other investment, or invest in such tangibles as gold, silver, oriental rugs or diamonds.

You can open your self-directed IRA at almost any brokerage house. It usually costs little or nothing to open such an account with a discount broker, and $30 or more at a full-service brokerage.

Besides these costs, you will have to pay commissions on any trading you do. For example, they will run to $70 or so on a $2,000 transaction with a full-service broker. So, if you plan on heavy trading, consider a discount broker who will trim a few dollars off small transactions — and as much as 75% off the posted commission rate on trades of $10,000 or more. But discounters sometimes limit their business to stocks and bonds. If you are interested in limited partnerships or commodities, you may have to go to a full-service broker.

When weighing whether to open a self-directed account, consider this: some money managers argue that it makes no sense to use your IRA for aggressive investments such as growth stocks. One of the advantages of such stocks is that much of their return is likely to be taxed at the lower capital gains rate. You throw away that tax break when the securities are placed in an IRA.

If that conservative kind of reasoning appeals to you, one of the best ways to invest IRA money is in ultra-safe corporate or government bonds. Double-A-rated long-term industrial bonds in mid-1983 were paying close to 11% interest, as were corporate bond unit trusts.

But there is another way to look at IRA funds, especially if you are in your twenties or early thirties. Over the long run, conservative investments such as bonds and bank certificates of deposit probably will not grow as much as stocks in up-and-coming industries.

An investor who will not be needing his cash for 30 or 40 years most likely would do better to invest in a diversified portfolio of the shares of high-technology and other innovative companies than to tie up his money in fixed-interest securities. Indeed, almost anyone who feels optimistic about the future of the stock market should keep at least some of his IRA money in growth-oriented stocks or mutual funds that invest in them.

IRAs

BANK AND S&L PLANS

I F you are looking for a worry-free and very nearly decision-free Individual Retirement Account, then you may be wise to open your IRA at a bank, a savings and loan association (S&L) or a credit union that is federally insured. An IRA account at any of those institutions has several advantages. You deal face-to-face with your banker; the fees are modest to nonexistent; and the federal government insures your balances up to $100,000. When your account gets near the insurance limit, just open *another* IRA at a different savings institution.

But there is a reason why not everybody is beating a path to his local banker. If you ever need to withdraw your money for some emergency, you will forfeit three months' interest on bank certificates of more than a year, and one month's interest on those of a year or less.

The closest equivalent to a bank or credit union for IRA investors is a money-market fund. Money funds are considered quite safe, but right now they are not federally insured. However, banks and savings and loan institutions do offer competitive money-market deposit accounts. They pay roughly the same interest rates as do ordinary money-market funds and they *are* federally insured, up to $100,000. Some institutions allow you to use these accounts for your IRA.

Banks and S&Ls also offer two types of longer term IRA savings certificates.

First, there are *fixed-rate* certificates. They lock you — and the bank — into the same interest rate for anywhere from six months to ten years.

Then, there are *variable-rate* certificates. They are adjusted at regular intervals in line with a pre-agreed market rate of interest. The certificates you choose depends on whether you think interest rates will rise or fall.

The interest rates that banks and S&Ls pay on IRA accounts vary from plan to plan and from bank to bank. The only accurate way to compare is to ask for the compound annual yield, also known as the effective annual yield. Trouble is, bankers are likely to quote you the so-called nominal interest rate, which does not reflect the differences in the way the interest is compounded. So, always ask for the effective annual yield, and don't open an IRA in a bank or S&L that will not tell you what it is.

IRAs

INSURANCE COMPANY ANNUITY PLANS

Y OUR friendly insurance agent probably will be calling you soon — if he hasn't already — to tell you all about his company's annuity plans for your Individual Retirement Account. It might be wise to listen.

An IRA annuity that you take out with an insurance company is a contract promising to pay you income for a specified time, usually from the day you retire for the rest of your life. Insurance companies offer you two kinds of IRA annuities.

First, there are fixed plans. They guarantee to pay you back all the money you put into them, plus either a variable or fixed rate of interest.

Second, many insurance companies are offering variable annuities. The value of the money you put in fluctuates along with the ups and downs of the stock market. So, you get a crack at capital gains, which you don't get in a fixed annuity. Of course, you can also suffer capital losses if the market goes down. Some of these variable plans allow you to move your money at will from one type of investment to another, typically into a stock-investment fund, a bond fund or a money-market fund.

On fixed annuities, some insurance companies have been guaranteeing relatively high effective one-year yields, after management fees. But watch out: a number of insurance companies announce a guaranteed rate on your *new* IRA contribution each year, but say nothing about the rate that they will pay on your deposits and reinvested earnings from previous years. So make sure you ask the insurance agent which rate he is quoting: the new money rate or the so-called portfolio rate, which applies to your recent contributions *and* all the money in your account.

The disadvantages to annuity plans are the high sales charges you will face if you want to withdraw more than 10% of your funds during the first few years. These charges come on top of the IRS penalties for early withdrawal. And yearly management fees on variable annuities can run high. But annuities offer you the largest choice of pay-out plans once you do retire, and most insurance companies have a good record for safety in managing pension money. (For more, see "Annuities.")

IRAs

YOUR OWN COMPANY PLANS

MANY companies have automatic payroll-deduction programs that enable you to contribute regularly to an IRA. If your employer does not offer such a plan, you can arrange for your bank to deduct a fixed amount from your checking account every payday. Either way, you will be automatically saving — and sheltering from taxes — up to $38.46 a week to reach the IRA maximum of $2,000 a year.

While payroll-deduction plans are convenient, they do cost you a little money. If you spread your contributions over a year instead of investing the whole $2,000 in January, you will be investing as late as December money that could have been earning tax-deferred income eleven months later.

Some employers let you invest your IRA money in company retirement programs. Others will allow you to decide whether to put it in mutual funds, bank certificates or annuities.

A better choice than an IRA for many people would be an ordinary company thrift or savings plan. Employees typically invest up to 6% of their pay in a mutual fund through automatic payroll deductions. Then the company matches some of that investment. Most plans offer a 50% match — if you contribute $3,000, say, the company adds $1,500. Immediately, then, your investment earns a 50% return.

A consulting firm that has compared company thrift plans and IRAs discovered that an employee who can't afford to put money in both will earn more, after taxes, with a company savings plan. That assumes that both investments pay the same rate of interest and that the company matches at least 25% of the employee's contribution.

IRAs

SOME BETTER ALTERNATIVES

THOUGH Individual Retirement Accounts are a worthy way of saving money and reducing your taxes, they are not the only way. You might do better with either a company savings plan, a nonprofit-group annuity, a salary-reduction plan or a Keogh plan.

To repeat: If your company has a savings plan, chances are you will be able to accumulate more money, after taxes, by contributing to it than by opening an IRA. You generally can deposit up to 6% of your after-tax income in the company plan, and your employer matches every dollar you contribute with an untaxed 50 cents. Most companies let you take your own contributions out at almost any time — without the tax penalty you would incur with an early withdrawal from an IRA.

Another nice shelter is the nonprofit-group annuity. Teachers, hospital nurses, social workers and other employees of nonprofit organizations can take advantage of nonprofit-group annuities. An employee of an eligible group tells his boss to put as much as 20% of his salary into an untaxed annuity or some other investment. Eligible employees get all the advantages of an IRA but usually can shelter more than $2,000 of their salary per year. There is no tax penalty for withdrawals.

Some companies are going the tax-sheltered annuities one better by offering their employees something called a salary-reduction plan. Again, a portion of the employee's salary is withheld — untaxed — and the money is invested in an annuity, in the company's stock or in some type of mutual fund. There's no penalty for early withdrawal of every penny you put up. (See "Tax Savings: Salary Reduction Plans.")

A person in business for himself can have both a Keogh plan and an IRA, so he needs to decide which to contribute to if he can't afford both. For those who have no employees, the Keogh wins hands down because you can shelter much more income in it than in an IRA.

IRAs

IRA ROLLOVERS

Y ou can save a lot of taxes on any lump sum of cash or stock that you collect from your company savings or profit-sharing fund when you leave the company. You do that by putting the proceeds immediately into a tax-deferring Individual Retirement Account. This transaction is called an IRA rollover.

You thus postpone paying taxes on your earnings from these company plans, and on your employer's contributions, until you start withdrawing the money from the IRA. If you then expect to be in a lower tax bracket, it's probably wise to make this IRA rollover.

But be careful; the taxman won't allow you to roll over any contributions that you made to the company plan, since these are not subject to income tax when you leave the company. However, if your employer made any contributions for you, you are liable for income tax on them — unless you roll the money over into an IRA within 60 days of receiving it.

Jewelry

HOW TO GET GOOD VALUE

A BIRTHDAY or anniversary or other special occasion is coming and you have a gem of an idea: you will buy some jewelry for your love. But you have no idea which gem to get. Like love itself, buying one of these glittering aphrodisiacs is often blind.

Fortunately, you are likely to get good value now. Although demand and prices have risen somewhat during the economic recovery, prices for diamonds and precious colored stones are generally still below their wild peaks of the early 1980s.

If you want more gem for less money, consider buying a semi-precious stone. Green garnets, which are often sold under the name of tsavorite, are a respectable substitute for emeralds and they cost far less — $500 or so a carat. Red spinels and red tourmalines, which are also known as rubellite, can satisfy ruby tastes on rhinestone budgets. Their prices range from $100 to $800 a carat. Tanzanites resemble fine blue sapphires, and they start at $800 a carat. But they are not as durable as sapphires, so don't buy them for a ring.

About 100 mineral and organic substances now qualify as gemstones, and as a buyer you will be choked with choices. Your criteria for judging whether a gem is really a gem include its sparkle, luster, freedom from flaws, rarity and hardness — the more of all these the better. The most important criterion is color. The richer and more intense the shade, the more valuable the stone — and the more you will pay for it.

The risk you take in buying a semi-precious stone is that it may go out of fashion as quickly as it came in, leaving you with jewelry that's pretty but hard to sell.

To increase your chances of selling a stone if you have to or just want to trade up, buy at least a carat. Buy the stone that has a better color and fewer flaws — even if it is the smaller of two you are considering. And whatever you can afford, buy the best. You are much better off with a top-of-the-line tourmaline than a run-of-the-mill ruby.

Bargain hunting for jewelry is a tricky business. Buying stones from a wholesaler can save you a bundle, but most reputable dealers will not sell to anyone not in the trade — unless you are a friend or a friend of a friend. Shopping in the bazaarlike jewelry exchanges of New York and Los Angeles is as risky as ordering a stone by mail. If you know someone, or have an expertise in stones, fine. Otherwise, you may not be able to find much of a bargain.

If you buy jewelry that costs $2,000 or more, ask your jeweler to let you borrow the piece for a few hours so that it can be independently appraised by a member of the American Society of Appraisers. Its members must prove their competence and bind themselves to a code of ethics; they charge from $20 to $100 an hour, depending on their experience. You can find members by writing to the society at P.O. Box 17265, Washington, D.C. 20041.

The jeweler you buy from should belong to the American Gem Society. Its members have to take courses and pass exams periodically to maintain their expertise.

Another clue to the quality of a jewelry store is the brand of watch it sells. One seasoned appraiser observes that if a store, no matter how small or drab, carries Rolex and Piaget watches, that is a good sign. It suggests a desire to sell to quality-seeking clients.

Wherever you shop, insist that a fine stone come with a certificate issued by an independent testing laboratory that describes the gem's properties. Your jeweler can send diamonds to the Gemological Institute of America in New York City or Santa Monica for certification. Meanwhile, the American Gemological Laboratories, Inc., 645 Fifth Avenue, New York, New York 10022, evaluates colored stones.

When you buy jewelry, you are not just buying a stone. The setting is important, too. Mother's white gold and platinum are passé now, and all that glitters is yellow gold of the 18-karat variety. That's 18 parts pure gold mixed with six parts of metals such as copper and zinc. Gold jewelry should be stamped with the manufacturer's trademark and the gold content. Don't buy any that isn't.

One reassuring point: it's hard to go wrong giving jewelry as a gift. Diamonds are seldom returned because they are too big. (See also "Investment: Gems for Investment.")

Keogh Plans

SHELTER FOR THE SELF-EMPLOYED

If you are in business for yourself or have any kind of free-lance income as, say, a writer, an artist or a carpenter, look into a Keogh plan. It's a government-sponsored tax shelter, and you can put a lot more into it than into an Individual Retirement Account.

In 1983, you could contribute as much as 15% of your self-employment earnings annually, just so you did not contribute more than $15,000. In 1984, you will be able to put away 20% up to $30,000. All your contributions are tax-deferred.

You can have both a Keogh and an IRA, in which you can shelter at least $2,000 a year. So, anybody who has both a Keogh and an IRA can shelter as much as $32,000 a year, beginning in 1984.

If you plan eventually to take all the money out of your retirement plan at one time, the Keogh will be less heavily taxed than an IRA. If you have contributed for five years, your withdrawal will qualify for 10-year averaging, which reduces your taxes. That is, you are taxed on the money as if you drew it out in smaller amounts stretched over 10 years. IRAs do not qualify for this tax break.

Lawyers

HOW TO FIND ONE

Whether you are buying a house, making a will or filing a suit, sooner or later you will need a lawyer. Finding the right attorney at the right price can be a trial.

You are probably better off not to search in one of the large, wood-paneled law firms. Most of those partnerships specialize in corporate work, and even if their members agree to defend you in traffic court, the meter could start ticking at $100 an hour, or more. Instead, scout for a general practitioner in a moderate-size firm that handles personal and small-business affairs.

To find one, the best advice is old-fashioned: ask people whose judgment you trust, for example, your banker, insurance agent or a member of your company's legal department. But make sure that the recommended attorneys have dealt with cases similar to yours. Your neighbor may have had a Perry Mason for his auto accident case, but that's probably not the right lawyer for your landlord-tenant dispute.

If you want additional recommendations, try your state or local bar association's lawyer referral service. You will find the number listed in the Yellow Pages. The referral service will give you the next name up on a list of participating attorneys. Trouble is, quality can vary widely. Some bar associations add the name of any attorney who wants to be included; others charge a fee or require only a minimum amount of experience. So ask the service what screening procedures are used. Also explain what kind of legal help you need, since many services break down their lists by specialties.

You can check the background of almost any attorney by consulting the *Martindale-Hubbell Law Directory,* available at most large public libraries. It describes the lawyers in your community and their educations. Sometimes it also gives evaluations by judges and fellow attorneys. If you need a foreign lawyer — to settle a relative's estate, for instance — write to the Overseas Citizens Service at the Department of State, Washington, D.C. 20520.

Lawyers typically charge $20 to $50 for an initial consultation, but many waive the fee if they do not take the case. Don't be shy about inquiring how much time and money your case will cost. Most attorneys charge by the hour; ask for an optimistic and a pessimistic price estimate.

For routine procedures, a lawyer may charge a flat rate — say, $50 to $200 for a simple will. For personal injury and damage cases, you might pay a contingency fee ranging from 20% to 50% of the amount finally collected, depending on how much work is required of your lawyer. Real estate closings are often charged as a percentage of the sales price or mortgage, typically ½% to 1½%.

Remember that the fee is only one factor. Some of the least expensive advice can be as sound as the costliest. But $100 an hour for a tough, experienced specialist may be well spent — if you stand to lose heavily in a property settlement or child-custody battle.

When your problem is relatively simple, you might turn to a cut-rate legal clinic for no-frills assistance. But even clinics offer low prices only on high-volume procedures, such as wills. Handling extras might be charged by the hour — at $75 per hour in some cases.

Prepaid legal plans are an inexpensive alternative. Most are organized as benefits for groups such as labor or credit unions. For a yearly fee, a subscriber can get unlimited telephone consultations with a lawyer. Most prepaid plans will not cover criminal cases or litigation costs if you want to sue through the plan. But you can get valuable prevention advice that might keep down your costs. It's cheaper to ask a lawyer what your options are if you break a lease, for example, than to pay him to go to court when your former landlord sues for a year's rent.

Leasing

SOME GOOD DEALS ON CARS

Whenmg prices for used cars are high, your cost of leasing a new car tends
to go down. That's because the projected resale value of a car often affects
the size of your lease payments.

In a so-called closed-end lease, your monthly payment depends in part on
how much the leasing company expects the automobile will be worth when
you are finished with it. If the company figures the used car will bring a
high price, it will charge you lower monthly payments.

In mid-1983, many of the best closed-end leases were available on foreign
cars. For example, one leasing company was offering a four-year lease on an
AMC Spirit DL for $142 a month. But a Nissan Sentra — which has the
same sticker price — was available at $122 a month. Another company of-
fered a five-year lease on a slow-depreciating Mercedes 240SD for $384 a
month — or about $40 a month less than some U.S. luxury models with
roughly the same sticker price.

There were also some leasing bargains among American cars, including
Chrysler's Dodge Colt and General Motors' Chevrolet Cavalier and Pontiac
Firebird.

Legal Disputes

SETTLING THEM OUT OF COURT

AMERICANS seem to sue by reflex action when they believe they have been wronged. Yet, as Abraham Lincoln once noted, "The nominal winner is often a real loser — in fees, expenses and waste of time."

When your impulse is to sue, you don't necessarily have to go to court and tell it to a judge. There are faster — and cheaper — ways to settle legal disputes. For example, you can rent a judge who is sometimes called a "dispute resolver." Or you can go to a so-called dispute mediation center to have a quarrel settled. Such innovations are cheaper, faster and simpler than traditional litigation. Basically, they offer third-party mediation — help in resolving differences.

The best-known alternative to going to court is the American Arbitration Association. Its 25 regional offices handle 38,000 cases a year. People who seek arbitration agree to abide by the decision of a third party.

An increasingly popular device for business people is the mini-trial. The idea is to let companies settle their own fights out of court. Representatives of two disputing companies argue out their case before top executives of both of those companies. If they then cannot reach a compromise, they bring in a third party to help, often a retired judge.

Similar mini-trials also are well suited for disputes involving, say, a home-owner and a contractor over faulty bathroom plumbing; or the owner of a wrecked auto who is claiming more damages than an insurance company is willing to pay. They hire a retired judge — and often he can sit down with both sides and work out a settlement in an afternoon. The fee might run $150 to $200 an hour.

The savings aren't only in money but also in damage to the disputants' feelings. An added benefit of resolving a case out of court is privacy. So is the fact that the remedy can be flexible, shaped by the plaintiff, the defendant and the dispute resolver. Although courts award money damages, they generally can't order a contractor to fix a leaky roof.

Most out-of-court settlements involve mediation — that is, third-party help in settling disputes. The savings can be large. For instance, in Denver, a mediated divorce usually costs from $215 to $1,300. A court divorce involving lawyers would run $1,000 to $10,000 — for each side. There are thousands of divorce mediators around the country. Many are lawyers with training in mediation.

To handle everyday disputes such as landlord-tenant and neighbor-against-neighbor disagreements, 180 mediation centers have popped up in some 40 states. They are sometimes called neighborhood justice centers, and they are usually state-supported. Not only are they fast, informal and effective, but they also cost nothing to iron out such problems as dogfights, broken windows and loud stereos.

For consumer complaints, state or local small-claims courts often serve you well. The maximum claims range from $200 in some rural counties of Washington and Georgia to $5,000 in Albuquerque, New Mexico. These courts are supposed to be simple, straightforward and free of lawyers. They are designed to make it easier for you to get justice without hiring an attorney, but because most states allow lawyers to represent either side, you might find that your opponent has hired one who outclasses you or ties you up in costly appeals. Even so, you might do very well on your own — and it will cost you only a few dollars to bring your complaint to small-claims court.

For more information on how you can help in settling legal disputes out of court, look in the Yellow Pages under "Mediation Services." Or phone an organization named Endispute, which has offices in Washington, Chicago, Los Angeles and San Francisco. Or contact the American Arbitration Association, which is in 25 cities.

Finally, the Better Business Bureau offers mediation and arbitration services to consumers at most of its 157 offices.

Life Insurance

COMPARING REAL COSTS

INSURANCE agents have something to say these days that's worth hearing: the cost of insurance is plunging. During the 1970s, according to the American Council on Life Insurance, the rates of 30 representative companies fell 16.5%. Rising life expectancy has allowed insurers to cut premiums.

The premium, however, is not totally reliable for comparing prices. There is a better way of stating your insurance costs. It's called the interest-adjusted index, and all agents can quote it to you. The interest-adjusted index takes into account three variables that affect your real insurance prices. Those three are the dividends on the policy, its cash value and the interest you could have earned if you invested your money elsewhere.

You should ask your agent what is the interest-adjusted cost index of your policy and then compare it with policies offered by competing companies. And you might shop around for an insurance firm that provides special discounts. There are discounts on insurance rates for women (because they live longer), for nonsmokers and for people who exercise. Occidental Life Insurance Company of North Carolina even offers a special saving up to 25% for marathoners, as long as they can prove that they have run one official 26-mile race to the finish. It has the same discount for people who regularly do other aerobic exercises, such as racquetball, squash, bicycling and cross-country skiing.

Life Insurance

HOW MUCH DO YOU NEED?

INSURANCE agents offer formulas for how much insurance you need, but they are flawed. The problem is that such formulas cram many different kinds of people, with different needs, into the same pigeonhole. Fortunately, there is a simple way to assess your needs.

First, you estimate your family's annual living expenses and how long you would want insurance to cover them.

Next you add in the amount you need, if anything, for your children's college education.

Then, when you have the total, you subtract from it the resources that you already have available. The answer is your insurance deficit — or surplus.

This fairly simple mathematical calculation is worth repeating periodically. It allows you to adjust for changes such as the birth of another child or an investment that pays off.

How much insurance you need hinges on what you want it to do for you. Many people expect it to do too much. In fact, insurance should be designed to maintain, not to raise, the standard of living a family has achieved.

You may already have more protection than you realize. Don't forget that the government pays monthly Social Security benefits to a widowed mother until her children are 16. But from her youngest child's 16th birthday until she qualifies at age 60 for Social Security retirement income, the widow is on her own.

You should use insurance only to protect dependents. People without children often make the mistake of listening to agents who recommend buying policies while both the premiums and the risks of being medically uninsurable are low. But neither argument is convincing. If you can't think of a beneficiary, you don't need life insurance.

Life Insurance

THREE KINDS OF POLICIES

Y OU'VE heard a lot lately about the three kinds of life insurance policies. They're whole life, term and the new universal life. But which of those three is best for you?

You need life insurance early in your career, when your children are young and your assets are low. But if you plan properly as you get older, your insurance needs should decline or even disappear.

The insurance that protects your family when you need it most for the lowest possible price is *term insurance.* Premiums are modest when you are young, but grow along with your age. Rates go up every year in the most popular plan. That's annual, renewable and convertible term. If you want, you can convert it automatically into whole life insurance.

Whole life insurance premiums, by contrast, never rise. But whole life buyers start out paying five or six times as much as they would for term. The excess premium goes into a cash reserve. When you retire, you can surrender your whole life policy and retrieve a fair amount of the cash in your reserve. If you have kept the policy 25 or 30 years, its cash surrender value will be about two-thirds the face value of the policy.

Whole life is a form of savings account. The earnings grow tax-deferred, but the policyholder usually gets little more than the passbook rate on his savings. Whole life has other disadvantages. There are heavy sales charges, typically 70% of the first year's premium, plus 7½% annually for the next nine years.

You can't permanently withdraw any of your paid-in cash and still remain insured. So if you need to get your hands on the money, you'll have to borrow against it, usually at 8% interest. You can't vary the premium or freely increase the insurance protection to suit your changing situation, either.

But you can do all that, and more, with a *universal life policy.* This policy combines term insurance with a tax-deferred savings account that pays rates as high as 12%. So, if you want to protect your family *and* build up tax-deferred savings, the best way to do it may well be to buy a universal life insurance policy.

Life Insurance

THE ATTRACTIONS OF UNIVERSAL LIFE

U NIVERSAL life insurance is barely three years old, but it has spread like Pac-Man, gobbling up 10% of life insurance sales in 1982. People buy it less for fear of dying than from dread of paying taxes.

Universal life combines insurance with a cash reserve, which is really a savings account. The earnings on these savings are tax-deferred. In that respect the policy is similar to whole life.

But unlike whole life, which often pays the policyholder little better than a 5¼% passbook savings rate on his cash reserve, universal life offers bond market rates of interest. In mid-1983, that was 8% to 12%. You would have had a hard time matching that kind of after-tax return anyplace else without taking some sizable risks or tying up your money for a long time.

The risk of losing money you invest in universal life is almost nil. And, with the best policies you can adjust the size of your premium to vary the amount you put into your cash reserve, just so you do not exceed the quite generous legal limits that Congress imposed to keep people from sheltering vast savings with tiny insurance policies. But those limits are quite generous. For instance, in one plan, a nonsmoking 30-year-old man buying $200,000 worth of insurance pays the maximum legal premium of just over $6,000 a year. Assuming that the policy continues to pay its 11% interest, then by the time he is 56, he could accumulate a legal maximum cash value of $839,500. You can thank the miracle of tax-deferred compound interest for that growth.

One warning: you have to shop for universal life with utmost care because these policies can carry large sales commissions amounting to 50% or more of your first year's premium.

Universal life doesn't always make sense for people who need less than $50,000 of insurance. That's because the smaller the policy, the more burdensome the fees.

Money-Market Funds

CHOOSING THE BEST ONE FOR YOU

M ONEY-MARKET funds have been a big bonanza for small investors. These funds buy short-term government, bank and corporate obligations, and though their yields declined from the stratosphere in 1982 and 1983, they were still far higher than the inflation rate.

Some safety-first investors flocked to money-market funds that buy only government securities, such as Capital Preservation Fund and Cardinal Government Securities. But these often pay less than do ordinary money funds and the new bank money-market accounts. Almost invariably, you can feel quite secure investing in a regular money fund, particularly if it is run by a well-established mutual fund group or brokerage firm. But to sleep more soundly at night, check that the average maturity of the fund's securities is 60 days or less by asking the fund or looking at "Donoghue's Money Fund Report Table," published in over 70 newspapers. Longer maturities do not give fund managers enough flexibility. If interest rates rise and the fund is locked into securities that pay lower rates, disgruntled shareholders might start a run for redemptions.

Choosing a money-market fund only because of its high yield can be a mistake. Since most ordinary money funds make the same kinds of investments, their returns are usually within one or two percentage points of each other. You might be wise to seek out money funds that let you shift your assets into other kinds of mutual funds when you think that interest rates are heading down and the stock market is heading up.

Some money funds have exchange agreements with independent mutual funds. Other money funds belong to one of the many fund families. These families also have mutual funds that invest in stocks, and sometimes in corporate and tax-exempt bonds.

Once you invest in a family, you usually can shift your cash from, say, a money fund into a stock mutual fund merely by making a phone call. Often the transfer costs nothing, and generally you can move your money around as often as you like. But a few fund families limit the switches in various ways to protect the fund against a sudden loss of assets in any one fund and to deter the shareholder from hasty decisions.

A number of companies have good reputations for performance and offer a variety of funds. A sampling of the families that meet those criteria would include American General, Dreyfus, Fidelity, Kemper, Oppenheimer, Putnam, T. Rowe Price, Stein Roe & Farnham, Value Line, Vanguard — and many more.

Your own selection of a mutual-fund family should be based chiefly on how well its stock funds have performed over the past decade. The most successful funds have been the so-called aggressive ones, which put shareholders' money in small or medium-size companies with big potential for growth. The time may come when you will want to transfer some assets from your money-market fund to your stock mutual fund. If you have chosen your fund group carefully, you will be able to keep it all in the family.

Money-Market Funds

HOW SAFE ARE THEY?

IF you have invested in a money-market fund, your savings are not only collecting relatively high interest, but most probably they are also quite safe. However, there are some risks. Although investors look upon money-market funds as reliable alternatives to the friendly neighborhood bank, even the soundest of them are a bit riskier than banks.

Certainly, money funds have most of the convenient attributes of bank checking accounts. Depositors can make withdrawals at any time by writing checks against their money-fund account. Almost always, you can take out, dollar for dollar, what you have put in, including dividends. They are declared daily and automatically credited to your account.

Could it be true that money funds are a golden exception to the iron rule that higher yield means higher risks? Not entirely. Deposits in them lack the protection of federal government insurance, which covers deposits in banks, savings and loan associations and credit unions against losses up to $100,000.

Furthermore, money-fund interest rates can plummet. In 1976, for example, they dropped below passbook savings rates. When interest rates fall, it's easy enough for you to pull your deposits from money funds. But this very freedom can hobble the funds' ability to pay off on the deposits dollar for dollar. Indeed, when interest rates drop, some depositors tend to take flight like sparrows off a wire. In a few rare cases, this can cause you trouble if you have your cash tied up in money funds. You may not necessarily get back every penny that you have put in.

Guardian angels do not watch over every money-market fund. In 1978, a small fund, the First Multifund for Daily Income, had to lower its share price from $1 to 93¢. That was like a bank coldly telling its depositors: "Sorry, but we will now return only 93¢ of every dollar in your account." Redemptions began accelerating, and First Multifund eventually merged into another fund.

In 1980, another fund, Institutional Liquid Assets, came close to a similar experience. But then its distinguished sponsors, which included the First National Bank of Chicago and the Wall Street investment banking firm of Salomon Brothers, pumped in new money — and so, investors could collect 100¢ on the dollar.

The lesson for investors is not to abandon money funds but to choose them with care. Here are three guidelines:

First, know the manager or sponsor. You needn't entrust your money to complete strangers. You may already do business with a firm that sponsors a money fund, say, a brokerage house, a life insurance company or a mutual fund group. A sponsor with an established reputation for financial responsibility will not jeopardize it by abandoning its customers. Strong sponsorship can give investors more peace of mind.

Second, to repeat, go for funds that invest in securities that have a low average maturity — 45 to 60 days at most. Funds with longer maturities may give cause for concern. The average maturities of large funds are published once a week in some newspapers. Also, most funds will supply the information via a toll-free telephone number.

Again, don't chase after the highest possible yields, or the hottest fund of the month. Over a year's time, the difference in interest payments between one fund and another is likely to be inconsequential. The customer shouldn't be greedy. He should expect a reasonable rate of return. But what is reasonable? Here's one tip: look at the yield on 90-day Treasury bills. Then pick a strongly sponsored fund which matches that yield.

You can look up the safety rating of your money-market fund in a newsletter called *Money Fund Safety Ratings*. It ranks 110 funds from Triple-A through D on the basis of the diversification, maturity and quality of their investments. For a free copy of this newsletter, write *Money Fund Safety Ratings*, 3471 North Federal Highway, Fort Lauderdale, Florida 33306.

Mortgages

A FREE GUIDE

IF you are a first-time home buyer or are returning to the housing market for the first time in years, you will need to educate yourself about the many new types of mortgages and real estate terms. A good way to start is by reading a free 16-page booklet titled *The Mortgage Money Guide: Creative Financing for Home Buyers*, published by the Federal Trade Commission. It defines the 15 most popular types of mortgages without endorsing any one of them and lists the pros and cons of each. The booklet also helps prospective buyers understand the fine print in mortgage contracts. There is also an easy-to-read page of mortgage payment tables.

To get your free copy of the guide, write to the Federal Trade Commission, 6th and Pennsylvania Avenue, NW, Washington, D.C. 20580.

Mortgages

ADJUSTABLE-RATE MORTGAGES

A VAST new array of mortgages is available today. If you are in the market for a house or an apartment, what kind of mortgage is best for you?

Your choice should be determined by your income and by your expectations about inflation and interest rates in general. If you expect interest rates will drop in the years ahead, you probably would be most comfortable with an adjustable-rate mortgage. As interest rates rise or fall, so will your monthly payments. These mortgages are also sensible for people who believe they will be able to refinance their loans at lower rates in the future.

On the other hand, if you expect that interest rates in general will rise over the next several years, you probably would be best off with a fixed-rate mortgage. Fixed-rate loans do not fluctuate. No matter how much interest rates may climb, your monthly payments will remain the same.

One incentive for your accepting an adjustable loan is that the interest on it is often one to two percentage points less than on a fixed-rate mortgage, at least at first. That seemingly small allowance is enough to let some buyers swing a purchase. In mid-1983, you could get adjustable-rate loans for about 12%.

The floating interest rates change anywhere from monthly to every five years, according to an index that you and your lender agree on. Before you make a deal, ask what index will be used. You should be able to find the index easily in the financial pages. Restrictions on how much an adjustable loan can rise or fall vary from state to state and from lender to lender. Federally chartered commercial banks and savings and loan associations can adjust as often as they want. The most common adjustables keep your payments fixed for one, three or five years.

Given the trend toward deregulation in the banking business, there probably will be fewer regulatory restrictions on adjustable mortgages than there are now. That means you will be able to dicker over the details of your mortgage loan even more in the future than you can today.

The most important point to bargain for is a cap, limiting the increase in your monthly payment after the one-year, three-year or five-year term is over. The next most significant negotiating point is the index that will be used in computing the rate of interest on the mortgage; often it is tied to the six-month Treasury bill rate. What matters most to you is how much this index fluctuates. Short-term rates gyrate much more than long-term ones do. So borrowers whose budgets cannot stretch to accommodate rising monthly payments should try to get the longest-term, least volatile rate they can. That is often the Federal Home Loan Bank Board's national contract mortgage rate.

A few state-regulated lenders are allowed to link their mortgage rates to measures of their own devising. Often that is the price they must pay for obtaining funds. You should avoid this type of loan, which critics say is "a license to rip you off."

Other kinds of adjustable loans can be even more insidious. The most dangerous is the payment-capped adjustable mortgage, also known as the dual-rate mortgage. Typically, the lender refigures your loan amount every six months as interest rates fluctuate. But your payments are fixed. The difference shows up in your loan balance. If interest rates fall, a larger share of your monthly payments goes toward paying off your principal. But if rates rise, your equity actually decreases. That's because your monthly payment is not large enough to cover the interest charged, so the unpaid portion is added to your loan balance.

Dual-rate mortgages alarm many real estate professionals. For instance, Richard Elbrecht, a mortgage specialist with the California Department of Consumer Affairs, recommends that lenders be required to limit changes in rates to 1% a year. As he says, "In the same way we ban unsafe cars and unsafe drugs, we should prohibit unsafe mortgages."

Mortgages

SELLER FINANCING

T HE excitement of home buying has shifted from a hunt for the right house to a search for the right mortgage, sometimes any mortgage that will fit your budget. But even in this era of daunting interest rates, hundreds of thousands of families have found ways to finance the home of their dreams. You should be able to do it, too — if you are willing to explore the vast new world of mortgages.

Look for a mortgage that not only falls within your budget today but also will be manageable in the future. Begin your hunt with the seller of the house you want to buy. Sellers have learned that offering financing is usually more important than cutting prices when trying to unload a house. Generally the seller will give you a bargain interest rate. Perhaps he will offer a so-called balloon mortgage, which lets you, the buyer, pay back the loan at a particularly low rate. The catch is you get that break for only three to five years — and then the entire loan becomes due. If interest rates fall by then, you will be able to refinance the mortgage at a reasonable rate. But if interest rates rise, balloonists can find themselves heading for a crash. In California, where rocketing real estate prices popularized the balloon mortgages early on, refinancing has become a serious problem. In 1981, for example, the foreclosure rate there tripled.

Assuming a seller's old, lower-interest loan is becoming tougher and in some cases riskier. Many mortgages have clauses that ban assumptions, and the U.S. Supreme Court has upheld the right of federal savings and loan associations to enforce those provisions.

Mortgages

SHARED-APPRECIATION MORTGAGES

A YOUNG couple in Phoenix spotted a house they wanted to buy. The price: a stiff $98,500. They figured that after putting 20% down they could get a $78,800 mortgage at interest rates then at 13½%. But monthly payments would have come to $950 a month, and that was more than the couple could afford. Their solution was to go to a mortgage company that offered them what is known as a shared-appreciation mortgage.

This new type of loan lowered their monthly payments by one-third. But in return the buyers promised to give the lender one-third of the profit they make whenever they sell the house. Because housing values have risen so dramatically in the past, offering to share your appreciation might sound like a pact with the devil. But by agreeing to share profits, the Phoenix couple were able to buy as their first house one that might have taken years to acquire. And when they sell, even though they will have to give the lender a third of the profit, they still stand to come out ahead. That's because their two-thirds share will probably amount to just as much as the full profit on a cheaper property.

Generally, these shared-appreciation mortgages help not only first-time buyers, but also elderly buyers, people who cannot afford to make big payments and who expect to own their houses for the rest of their lives.

If you consider a shared-appreciation mortgage, be aware of the risks. Under some agreements, a lender can collect his share of the appreciation after 10 years, even if the homeowner has not sold. If the homeowner does not have the cash to pay, he will have to borrow and perhaps take out a new mortgage. This could zap him with exploding monthly payments.

The shared mortgage is a poor choice for a do-it-yourselfer, too. If you make home improvements yourself, the value that you add to your house is shared with the lender.

Mortgages

"RICH-UNCLE" MORTGAGES

For people who cannot raise a down payment for a house of their own, there is a shared-equity mortgage for which bankers have an apt name. The loan depends on an outside private investor to put up all or part of the down payment in return for a share of the tax benefits from home ownership and a part of the profit when the house eventually is sold. It is called a "rich-uncle" loan.

Most homeowners would hate to give up the tax advantages of having a house. But people who face difficulty buying a house often find that the tax deduction is not as important to them as it would be to a more affluent investor. Here is how the shared-equity mortgage works:

For example, Eldon Johnson is a garbage-truck driver in Fort Myers, Florida. On his $18,000 annual pay, he could not have bought a house without the benefit of a "rich-uncle" loan. After the owner of a local stereo store put up $5,500 for a down payment, the Johnson family were able to buy the $55,000 three-bedroom house. They make the $529 monthly payment, and their investor gets roughly two-thirds of the tax deduction at the end of the year. The investor is in a much higher tax bracket, so the arrangement benefits both.

Thanks to their "rich-uncle" loan, the Johnson family is living in a house they otherwise could not have purchased. If they sell the house for a profit, their affluent investor gets a cut of it. They can buy him out at any time they can afford it, but he cannot turn the tables on them. If they do not buy him out, he signs his interest in the house over to them at the end of the 12th year. By then, their "rich uncle" will have recouped his investment.

Mortgages

STILL MORE ALTERNATIVES

An increasingly popular method of reducing your mortgage payments is the so-called buy-down. That happens when desperate builders who have a house to unload make a lump-sum payment to the lender — and the lender in turn reduces his mortgage interest enough to tempt people actually to buy those houses.

For example, a California developer spent $4,600 to reduce the interest rate to 9¾% on a mortgage that a buyer got on one of his homes. The rate rises one percentage point every year, until it levels off at 12¾%. In that period, the buyer's monthly payment will go up by $300. But the couple who bought the house hope their income will rise substantially by then — or that they will be able to refinance the mortgage at a lower rate.

If you are confident that your income will rise a lot in the next few years, you may find a so-called graduated-payment mortgage attractive. You start out paying a small monthly amount that keeps growing at an agreed-upon rate until it levels off. Sounds good, but such a loan ends up costing you more than a conventional mortgage in the end.

If you have a lot of liquid cash, you may be interested in one of the new zero-interest-rate loans. They are commonly used by developers to move unsold houses. You make a very large down payment, usually 30% to 50% of the purchase price, and then pay off the principal over five to seven years. Even though you're charged no interest, tax lawyers believe you're still entitled to the income tax deduction that a loan ordinarily generates. That is, you may be able to deduct an amount equal to 10% of your mortgage payments every year. But zero-rate mortgages can have one major drawback. Sometimes developers will increase house prices by as much as 25% or add on a loan fee of about 5% for buyers who use the zeroes.

Mortgages

THE PROFITS AND PERILS OF SWAPPING YOUR MORTGAGE

WITH interest rates down from their peaks of the early 1980s, this may be the time to swap your old, high-interest mortgage for a new one. If you bought a home in the last few years, you may well be able to lop a lot off your monthly payments.

You may be carrying a mortgage with rates as high as 18%. But don't assume that your mortgage lender has locked you in and thrown away the key. Other lenders are eager to spring you. There is much mortgage money around now, and lenders are competing eagerly to get your business. In mid-1983, for example, you could refinance and get a loan for 11% to 13½%.

Swapping a peak interest loan may — or may not — be a smart move for you. Everything depends on your up-front costs.

Looked at over the full term of the loan, a saving of even one percentage point would seem worth grabbing. A decline of one point on a 30-year, $100,000 mortgage saves you nearly $13,000 in monthly payments. And if you can lower your interest rate by two points, it is possible to break even on your refinancing costs in less than two years.

Even so, many people would do best to wait for an even wider point spread before they run to the bank for a new loan. Unless you can reduce your mortgage interest by two to three points, it is probably not worth the hassle and the immediate up-front costs. For example, if there is a prepayment clause in your mortgage, you will have to pay plenty to get out of it — as much as 3% of the unpaid balance. That's on top of the usual costs of refinancing. If you get a new mortgage from a lender different from your original one, you will have to pay as much as 1% of the loan for a new title search, plus fees for such things as a reappraisal and the lender's legal expenses.

So, you should check carefully to see what these real front-end costs will be, after you figure in your income tax deductions for them. Then compare them with what immediate and long-term savings you can expect by refinancing your mortgage. And if your present lender balks at refinancing, go to another source of funds, either a different bank or savings and loan association — or a mortgage company.

Moving

GETTING HELP WHEN YOU RELOCATE

Moving to a new state or city does not have to be a journey into the heart of darkness. You will have to do a fair amount of letter writing, library reading and talking to strangers, however. And eventually you should visit the place where you think you'd like to live.

Anyone contemplating a move would do well to read *Places Rated Almanac*, published by Rand McNally for $11.95. This useful book compares the climates, crime rates, housing, education, recreation, arts, economic conditions and transportation systems in 277 metropolitan areas. Its first choice of a place to live is Atlanta.

United Van Lines has a free kit describing any one of 7,000 U.S. and foreign cities. Just call 800–325–3870 in most states. The *Book of the States*, which you can find in most libraries, gives you the tax rates of each state, county and municipality. The local Chamber of Commerce, of course, is another good source of information.

To get a feel for life in a community, subscribe to local newspapers and city or state magazines and talk to people who live there. You can come closest to experiencing life in a strange city by visiting or becoming a paying guest of someone in town. One way to do that is to seek commercial bed-and-breakfast accommodations in private homes.

Once you arrive, walk through the neighborhoods. A stroll past shuttered shops on Main Street may tell you more about the state of the economy than any Chamber of Commerce brochure. Seek out real estate agents. They know the virtues of various neighborhoods and they are willing to spend a lot of time with serious sales prospects. (See also "Home Movers: How to Find One.")

Mutual Funds

HOW TO MAKE MONEY IN THEM

J UST as there is no perfect person or painting or poem, so there is no perfect investment. But the one that comes closest for most people is the mutual fund.

What you get from a mutual fund, at relatively low cost, is professional management of your money. Your investments are handled by people who devote their full time and attention to them.

A mutual fund buys a wide variety of securities and then sells its own shares to the public. The price of a share rises or falls every day, along with the rises and falls of the total value of the securities the fund owns. And you can sell your shares back to the mutual fund at any time.

Many funds have been rising even faster than the market indexes since stocks started bounding up in August 1982. And, in the five years ending in 1982, funds that invest primarily in stocks had average gains of 120.5% compared with a 93.2% total return for Standard & Poor's 500 stock index.

Once you invest in a fund, you receive dividends every quarter and capital gains distributions annually, if the fund has earned either. A fund earns and distributes capital gains if and when it sells stock at a profit. Then you pay tax at the long- or short-term gains rate. Almost all mutual funds offer to reinvest your earnings automatically in additional shares.

You also can use mutual funds for your Individual Retirement Accounts and Keogh plans. And simply by making a toll-free phone call, you can switch your money from, say, a stock mutual fund to a bond fund or to a tax-free bond fund or to a money-market fund. You can do that if you patronize one of the many mutual-fund companies that offer several different kinds of funds.

What kind of mutual fund should you choose? That depends in part on how much time you are prepared to spend every week studying the stock market. Let's say you follow the financial news but you certainly do not want to re-examine and make changes in your investments as often as every week. What you need is a mutual fund that over the years consistently has climbed more than the stock-market averages during good times while not falling more than the averages in bad times. Quite possibly that will be one of the so-called growth funds or growth-and-income funds.

On the other hand, what if you are willing to pay really close attention to your investments and try for spectacular gains during rising markets? Then you are a candidate for so-called maximum-capital-gains funds. They are aggressive funds that buy the fast-moving stocks of small, potentially rapidly rising companies.

But be ready to bail out of such a high flier quickly. Maximum-capital-gains funds tend to rise fast — and then fall fast when the market starts to turn down.

Let's say you're essentially optimistic about stocks but also wary about a possible resurgence of inflation. In that case, you can invest mainly in a fast-growing technology-stock fund — which buys into promising but risky technology companies — and simultaneously keep, say, 10% of your money in a fund that buys gold-mining shares. They most likely will jump if inflation threatens.

The Great Divide in mutual funds is between load funds, which charge sales commissions up to 8½%, and no-loads, which have no sales charges. Load funds pay stockbrokers and their own salesmen to sell shares in funds. The no-loads sell theirs through the mail. But whether the load buys better performance is highly questionable. Before you buy anything, study the prospectuses of several funds carefully to see how they've performed over the past years.

For a directory of no-load funds, send $1 to No-Load Mutual Fund Association, 11 Penn Plaza, Suite 2204, New York, New York 10001.

Mutual Funds

SWITCHING AMONG THE FUNDS

Today's fast-rising mutual fund can easily turn into tomorrow's loser.

So, the trick to making money in mutual funds is to be a fair-weather friend. You want to get out of the losers and into the winners by switching around from fund to fund.

Aim to move just before big up or down swings in the stock market. When it is advancing rapidly, invest in the speculative funds. Then at the merest flutter of danger, you can switch to the safety of a more secure money-market fund. Investors also quite often have the option of switching to tax-free municipal-bond funds or corporate bond funds within a group managed by the same fund company.

But you need to know when to switch and more specifically which fund to switch to. For this reason it probably pays to subscribe to a monthly newsletter advisory service that tracks the performance of the various funds. Among those newsletters are *Growth Fund Guide* (Growth Fund Research Building, Yreka, California 96097); *Mutual Fund Specialist* (P.O. Box 1025, Eau Claire, Wisconsin 54701); *NoLoad Fund°X* (235 Montgomery Street, San Francisco, California 94104); *Switch Fund Advisory* (8943 Shady Grove Court, Gaithersburg, Maryland 20877); *Telephone Switch Newsletter* (P.O. Box 2538, Huntington Beach, California 92647); and *United Mutual Fund Selector* (210 Newbury Street, Boston, Massachusetts 02116).

These newsletters rank the mutual funds according to how much the prices of their shares rise or fall in value over one-month, three-month, six-month and one-year periods. The strategy of switching is to (1) buy into the mutual fund that is on top of the rankings for performance over the past year, and (2) keep your money in that fund as long as the advisory service tells you it is among the top five in its category for the past year. The various categories that the funds are divided into include growth, aggressive growth, and growth and income.

When your newsletter arrives — usually a week to 10 days after the end of the month — a quick glance will tell you if the fund you are invested in is still on top. If it is not, the rankings will tell you which one is.

An easy way to switch among mutual funds is to put your money into a fund company that offers a big variety of different kinds of funds. Then when your advisory service tells you just which one is the company's current star fund, you can move your money into it by making a simple phone call to the fund company.

You often can do even better at switching if you are willing to go to the trouble of closing your account with one mutual-fund company and opening a new account with a different company that offers the currently best-performing fund in its category. According to one study, if you had followed such a switching strategy between August 1976 and July 1982, you could have had an annual compounded rate of return of almost 28% — and your investment would have quadrupled.

Leapfrogging from fund to fund in search of the best return does require a bit of work. The first step is to call the toll-free 800 number of the new fund you want to invest in. You can get these numbers from mutual-fund newsletters or mutual-fund companies' ads or merely by dialing 800 information at 800–555–1212.

When you reach the mutual-fund company, ask for shareholder services. Say that you want to open an account and then request an account number for yourself.

Next, write to the head of shareholder services at your old fund, that is, the fund you are presently invested in. Your letter should say, "Please sell all full and fractional shares in the account of . . ." and then give your name and your old account number. Ask that the redemption check be made payable to, and sent to, the new fund you're moving to. And, be sure to request that the words "for the benefit of" appear on the check, followed by your name and your new account number.

Probably it will take one to two weeks for your money to arrive at your new mutual fund. You can short-circuit this process if you have a money-market account. Then you just send your own money-market check to open your new mutual fund account. And to cover that check, tell the mutual fund that you are leaving to mail the cash that you have withdrawn directly to your money fund.

If you do not want the anxiety of having to call turns in the market, one sensible strategy is dollar-cost averaging. You just invest the same amount every month. When the market is low, that amount buys you relatively many shares; when the market is high, you get fewer shares. If you have, say, $1,200, you might invest $100 a month for a year or longer in an aggressive stock fund. This lets you get in on the action of an aggressive fund without having to pick the single best time to buy.

Another technique is to invest in a portfolio of several funds and to alter the mix whenever you sense a change in the market. If you figure the market will rise, you might want to place 75% of your capital into aggressive growth funds and only 25% in money-market funds. But as soon as you sense a sharp decline ahead, you can reverse your investments, putting more of your cash into the money-market funds.

Mutual Funds

AGGRESSIVE GROWTH FUNDS

Now that the experts figure that the stock market will do well in the mid-1980s, the time may be opportune to invest in mutual funds that aim for aggressive growth. But if you do, stand ready to move out again fast.

Aggressive growth funds invest heavily in stocks of small companies that have large potential, such as those involved in high-technology, health care, and certain other services. Like the firms they invest in, these funds are volatile. They tend to jump, and plunge, faster than the market itself.

Led by these growth funds, mutual funds invested in stocks have risen impressively even when the market performed unimpressively. For example, with all dividends and capital gains reinvested, they grew by an average of 157% from 1974 to 1979. By contrast, the Dow Jones industrial average rose 77% and the Standard & Poor's 500 stock index increased 99%. The mutual funds even outperformed real estate; the average price of a one-family house, for instance, climbed 81% during that period. The best funds were the most speculative. In general, funds emphasizing capital appreciation outperformed more conservative funds by almost 50%. Of course, during the bull market that began in August 1982, the stock funds did even better. Some rose more than 100% in less than a year. But even the most optimistic analysts of speculative mutual funds stress the importance of moving quickly out of the volatile funds at the first sniff of a decline.

Mutual Funds

THE MOST SUCCESSFUL FUNDS

IF you are thinking of investing in a mutual fund, you probably will favor one that has performed well in the past. But which funds have done best?

Money magazine has ranked 284 individual mutual funds according to how much they rose over one, five and 10 years through March 1983.

The star 10-year performer was Twentieth Century Select of Kansas City. It had a fabulous rise of 710% in the 10 years from March 1973 to March 1983.

The five-year winner was Fidelity Magellan of Boston, up 577% since 1978.

Which mutual-fund families have earned the most for their investors during the recent turbulent years in the stock market? *Money* magazine studied 97 funds offered by 25 different fund companies; then it rated these families according to the gains their major member funds made from early 1974 through December 1982 after all sales charges and commissions were deducted.

By *Money*'s standards, the top-rated family overall was Value Line (711 Third Avenue, New York, New York 10017). Two of this family's mutual funds came in first in their particular categories. The Value Line Income Fund was the highest riser in the category that aims for high dividend-and-interest payments. And the Value Line Fund was first in the category that aims for a combination of long-term growth plus immediate cash income.

In second place among the fund families was the Kemper group (120 South LaSalle Street, Chicago, Illinois 60603), which is part of the Kemper insurance and investment empire. Both Kemper's long-term growth and its growth-and-income funds ranked relatively high. But its maximum-capital-gains fund, which aims for very fast growth by buying smaller companies, finished fairly low.

The third-ranked group was Oppenheimer (2 Broadway, New York, New York 10004). The Oppenheimer Special Fund was in first place in the maximum-capital-gains category. Its long-term growth fund, called Oppenheimer Time, was also very high.

In the overall family rankings, the Security fund group (700 Harrison Street, Topeka, Kansas 66636) finished in fourth place. The Sigma family (3801 Kennett Pike, Wilmington, Delaware 19807) was in fifth place. Other fund families that also did notably well were Neuberger & Berman, Vanguard, American General, Delaware and Dreyfus.

[241]

Mutual Funds

"HUMANISTIC" FUNDS

ARE you looking for "humanistic" mutual funds? There are several of these funds, which do not invest in companies that make weapons or pollute the environment.

They are Pax World Fund of Portsmouth, New Hampshire, the Dreyfus Third Century Fund of New York City, and the Calvert Social Investment Fund of Washington, D.C. All of them are no-loads. That means you do not have to pay any salesman's commission to buy into the fund, and almost all your money is put to work for you.

The trouble is, idealism has its price. For the five years that ended June 30, 1983, only one of these funds did better than the Lipper mutual-fund industry average gain of 149%. The good performer was Dreyfus Third Century, which was up 152%. Meanwhile, the Pax World Fund rose only 93%. Calvert, which started in October 1982, had gained about 18%.

Oil Lotteries

A LONG-SHOT CHANCE TO WIN A LEASE

F EW people are willing to trek through the Badlands of North Dakota or the bayous of Louisiana in search of the right spot to drill for oil or gas. And few would spend hundreds of thousands of dollars to sink a hole that could easily turn out to be dry. But anyone can experience the thrill of wildcatting by participating in the oil and gas lotteries sponsored by that great gambler, the U.S. government.

Every two months the Bureau of Land Management offers up between 1,200 and 1,800 tracts of land for drilling. And any adult U.S. citizen can apply to lease these parcels at the cost of $1 an acre a year for the first five years and $3 an acre a year to the tenth year — payable in advance. The parcels range all the way from 40 to 10,000 acres. Naturally, there are more applicants than parcels. As many as 7,000 people may seek a single promising tract, so the Bureau of Land Management holds lotteries at eleven regional offices to determine which applicants will be awarded a lease. Bureaucrats use a computer to pick the winner.

The possibility of winning is slight, but then, too, the cost of entering a lottery is not overwhelming. The filing fee is $75 a parcel. Of course, most people entering the lottery don't have any intention of drilling wells themselves. Instead, they hope that an oil company will buy the lease from them.

For a lease, companies offer anywhere from practically nothing to several hundred dollars an acre — plus a royalty. That's typically 3% to 5% of the value of any oil or gas that is ultimately pumped out. A lottery winner might be able to sell a lease on a 1,000-acre tract for $100,000 up front. Then, if the buyer drills on the property and finds oil or gas, royalties could add up to several times that amount.

If you decide to enter a federal oil and gas lottery, you must recognize that the chances of scoring are quite small. In 1982, for example, 2½ million applications were filed for 9,000 parcels of land put up by the government. That meant the chances of winning were about one in 278. But since it costs only $75 to get into a lottery, it's not bad as a romantic gamble — and it might pay off.

One way to get in is to use one of the big commercial filing services. They often advertise in national financial publications. A service will apply for a lease in your name on one of the most desirable parcels of land. The charge is usually $300, which includes the $75 federal application fee. A disadvantage is that these filing services tend to identify the best leases and then direct all of their clients to them. If you file through one of the services, you'll probably be applying for the most hotly contested parcels, and thus face the worst odds against winning. Beware of any company that guarantees you will win a lease.

The alternative is simply to file on your own. You can get information by writing to the Bureau of Land Management, Washington, D.C. 20240. The system works like this: Each B.L.M. office posts a list of parcels on the first day of January, March, May, July, September and November. If you pay a small fee in advance, the B.L.M. will mail you a copy of the list. Then, by the 15th business day of the month, the B.L.M. must receive your completed application form — including $75 for each tract you are applying for.

If you decide to apply on your own, you have two choices. You can file blind and take the risk that you'll win a valueless parcel. Or you can try to choose the most attractive parcels yourself. That can be complicated and expensive. You can buy maps, guides and other information about the parcels offered from companies that cater to oil lottery applicants. But some people who work hard at it, file a lot of lottery applications and even win quite a few of them say their oil and gas profits just about cover their costs.

Even if you win a federal oil lottery, there's no guarantee that oil companies will be interested in buying the tract you might win. And even if they do buy, your chances of making really big money from a royalty are small. Only about 10% of the parcels awarded in oil lotteries are actually drilled on. Still, oil lotteries can be a fascinating speculation.

Personal Finance

HOW TO AVOID MISTAKES WITH YOUR MONEY

Everyone makes financial mistakes — like the man who died before he told his new bride the location of his safe-deposit box, or the low-income fellow who invested the family savings in tax-exempt bonds instead of money-market certificates, which would have paid him much, much more.

The most common financial mistake is a failure to define your goals. Few people know what they really want their money to do. Several years' accumulation of savings or a sudden inheritance or other windfall leaves them with money to invest and no idea of how to make it best work for them.

What is *your* goal? For example, are you saving for college tuition, or future security? A necessary first step to accomplish your goal is to estimate just what you want your money to do and how much you will need to do it. The next step is to figure out how much you must put away each week — or month — to reach your goal.

Another common mistake is failure to follow through on your financial goal. The cost of not making investment moves immediately can add up. Say that, after a check of your personal finances, you decide to shift some money from your low-paying savings account into higher-yielding Treasury bills. If you delay just a few months, your procrastination will cost you a bundle of money.

A third financial mistake is the failure to maintain careful records. You have to keep — and keep updated — lists of your investments, your bank accounts and any financial advisers you might have. Your personal financial file should list names and amounts of all your securities, money-market funds, hard assets and life insurance policies. It also should give the location of your safe-deposit boxes and contain your tax records and credit-card information, as well as wills and deeds.

Doing that is not only a wise precaution in case anything happens to you; it's also a constant reminder of your financial position. If you are always aware of where your money is, you can take advantage of tax changes and map out new investment strategies. Keeping such information complete and correct makes it easier for you to switch around your investments and eases the burden on your family if you become ill or injured.

Still another common financial mistake is greed. Some people are so obsessed with making tax-exempt or sheltered investments that they often miss much more lucrative, if taxable, investments. Tax shelters make sense only if they are worthwhile investments even without the tax break. Avoid shelters that are unduly risky or that cost much more than a nonsheltered investment. And it doesn't pay to invest in a shelter if there is even a slight chance the IRS will not allow the deduction. Before you invest in a tax shelter, read the prospectus to check the past performance of the sponsors. What were they selling last week? You also should consider whether you are already oversheltered and whether your tax bracket will be higher some years from now, when you begin to receive taxable investment proceeds.

It is a mistake to heed advice from people who are not qualified to give it. Amateurs — like your next-door neighbor or your cousin's son-in-law — can do more damage than good. You are better off soliciting and then carefully considering professional advice from brokers, bankers, attorneys, accountants or financial planners. Fees should be agreed on in advance, but sometimes the advice is free.

Another common mistake is a failure to keep an open mind about investment opportunities. Many people invest in just one thing and stick with it. Huge sums of money are still locked away in passbook savings accounts, which pay interest of only 5¼% or 5½%. Much higher-yielding money-market funds, Treasury bills, short-term income trusts or tax-deferred annuities are safe as well as rewarding, but many people are — in the words of one savings bank president — too lazy or afraid to move their money.

The biggest mistake most people make with their money is not hedging their assets and not diversifying their investments. If you have a variety of investments, you stand a better chance of riding out any financial storm.

Say that you're a middle-income person with a good job, and your goal is to build an estate for the future. No matter how much or how little you can afford to invest, you should spread your investments around. You might be wise to put 50% of your investments in stocks and stock mutual funds; another 10% into real estate, such as shares in real estate investment trusts; 10% into bonds — high-rated corporate bonds, if you are conservative, deep-discounted intermediate-term bonds if you are aggressive, and municipal bonds if you are in a high tax bracket; 10% into tax shelters of the conservative kind that will not "burn out" and leave you with huge tax liabilities to pay off in the future; 5% into precious metals, 10% into such cash assets as money-market funds that you can shift into new investments as opportunities arise; and finally, about 5% into assets that suit your fancy, anything from stamps and coins to art and gems.

If you are nearing or already in retirement, you have different goals. You want an assured income to live on month after month, so you would split up your investments differently. You might divide your assets into four roughly equal parts: one-quarter in high-grade stocks or stock mutual funds; one-quarter in bonds; one-quarter in real estate; and one-quarter in such cash equivalents as money-market funds. But whatever your age or stage, you can protect yourself better against financial adversity by diversifying.

The worst mistake an investor can make is to assume he will not make a mistake. We all do. But here, to recapitulate, are ways you can head off serious losses in your personal finances:

— Define your goals. Give careful thought to what you want your money to do for you. Then follow through, by saving and investing.

— Keep careful records and review and update your financial plans regularly.

— Don't get carried away with tax-sheltered investments. Remember: they make sense only if they would be worthwhile investments even without the tax breaks.

— Get your advice from professionals — stockbrokers, bankers, attorneys, accountants, insurance agents and financial planners. Make sure they coordinate all the advice they give you.

— Keep your knowledge of investments up to date by reading widely and asking questions.

— Finally, put your money in a variety of investments that can flourish in different financial climates. This way you can minimize the cost of any errors.

Personal Finance

FACING UP TO YOUR FEARS

Let's face it: many people's personal finances are a mess. They don't keep records, their savings are scattered and not earning nearly as much as they could and their family budget is all bull and a yard wide. But you *can* get your personal finances together.

Your greatest obstacle is fear. But when people recognize their fears of finance, they often choose to confront and conquer them. Fortunately, the three most common fiscal fears are easy to identify. They are fear of responsibility, fear of risk, and fear, believe it or not, of wealth.

Victims of fiscal irresponsibility are plagued by inaction. What they really yearn for is someone who will make all their financial decisions for them. So, often they unquestioningly invest in what some broker or banker — or even some fairly successful friend — advises them to invest in. And often they get stung.

Then there is fear of risk. Victims are afraid to do anything with their assets for fear of doing the wrong thing. So they keep their money in low-yielding passbook savings accounts when they could easily earn much more interest by transferring at least some of it to high-paying money-market funds or U.S. Treasury securities or federally insured bank certificates of deposit or bank money-market deposit accounts.

As for fear of wealth, people sometimes feel undeserving of increased incomes or substantial inheritances. If they have investments, they're afraid to change them even when a security plummets. They feel guilty about earning more than their parents did. And their guilt translates into immobility.

Facing up to your fears about money and then taking steps to act and put your finances in order is one way to sleep free of worry or guilt. And, in a world where so much seems to be sliding out of control, it's reassuring to know that, if you're willing to make the effort, it's still possible for you to determine your own financial destiny.

Personal Finance

CALCULATING YOUR NET WORTH

THE first step toward taking control of your personal financial life is to calculate your net worth. That's what you own minus what you owe. Once you figure out what you're worth, you can set your goals — for example, to take a vacation, buy a house or secure a comfortable retirement. Then you can devise strategies to reach those goals.

Your net worth is your financial mirror image — what you look like on a given day. Anyone with a simple pocket calculator can figure net worth. Add up the current value of your checking or savings accounts and money-market funds. Don't forget the current market value of any stocks, bonds or other securities you may own. Your insurance agent can supply the current cash value of your life insurance if it's not in the policy. To find out what your house or condo is worth, consult a real estate broker or note the asking prices of similar homes for sale in your neighborhood.

When adding up, don't overlook the current worth of your employee benefits, such as profit sharing and thrift programs and unexercised stock options. Often these assets are second in value only to your house.

If you own some art, antiques, jewelry or other collectibles, you may need to call in an appraiser to give a good estimate of their current resale price. No matter what kind of collectible you have, you can expect to pay an appraiser an hourly fee of $50 to $125. If you don't have many collectibles, you don't need an appraiser. Just ask an antique dealer what he thinks you could sell them for. But remember: your possessions are worth what you could get if you had to sell them immediately — not what it costs to replace them.

You should recalculate your net worth at least once a year. Some debt counselors urge their clients to take their financial reading immediately before they start Christmas shopping. But if you've never done a personal balance sheet or yours is as old as an 8% mortgage, the best time to start is now. You might discover that you are better off than you thought.

Personal Finance

MAKING A BUDGET

WHETHER you are a student whose money runs out long before the month does or an executive with a comfortable income, you need a budget. If you don't have one, start now. In just three months' time, you can win the battle of the budget. If you devote only a few hours during each of those months to considering and correcting your income and outgo, then you can reduce overspending, free up money for savings and investments and build a cash reserve for any sudden urge to splurge.

To figure out your monthly income, add up your annual salary and any other money you receive — such as dividends, interest or child support — and divide by 12. Then do the same thing with your expenses, adding up all your bills for the year. The purpose of this exercise is to smooth out your expenses and prepare for them so that you never have to invade your savings for unexpected bills. If you want to get a handle on where your money is really going, try to keep a journal and jot down all your expenses as they hit you every day.

Once you have figured out how you are spending your money, devote the second month of your program to trimming any excesses in your budget so you can build up savings and investments. Some financial advisers recommend that you allocate no more than 65% of your take-home pay for fixed expenses, including rent or mortgage payments, utilities and food. Allow another 20% for such variable outlays as household repair, recreation or clothing. Put aside 10% for insurance premiums and property taxes, and the last 5% — or more than that, if possible — for savings.

During the third month, you should carefully evaluate your income-and-outgo statement and make any changes so you can live on it. Successful budgeting depends on being neither too rigid nor too loose. If you are passionate about movies and want to see three or four films a week, then adjust your spending in some other area.

Aim to build up savings that eventually will amount to at least three months' worth of your after-tax income. Put that cash away in a money-market fund, Treasury bills, short-term bank certificates or other liquid savings.

You are in good shape if 10% or less of your after-tax income is going to pay off installment loans, such as car payments, or bills for furniture and appliances that you bought on time. If those expenses creep beyond 15% of your income, you are losing the battle of the budget.

Personal Finance

WHERE TO GET HELP

IF the thought of organizing your personal financial affairs overwhelms you, take heart. You need not — indeed, should not — do it all by yourself.

Help in getting your finances together ranges from books that can motivate and educate you to personal financial planners who can compile voluminous studies of your economic life. Or you can take courses, attend public seminars and ask the advice of a stockbroker, an insurance agent, attorney, accountant or banker.

Yet there is no reason why you cannot at least decode the simple ciphers of money management in a weekend of dedicated reading. Some books can give you a grounding in money matters. Among the best are *The Power of Money Dynamics* by Venita VanCaspel, *Everyone's Money Book* by Jane Bryant Quinn and *Money Talks: Bob Rosefsky's Complete Program for Financial Success.*

Also, financial institutions often publish material that can help you, and it is usually free at their offices. Look for publications put out by banks, life insurance companies and stock brokerages.

You might benefit from studying financial planning in a classroom setting. Courses on personal finance are offered by colleges, universities, community service organizations and other sponsors of adult education programs. The charge is often minimal — perhaps $30 or $50 — or even free. The chance you take in any course is that your teacher is merely a salesperson in the guise of an educator, so check his or her credentials closely. Avoid instructors whose expertise is limited only to selling stocks, bonds, insurance or other so-called investment products.

If you want extensive personalized advice about investing, budgeting and getting your finances together, you can always hire a professional financial planner. You can get names of planners from bankers, accountants and stockbrokers.

If you normally progress unimpeded down your private road of good intentions, you probably won't have to hire a professional adviser to make a full-scale financial plan for you. The more help, discipline and encouragement you require, the more you'll have to pay. But people who have trouble getting started may discover that the professional help of a financial planner — even just at the beginning — can make the difference between success and failure.

You can spend from a few hundred dollars for a one-shot diagnosis of your

[251]

financial ailments and opportunities to several thousand for a complete analysis. For ongoing consultation, planners either charge you a flat fee, or else they earn their income from commissions on the investments they sell to you. The advantage of hiring a fee-only planner is that you know he won't recommend stocks, bonds or life insurance to you just to receive a commission on the sale. But these fee-only planners tend to be costly.

Financial planners sometimes offer public seminars to expand their market. These meetings usually are advertised in local newspapers, and they can be worthwhile. Often the planners charge nothing for the first hour or two of consultation, then $50 to $150 for each additional hour.

Finally, you can get an inexpensive education in investment by joining an investment club. They are located in many cities. For more information on how to join — or even start — such a group, write to the National Association of Investment Clubs, P.O. Box 220, Royal Oak, Michigan 48068. (See "Investment: Investment Clubs.")

Personal Finance

BUDGETING FOR STUDENTS

W HEN heading off to college, an extracurricular activity that every student should master is personal money management. But a student's day-to-day spending is typically as ad lib and unbuttoned as a fraternity beer blast. That doesn't mean you can't keep your undergraduate from overspending.

During a school year, the average college student will lay out $1,455 for books, other supplies, transportation and personal expenses. There's plenty of room for economizing, and the first place to look is at food and phones. Two recent surveys illustrate the point. At Penn State, boarding students forked out an extra $415 a year for all those 2 a.m. pizzas and their accompaniments. And at the University of Connecticut, students spent more than $50 a month each on long-distance phone calls.

While many students seem to think that it costs less to live off campus than in a dorm, they may be wrong. In college towns with a lot of demand for off-campus housing, accommodations within walking distance of campus tend to be expensive. Of course, off-campus students can save money by sharing housing and doing their own cooking. If landlords demand a one-year lease, students should hold out for subleasing privileges.

Fraternity living is back in style on many campuses, and it is costly. Dues range from roughly $60 to $150 a month, and there's a certain social pressure to do things with friends that usually involve spending money.

Most parents have to send money at one time or other. But doling out funds regularly by the week or month may tend to foster an unhealthy dependence. Instead, try giving your undergraduate a lump sum each semester and make it clear that the money will have to last. If you give your children spending money, be certain to sit down and discuss your mutual expectations. To avoid unnecessary strife, you need to know the student's assumptions about spending. And the student, in turn, should know when a check is coming, for what amount and any rules about its use.

Whether students rely on parental subsidy, use their own money, or both, most have their own savings and checking accounts. Unhappily, few seem to know or care enough about how they work.

Many undergraduates keep their checking accounts in their home towns. But long-distance management of financial affairs is hard. For instance, it's tough to verify your balance quickly if you use an out-of-state bank. So it's a good idea to have an account on campus.

Some people strike a compromise by maintaining a checking account at school and a savings account at home. That can encourage self-discipline by making it difficult to dip into savings. Keeping a savings account far away is especially helpful for students who are tempted by automatic teller machines that make cash available at any hour, day or night.

Although some parents feel that a credit card might wrongly cushion a student who manages his or her affairs badly, others find that the piece of plastic can provide a good back-up for college kids. It helps with car rentals, plane fare and railroad tickets. Trying to get money to college-age students in various locations can be frustrating. And it's often impossible for people of any age to cash personal checks away from home. Most parents who give their college-age children credit cards do so strictly for use in emergencies and they expect repayment.

Undergraduates who want to establish their own credit identity can do so in a couple of ways. One is to open a charge account at a local store. Another is to apply for a student credit card such as the Blue Key Card, which is available at about 30 colleges, most of them east of the Mississippi.

Ideally, college students should take full charge of a semester's spending. If the first semester seems too soon, put it off until the next term. But it won't get any easier until the student runs his or her own finances.

Pets

HOW TO BUY — OR ADOPT — A PET

Pᴇᴛs outnumber people in the U.S., and Americans spend more money on them than they do on their babies. The purchase, feeding and maintaining of household animals is a $6 billion-a-year industry.

What are we spending that $6 billion on? In a nation of working wives and tight housing, the trend in pet ownership is toward smaller, quieter animals that require little care. Pet shops across the land are reporting brisk sales of birds, especially parakeets, and finny creatures like angelfish, guppies and swordtails. The amount spent on fish alone is close to $1 billion a year.

The dog is still top dog in the pet world. Poodles are the most popular breed, probably because they are intelligent and adapt well to apartment living. Defying the trend to small, easy-care animals is the second most popular breed, the Doberman pinscher. A large, ferocious-looking animal, it is much in demand as a guard dog for nervous city-dwellers.

Companionship is the most common reason why people own pets. And it is no accident that the Siamese is the most popular breed of cat. Once it gets to know you, this chummy feline will "talk" to you, trail you around, play games with you and even jump into your lap uninvited. Animals encourage conversation, which is why they are sometimes used in therapy for the mentally ill. And, as any woman who is trying to meet men knows, the first rule is get a dog and walk it. If you need any further rationalization for owning a pet, you can claim it is good for your health. University of Pennsylvania researchers have discovered that when people quietly watch fish swishing around in a tank, tension eases and blood pressure goes down. Heart-attack victims with pets actually live longer than those without them.

Because animals can improve the quality of their owners' lives, pets' lives are now worth more, too. Settlements are rising in malpractice suits brought against veterinarians when animals die under their care. The vet used to be liable only for the replacement price of the animal; now owners sue and collect for mental anguish as well. Court awards to grieving owners have run as high as $13,000.

If you are thinking of buying a pet for yourself, or giving one to a friend or relative, be prepared to spend some money. The days of the $1.98 canary are long gone; today's price is $20 and up. That purebred doggie in the window will set you back $200 or more, and you could buy a new car for the price of a palm cockatoo — generally $12,000 and up.

The purchase price is often the cheapest thing about owning a pet. Care and feeding can run into hundreds of dollars a year. So it's important to select the right kind of animal. If you suffer from allergies, forget about long-haired cats and dogs. If exercise is anathema to you, don't buy a leggy Irish setter. As a rule, the longer the leg, the more exercise the dog will need. Never buy a pet you don't like or are afraid of just because it is popular. Boa constrictors are enjoying something of a vogue, but Miss Piggy said it best: "Never pet anything that can be made into a handbag or shoes."

If you don't want to spend a lot, you can adopt a cat or a dog from an animal shelter for a fee of from $5 to $40. Look for an animal that is alert and curious. The coat should be glossy, the eyes clear and the tail wagging. For a purebred cat or dog, go to a breeder; he will sell you so-called pet quality animals for $200 to $400 on average, but breeding or show animals will be more.

If you're interested in birds, fish or rodents, visit a good pet shop, but be selective. An active bird with glossy, brightly colored features and no discharge from the ears or nostrils is usually healthy. Be sure to get a written guarantee giving you a few days to return it if any serious defect or ailment should show up.

Plumbers

HOW TO FIND ONE

Finding a reliable, affordable plumber can be one of life's little trials. But don't wait for the pipes to burst before you begin looking. Every householder needs a list of good servicemen, including a plumber or two, and the best way to avoid panic is to have them lined up before you need them.

When checking a plumber's reputation, you should ask how quickly he responds to emergencies, if he can be reached at night and on weekends and, of course, how much he charges. But how do you find the name of a plumber to check out? If asking your neighbors doesn't turn up a satisfactory specialist, the first place to try is the local affiliate of the National Association of Plumbing-Heating-Cooling-Contractors. Sometimes it is listed as the Plumbing Contractors Association or the Master Plumbers Association. Most members are licensed and covered by liability insurance and workers' compensation. Their records probably will be fairly clear of complaints. The association often works with city agencies to resolve disputes that arise over a plumber's work or charges.

You pay less if you use an unlicensed, unaffiliated plumber, but if something goes wrong, you're more likely to be stuck.

So-called master plumbers are the most seasoned and best trained and can handle the toughest assignments. They have at least five to 10 years' experience and must pass a state exam. When you have a major job, the master plumber gets the appropriate building department permit. He also hires the apprentices and journeymen who do simpler repairs and installations, and he is responsible if anything goes wrong.

You also may locate reputable plumbers by calling the United Association of Journeymen and Apprentices of the Plumbing and Pipe Fitting Industry of the U.S. and Canada. In plain English, that's the plumbers' union. It will not recommend a specific plumber, but it will give you names of contractors who do use union plumbers.

Another good source is the building or plumbing inspection department at city hall. Inspectors see the work of every plumber in town, so they know good craftsmanship firsthand. If they don't want to recommend a plumber, at least they'll give you an opinion about any whose names you have.

And what can you expect to pay a reliable plumber? You've probably heard the old story of the brain surgeon who calls in a plumber to fix a leaky faucet. The plumber tinkers around for a few minutes and then announces, "That'll be $50."

"Heavens!" exclaims the customer. "I'm a brain surgeon, and I don't get $50 for a few minutes' work."

"Neither did I," says the plumber, "when I was a brain surgeon."

Plumbers have a well-earned reputation for high prices. You can expect to pay them between $25 and $50 an hour — and more than that at night and on weekends. That $25 to $50 charge can be deceptive; often it applies to plumbers' travel time as well as the time they spent on the job. And rather than raise their already steep hourly rates to cover boosts in the cost of insurance and their other expenses, many plumbers chose the artifice of a so-called cartage charge of $2 to $3 tacked on to the bill for each visit. Not surprisingly, the prices are highest on the East and West coasts and lowest in the South and Midwest, notably in rural areas.

You will not be able to negotiate the price on an emergency repair job. But if you have work that can be planned in advance, you should get bids from several contractors. Plumbing is highly competitive, and you would be surprised how much the bids differ.

Some people try to save money by buying parts for their plumber. That makes no sense. You will have to buy at retail, and plumbers buy at wholesale. You will not save any money, but you will run the risk of buying the wrong parts.

Don't assume all plumbing repairs require a plumber. There are many jobs you can tackle yourself. Anyone mechanically inclined can patch small leaks, warm frozen pipes, unclog drains, repair faucet drips and replace ceramic tiles.

But beware of getting in over your head. A workman who did was cleaning the filters in a Cincinnati winery one December when he accidentally knocked open a water valve connected with the vats of wine. The rising pressure of fermenting wine caused a backflow into the municipal water system. The resulting Christmas present for the people of Cincinnati: sparkling Burgundy on tap, somewhat diluted.

Psychotherapists

HOW TO FIND ONE

Thousands of Americans make a major and very important investment in psychotherapy. But picking a therapist can itself be a source of anxiety: Psychotherapy is expensive and practitioners range from geniuses to charlatans.

About 90,000 therapists practice in the U.S. today, offering more than 250 types of treatments. Anyone can hang out a shingle as a psychotherapist, and, with a little knowledge and a lot of brass, can succeed. Consequently, credentials are critical. Accredited mental-health professionals fall into five classes: psychiatrists, psychoanalysts, clinical psychologists, psychiatric social workers and psychiatric nurses.

Psychiatrists and most psychoanalysts have M.D.'s, which means they can prescribe drugs and hospitalization; they are needed to treat severe illness. Clinical psychologists have Ph.D.'s in psychology; clinical social workers must have at least a master's degree, and psychiatric nurses are registered nurses who have at least a master's degree in mental-health nursing.

The best way to find a therapist is to ask your family doctor for a referral. You also can consult state offices of professional societies, which give out the names of members by phone. Other good sources for specialists are mental-health associations, hospital clinics or self-help groups such as Alcoholics Anonymous or Parents Anonymous or THEOS, which is a group for widowed people.

To check a therapist's credentials, contact the state chapter of the appropriate organization — for example, the American Psychiatric Association or the American Nurses Association. A few professionals might not belong, but it's safer to stick with those who do.

When you first meet a therapist, remember — you are a customer as well as a patient. Ask about credentials and fees. Some therapists will reduce charges if you are unable to pay the full rate. Feel free to get a second consultation or to change therapists.

Fees depend largely on the type of therapist the patient chooses. Psychiatrists charge the highest. In private practice, their sessions of 45 to 50 minutes cost $40 to $100. Psychologists charge an average $60 for a session, while social workers bill $15 to $40.

Since therapists often practice in clinics as well as privately, you can visit someone at a clinic and save 50% compared with a visit to the same practitioner's private office.

[259]

Another way to save is group therapy. Many therapists and clinics run group sessions, in which several patients talk with a professional for about 90 minutes. The cost may run $15 to $50 a session, and group therapy is often used in conjunction with private sessions.

Medical insurance coverage for psychotherapy can vary greatly, so before beginning treatment, it is smart to check with your insurer about what is reimbursed.

Real Estate

THE TAX BENEFITS

Y OUR search for tax shelters should begin at home. If you are in a fairly high tax bracket and do not own a house or a condominium, it probably makes sense to buy one. Then you can deduct your mortgage interest and property taxes.

You also can claim those immediate tax advantages *plus* deductions for depreciation if you also buy real estate for *investment*. Being a landlord isn't for everyone, of course. Many busy people simply do not have the time or temperament to cope with tenant complaints and broken boilers. Instead, these people can buy into blocks of commercial property — for example, stores, offices, warehouses or apartment houses that are assembled and managed by real estate specialists.

The benefits of investing in real estate were substantially enriched by the tax law of 1981, primarily because it introduced the so-called accelerated cost-recovery system. This means that you can depreciate all investment property over 15 years instead of 20 to 40 years, as under the old law.

You choose between one of two ways to depreciate your investment:

First, you can use what is known as straight-line depreciation. With that, you divide the cost of the property by 15 to get your annual depreciation allowance.

Second, you can use rapid write-offs and deduct much more at the beginning of the investment's life than at the end. For example, on a $100,000 building, straight-line depreciation over 15 years gives you deductions of $6,666 each year — twice as much as under the old law. But the accelerated write-offs give you $12,000 in deductions for the first year — and less in succeeding years.

Investors who fix up and sell or rent old commercial buildings will also make out well under the 1981 tax law. If you buy a building that is more than 30 years old, you can take a credit equal to as much as 20% of the cost of the improvements. But to qualify for the credit, the improvements must cost either more than $5,000, or more than the price you paid for the building.

If you rehabilitate an old inner-city apartment house and then live in one of the apartments, you also can take a credit for fixing up the income-producing section. But here again, the fix-up expenses must exceed the cost of the building. (See also "Urban Homesteading: Bargains in Inner-City Houses.")

Real Estate

BUYING PROPERTY FOR YOUR COLLEGE-BOUND CHILD

Have you heard about my son — and daughter — the landlords? Some parents are managing to make money on their children's college education by buying houses for them to live in.

When Bill Nelson was a sophomore at the University of California at Santa Barbara, he and three of his classmates couldn't find a house to rent. So his mother bought one. The boys got a good deal. For a four-bedroom house, they paid $450 a month — exactly what they had paid for a cramped three-bedroom apartment the year before. The $450 almost exactly covered Mrs. Nelson's monthly mortgage payments, and the boys also promised to handle the repairs.

After Bill Nelson graduated, he rented the house out for $775 a month. The house cost Mrs. Nelson $85,000; five years later it was worth $250,000.

Buying a house in a college town can be an excellent investment, but it does present risks. Not all students are really cut out to be landlords. Some are too immature, or may see their parents' real estate venture as an opportunity to shelter friends. These youngsters may be reluctant to collect rent from their pals. Besides, owning a house requires constant attention. Sometimes the student landlord has to make a tough choice between mopping up a flooded basement or studying for an exam.

If you like the idea of buying a house or condominium for your college-bound youngster, you may be wise to let your child spend his first year getting used to his surroundings before you commit your money. If you then decide to buy, choose a larger, five-bedroom house over a smaller, two-bedroom one; the extra rental income is usually worth the additional expense.

Avoid a rattletrap house that needs a lot of work — unless you're prepared to spend a lot of money to fix it.

Pick a property as close to the campus as possible. But if housing demand is really high, don't rule out anything up to five miles away.

Think twice about buying in a small town that doesn't have many year-round residents. After all, you've got to find people who will be temporary tenants during the summer vacation.

Real Estate

INVESTING IN VACATION HOMES

SECOND homes are bought primarily for recreation, relaxation and retirement, but they can be profitable real estate investments, too. If you buy in the right place at the right time, the value of your vacation retreat can go through the roof. You stand the best chance for gain if your second home has two characteristics.

First, it has to be fairly easy to get to. The choicest turf is no more than a gas tank away from a big population area.

Second, the land surrounding the property should have limited potential for development. That automatically limits the supply of houses. Environmental laws that put a lid on construction have made waterfront properties especially good, though costly investments. In 1977, the state of New Jersey stopped a developer from filling in and building on some wetlands. In the three years after that ruling, prices of second-home plots in the area surged 300%.

Buying into a managed resort community can give you accessibility, planned development and a wise investment. One recent summer, for instance, a young couple paid $39,000 for a house in one of these communities north of Atlanta. The following April, they sold the house for $56,000 and bought a larger, $68,000 house in the same development.

Timing is critical in both the purchase and sale of vacation real estate. Because it is a discretionary purchase, prices fluctuate more widely in economic booms and busts than the prices of other houses do. Lately, buyers with cash in hand have been finding quite a few bargains. Though conventional financing can be expensive and tough to get, many sellers will take back the mortgages themselves. This means they, in effect, agree to receive payment for the house over a period of 10 years or so.

One way to beat the cost of second houses is to divvy up the ownership — and expenses — with several families. For example, four couples share a $100,000 ski condominium in Keystone, Colorado. Each couple arranged their own financing and borrowed from private sources, since banks do not give mortgages on a quarter of a house. Under a legal agreement, if one couple wants out, the others get first crack at buying their share.

To help pay for the mortgage, taxes and upkeep, more and more owners are renting out their second homes. Local real estate agents find tenants, and keep an eye on the property once it is rented. The agents' fees range from 10% to 20% of the rent. For higher fees, managers of some resort communities not only find tenants but also collect the rent and take care of repairs.

Like owners of any house, people with vacation real estate get tax deductions for mortgage interest and property taxes. An owner who rents out his property may qualify for additional deductions as long as he also uses the house himself some times. Those who rent for part of the year can deduct from their rental income a fraction of the expenses of ownership, according to a complicated IRS formula.

Repairs

SERVICE CONTRACTS

RIGHT after you agree to buy a car, refrigerator, TV set or other major appliance, the salesperson may startle you by warning that it could break down. Ah, but he'll add, you can insure against any repair cost by buying a service contract. Watch out: it may not be worth the money.

You generally can expect to pay far more for a service contract than for any repair bills it might cover. A study by the National Science Foundation showed that the cost of service contracts for color TV sets ran almost 10 times the probable cost of repairs for the average user. For refrigerators, service contracts cost 16 times as much as probable repairs.

If you feel that you must buy a service contract, the best time is a year or two *after* your purchase — once the warranty has run out and you have some idea of potential repair problems. Check newspaper ads for discounts that manufacturers sometimes offer. Be wary of contracts that are not sold by manufacturers. As one executive in the service contract trade warns, it's a fly-by-night business.

One way to avoid throwing away money is to compare the service contract with the manufacturer's warranty that comes with the product. Check the two for overlap, and satisfy yourself that you have complete protection.

A contract that covers only the power train of a car, for example, overlooks too many possible trouble spots. A useful service contract for autos does not exclude the electrical system and brakes. Also, it should allow you to get service at an independent repair shop in an emergency and reimburse you for towing costs. Many contracts sold by independent firms don't cover towing at all.

For TV sets, you will find that there is little advantage to buying a contract that starts before the year-long warranty expires. Read the fine print on TV contracts in any case — they may well require you to pay the first $75 for every repair job.

Service contracts are just not economical. They are a bargain only if you bought a lemon. When you buy a service contract, whatever its terms, you can be reasonably sure it's you who will be taking the financial risk.

Restaurants

EAT WITH THE ELITE — CHEAP

Rising costs are threatening to cook the goose of many a restaurant owner. But some enterprising dining spots have responded by luring more customers with off-hour prices. So one way for you to beat the steep costs of restaurants is to dine earlier. It is equally elegant — and often half as expensive.

If you want to go where the elite meet to eat cheap, then look for restaurants that offer early-bird specials. They are known variously as pre-theater, table d'hôte or sunset dinners. These discount dinners usually are served from about 5 p.m. to 7 p.m., and in some places also between 10 p.m. and 1 a.m. Prices during these off hours are 25% to 50% lower than usual.

There is often a special menu, with fewer choices than during peak times. But the fare can be first-class. A few restaurants even toss in extras such as a free aperitif or a ride to the theater. Some neglect to mention the discount unless you make it a point to ask. Still other discounts are short-lived promotions. Discounts are usually available every night of the week, but not always, so it is wise to call ahead to be sure the offer is still available, as well as to reserve a table.

You can find off-peak dining in almost all large cities, sometimes in the best restaurants. And for some reason, it is particularly common in rooftop restaurants atop famous skyscrapers.

Retirement

SAVING FOR YOUR RETIREMENT

IF you are under 45, you can look forward to an even longer average life span and better health than today's retirees. What you probably will not be able to do is retire as early as your parents could, or quit working completely when you do retire, or count on the government for most of your support in great age, or rely as heavily on your pension for the rest. Because you will have to do more to take care of yourself when you are old, you will have to start saving and investing while you are reasonably young.

Inflation and population trends are already straining the Social Security System and private pensions. By the year 2010, half of all Americans will be 40 or older, whereas today the median age is 30. A major reason for the aging of America is the lengthening of life spans. If a man makes it to the age of 65 in the year 2010, he will have a 50–50 chance of living several years into his 80s; women will live even longer — into their 90s.

With fewer young people and many more elderly, the few will have to support the many through Social Security taxes. The United States probably will have to scale back government-paid retirement benefits. They will be lower in real dollars, and they will start later in life. Corporate pensions may not be any more generous than they are now, and the age of eligibility will rise.

Today the combination of your pension and your Social Security benefits typically add up to 60% to 75% of your last few years' average salary. But pensions differ sharply from one industry to another. The best private pensions are provided by banking, chemical, insurance, petroleum and utility companies. But retailing, food processing and garment manufacturing firms tend to have the worst.

The very finest pensions go to government employees — military personnel and federal civil servants. A cost of living escalator makes many of their retirement plans especially generous. One study found that a federal civil servant who retired in 1969 at age 65 with a final salary of $25,000 had a pension that climbed to $35,000 in 10 years. Under similar circumstances, a person retired from a corporation would be collecting about $19,000, including Social Security. Almost no private plans are indexed to inflation, though some companies have given raises to their pensioners.

Happily, great new opportunities to save and invest for retirement are opening up. The number of tax-deferred corporate pension and savings plans has more than tripled since 1967, and new variations of those plans are appearing every day. Tax-saving Individual Retirement Accounts are now available to everyone who works for money. Meanwhile, the limit on tax-deductible contributions to Keogh plans for the self-employed has been raised dramatically. Add in the proliferation of new investments, from small-saver bank certificates of deposit to zero-coupon bonds, and you have a wide assortment of investment opportunities that can provide for your later years.

Qualifying for a pension should be easier in coming years. Today, you usually have to work at the same company for 10 years to become vested, which means that you are guaranteed benefits when you retire. But before the 1980s are over, Congress probably will require only five-year vesting for all employees who have pension plans.

To be financially secure later on, you will have to concoct a recipe for retirement income that will provide the same 60% to 75% of last earnings that are now typically provided by pensions and Social Security. The time to start saving and investing, of course, is now.

It's wise to get into the habit of investing in your tax-sheltering Individual Retirement Account beginning at age 30, so that time and compound growth can work on your behalf. Aim to save and invest 5% of your pretax income between the ages of 30 and 40. Then, increase that amount by one percentage point a year between the ages of 40 and 45. After 45, save 10% a year.

If your employer offers you a savings plan where the company kicks in 50 cents or more for every dollar you invest, that's an offer you shouldn't refuse. There are, however, two exceptions. First, if the plan invests exclusively in the company's own stock and you are not confident about the company's future, hang onto your money. Second, don't rush to invest if you don't expect to become vested, which in such plans could take four years or more.

In contrast to the safe and steady company savings plans, company profit-sharing plans can be chancy. The employer's contribution depends on the company's ability to turn a profit. As a result, there is no guarantee the plan will be funded from year to year. Even if you are sure about the profits, you still have to decide whether you could earn a higher return on the money you put in if you invested it on your own than if you left it with your employer's investment managers.

Nearly all companies with profit-sharing or savings plans let their vested employees leave with a lump-sum benefit. What comes next can be a real bonanza. The employee can take the employer's contributions plus any money that he has earned in the plan and defer paying taxes on the total by depositing all of it in an Individual Retirement Account. There the money can be invested, just like a regular IRA, and will compound tax-free until it is withdrawn.

[268]

Retirement

HOW TO CHECK YOUR COMPANY PENSION

IT's too late to start preparing for your retirement on the day you pick up your gold watch. You should be looking into the pension plan that your company provides right now.

Pension plans come in two kinds. First, there is the *defined benefit* plan. It promises you a set benefit upon retirement. Your pension is related to your salary and to the length of your employment, no matter what it costs the company to provide it. This means you can count on at least a certain minimum benefit. But if you change jobs before you're vested, you lose the benefits you have built up.

Second, there is the *defined contribution* plan. It promises you that your employer will invest a certain sum every year on your behalf. You are entitled to this money when you retire. Defined contribution plans are commonly company thrift or profit-sharing programs. Your employer agrees to match and invest a portion of your savings, or to set aside for you a percentage of profits pegged to your salary. If the company invests or performs poorly, the losses eventually come out of your own pocket. So it pays to monitor closely the income of a defined contribution plan.

Your pension is probably safer under a defined benefit plan than under a defined contribution plan. Even if your company runs into grave financial trouble, the Pension Benefit Guaranty Corporation, a government agency, insures these plans against termination. You are at least guaranteed of receiving some pension, up to the maximum insured benefit of $1,381 a month.

Even if your pension plan is well run and adequately funded, you may be in for a shock when you retire. Your monthly payments could be substantially less than your individual benefit statement has led you to expect.

The best way to calculate your pension benefits is to read the summary plan description that your employer is obliged to give you once a year. Turn first to the summary plan's section on Social Security. You may discover that your company reduces your monthly pension benefit by a percentage of the amount you will receive from Social Security. That percentage could be as much as 83%.

If you are married, check out the joint and survivor benefits section of the plan. Your monthly payment could be reduced while you are alive — if you have elected to let your spouse receive your pension after you die.

If you are thinking of taking a leave of absence or quitting and coming back, then you had better examine the provisions for interrupted service. You want to be sure you don't jeopardize your vesting. And if you are considering taking all your benefits in a lump sum, see if the actuarial assumptions are as favorable as if you choose monthly payments for life.

If you want to know more about your pension than what you can see in the summary plan description, ask your company for a copy of its fuller pension-fund tax return. It is called Form 5500. The Department of Labor also will send you that form if you call 202–523–8771. You can speed the shipment by giving your employer's identification number and the plan identification number. You will have to get these from your company.

Once you have a copy of Form 5500, give it a careful reading. The first thing you want to know is has the company told the IRS that it might terminate the plan? If so, the information will appear on line 9.

Line 12 gives the names of the fund's professional advisers. Watch out for lavish duplication of services — for example, four or five different lawyers or actuaries. That costs you money.

Line 13 lists the fund's investments. Notice if considerable sums languish in noninterest-bearing bank accounts. Look for diversification and degree of risk. More than a third of the assets invested in a single kind of real estate, for example, could be a sign of unnecessary risk.

Line 21 will tell you if the company is up to date on its payments to the fund. If it isn't keeping current with its obligations, the next step could be termination of the plan.

Your company's employee benefit managers should be happy to answer any questions you have about Form 5500. Their attitude ought to be completely open and above board. But if you get the feeling they are trying to hide something, take that as a warning about the future of your pension.

Retirement

SHOULD YOU TAKE EARLY RETIREMENT?

COMPANIES are offering some tempting sweeteners these days to encourage employees to take early retirement. Rather than close plants or lay off people, hard-pressed corporations offer financial inducements to employees who leave voluntarily, usually between the ages of 55 and 62. But you would do well to look hard before you leave. Early-retirement sweeteners can carry you only so far. The pension that seems so high today may be gobbled up by inflation tomorrow.

Almost every company pension plan provides for early retirement. About 85% of major plans contain terms that cut early retirees' pension checks by less than the actuarial tables would mandate. Yet the difference in payments can be substantial. In some cases, if you quit at 55 — when your earnings may well be on the rise — you might get only 25% of the monthly pension you would have received had you worked to age 65.

When deciding whether to retire early, you have to figure out what you want to do and whether you can afford to do it. Sit down with a pencil and paper — or personal computer — and analyze expected income and outgo. Your company's personnel department should provide individual or group counseling to help you. But it's wise to beware of the arm-around-the-shoulder manner of some company-paid consultants. They may make retirement seem more flowery than it will be.

Most retirees need at least 60% to 75% of their pre-retirement salary to maintain their standard of living. You can shade toward the lower end of that spectrum if your major outlays such as your housing costs, children's education expenses and medical bills are under control. If not, you will need more. In any case, if the combination of your pension and Social Security falls short of your requirements, you will have to make up the difference through savings and investments or a second career.

Social Security penalizes workers for early retirement. At age 62 — the earliest you can begin drawing benefits — the monthly payment is about 20% less than it would be if it were started at age 65. And the gap is never closed. The maximum annual benefit at 62 is about $6,360 per worker, or $9,336 for a couple with a nonworking spouse also 62. However, if you're retiring early from one job but intend to keep working in another job, you can postpone receiving your Social Security benefits and thereby increase the size of checks when you start accepting them.

About 20% of pension plans permit you to take your pension in a lump, up front, and it's a good option. Quite often you also have the choice of taking any severance pay in installments or in a lump.

The lump-sum method is usually better. You can pay taxes on the money at a favorable rate, and then you can reinvest the rest or use it as seed money for a second career. If you invest this money prudently, its earnings can take the edge off future inflation.

One appealing investment choice is to roll the whole lump-sum pay-out into an Individual Retirement Account. This allows you to defer taxes on the money until you withdraw it later on. Many early retirees find that their biggest nest egg is in their company's tax-deferred thrift or profit-sharing plan. You also can directly transfer the company's contributions and all the earnings from such a plan into an IRA.

But that is not your only tax-saving choice. You can take out all that money right away and reinvest it elsewhere — say, in real estate. Often you can use the special 10-year income-averaging rule dramatically to reduce your taxes on these funds from the company plan.

In any case, if you accept early retirement you most likely will want to reorient your investments toward assured income instead of capital accumulation.

Rugs

INVESTING IN ORIENTALS

AFTER gaining an average of 20% a year in value during the 1970s, many oriental rugs are worth a pasha's ransom. But the prices of all but the rarest rugs dropped about 15% in 1982. Americans have been lured away from oriental rugs to less exotic, more liquid investments. At the same time, once-insatiable European buyers have been priced out of the market by a strong U.S. dollar. People are either going for the best rug or are buying medium-quality nine-by-twelve decorative rugs that sell for $2,000 to $7,500. With prices down, now may be the time to make a deal.

Dealers are convinced that prices have nowhere to go but up. Older handmade carpets are in short supply. As a result of political upheaval in Iran, Afghanistan and other traditional carpet-weaving centers, the supply of newer rugs has decreased, too.

A nine-by-twelve antique rug can easily cost $30,000, but the best buys are the so-called middle-range rugs that include imperfect antiques or somewhat newer used carpets of medium quality. Rug dealers advise the purchase of Kirman, Kashan, Heriz, Sultanabad and Bidjar rugs. You can get a nine-by-twelve Gorevan, which is a floral-patterned Persian rug, for about $3,000 — that's $1,000 less than three years ago. And that's about one-fifth of what you would have to pay for the most coveted new Persian rugs — the Isfahan and the Nain types.

As a rule, the older an oriental rug is, the more valuable it is. But before you buy, carefully check the condition of an older rug. Look for moth-eaten spots and dry rot, which causes a rug to crack when you bend it. Also, look for seams in the back to see if the rug has been cut down or if new sections have been added. Weaving repairs cost from $50 to $500 — and that's for just a two-inch-square spot.

Finding the best rug merchant in your area may be a challenge. It's wise to steer clear of fly-by-nighters. Most commonly, these are auctioneers who work out of motels. Rely instead on department stores, reputable auction houses and established dealers. You can get a free directory of top dealers by writing to the Oriental Rug Retailers of America, P.O. Box 1333, Stamford, Connecticut 06905.

Safe-Deposit Boxes

PRIVATE VAULTS FOR YOUR VALUABLES

Rısıng crime has made more people than ever look for a safe place to put their valuables, whether they are jewelry, collectibles or important papers. For most people, the most economical place to store precious possessions is a bank deposit box. The smallest cost $12 to $25 a year and are large enough for documents, securities and real estate deeds and appraisals. If you have anything else, you probably will want a bigger box. Those larger boxes are in short supply and anyone with a lot of jewelry, a stamp collection or anything bulky may face a long waiting list.

One solution is to find one of the many private safe-deposit companies. They are spreading fast, particularly in the South and West. They have no connection with banks, but they do have security. To get in, you usually need to pass a complicated screening process.

Commercial vaults offer total privacy. Vault operators are not subject to banking regulations, so they are better able than banks are to keep the IRS from sealing boxes or prying into contents in cases of suspected tax evasion. On the other hand, a lack of regulations could mean some risks — a clever operator could start a business, then clean out the vaults and disappear.

The private vaults have the advantage of offering flexible storage space. Lockers can be fitted with special shelves and racks for stamp collections, rare books, wine, even computer tapes and disks. Works of art can be kept in rooms that have temperature and humidity controls and special fire-fighting systems designed not to damage art.

These commercial bulk storage facilities are sensible for two-home families who wish to lock up valuables when they are out of the area. Owners of vacation homes, for example, may want to store special possessions during the off-season.

Private vaults can be more expensive than banks for small spaces, but they're often cheaper for bulky storage. A private five-by-three-by-five-foot locker costs about $1,500 to $2,000 a year.

For more information about private vault companies, write to the National Association of Independent Security Vaults, 2294 Carroll Avenue, Atlanta, Georgia 30341.

Salaries

WHERE THE BIG PAY IS

How can you get the best salary — and where can you get it?

Some companies have a tradition of paying well, notably those exploring the frontiers of science and the new technologies. But within any industry, salaries commonly are 15% higher at the most open-handed firms than at the most tight-fisted ones. The principal factor is size: the higher a company's sales volume, the greater its pay is likely to be.

Many fields offer impressive rewards for accomplishment. Among the standouts are investment banking, stock brokerage, executive recruiting and law. Yet in a number of fields, mostly those that are considered glamorous, starting salaries are small. But they climb sharply in the upper-middle to upper ranks. Television and advertising are examples.

Starting pay at law firms ranges all the way from the teens to the mid-forties. Although a handful of big-city firms offer stratospheric salaries, that remuneration has less to do with an individual's immediate performance than his or her future promise.

Market conditions also influence pay. Partly because rich oil companies bid up the going rate for secretaries in Houston to around $20,000 in the early 1980s, less lucrative businesses there were forced to pay more for secretaries, too. Geography, however, has less influence than it once did. More than three-quarters of all companies adhere to a national schedule, paying the same amount for the same job regardless of location.

Bigger companies tend to pay better than smaller ones. Low-profit companies pay low or give meager raises or both. Old companies or those in established fields such as steel and autos tend to offer a larger share of total pay in the form of fringe benefits than those in new businesses do.

It's unwise to sell your skills short, even in a sluggish economy. In bureaucratic corporations with ossified pay systems, employees who start out cheap may never catch up.

Savings

THE BEST PLACES FOR YOUR CASH

T HIS is no time to be taking needless chances with your money. But it is possible to put your money into sound investments which offer returns that are safe, big and guaranteed.

Where is the best place to put your savings now?

Among the many safe and rewarding places to put your money are money-market funds, government securities and bank certificates of deposit. While bonds are somewhat riskier, they, too, hold out tempting yields.

The interest rates that all these savings devices and investments pay you are finally adding more to your earnings than inflation is taking away. At the same time, the income tax cuts of recent years let you keep more of what your money earns. So, after figuring in inflation and taxes, your "real" return on the savings is close to a postwar peak. This is the savings decade. Unlike the high-inflation 1970s, in the high-interest 1980s, you will do much better by saving than by borrowing.

No investment is absolutely riskless. So, when determining where to put your savings now, you have to weigh and balance off the three traditional concerns of yield, liquidity and safety. You also have to judge the extent of credit risk — which is the possibility that the borrower may default on your principal or interest. And you have to think about market risk — the chance that your investment may have declined in price when you want to cash it in and collect.

Savings

GOVERNMENT SECURITIES

IF you are looking for the safest place in the world to invest your money, then look to the federal government. Uncle Sam borrows more than $200 billion a year, and if he can't pay his debts, he can always print more money.

The government securities with the most appeal for individual investors are Treasury bills, notes and bonds.

Bills are sold in minimum denominations of $10,000, and they come in three-, six- and 12-month maturities.

Notes are usually sold in minimum denominations of $5,000 when they have maturities of less than four years — and in minimums of $1,000 when they have maturities of four years or more. You can get them in maturities ranging from one year to ten years.

Bonds also sell in minimums of $1,000 but have maturities of more than 10 years. If you were grading these bonds on a report card, their yields of 10.9% in mid-1983 would earn them marks of A-minus. They pay a percentage point or two less than similar debt issues of top-rated corporations. But all government securities rate an A-plus for safety.

You can buy Treasury issues through any of the 12 Federal Reserve banks or 25 branch offices. Or, you can order them by mail, using forms that you get from your local Fed Bank.

The securities come to market at various intervals. For example, three- and six-month bills generally are auctioned off every Monday; 12-month bills are sold every four weeks on Thursday; two-year notes are sold at the end of each month; four-year notes are auctioned off in March, June, September and December; five-year notes and 15-year bonds are sold in January, July and October.

You also can buy Treasuries from a commercial bank or your broker. This eliminates much of the hassle, but costs $25 to $50 and can wipe out a big part of your return.

Another problem is that you will pay a rather stiff penalty if you ever want to sell your government securities before they mature. Just as brokers will charge a small investor substantially more than the market price if he is buying, so they will pay him substantially less if he is selling. Thus, you are best off sticking to new government issues and holding them until they mature.

One big benefit: The interest earned on Treasury securities is exempt from state and local taxes.

[277]

And when you buy a Treasury bill, you get another nice extra. Let's take one example with round numbers for easy calculation: If you bought, say, a $10,000 10% one-year bill, it cost you only $9,000 — that is, $10,000 minus 10%. A year later you will get paid the full $10,000. The real interest that you will collect is your $1,000 profit divided by your $9,000 investment. In fact, that's not 10%, but a fat 11.1%.

Savings

MONEY FUNDS

MONEY-MARKET funds are like checking accounts that also pay you high interest. But how do money funds really rate as investments, in terms of the yields they pay and the safety they offer?

If you were filling out a report card on money-market funds, you would give them a B-plus for yields compared with other places to put your spare cash and your savings. They certainly pay you more than the 5¼% available on NOW checking accounts. Unlike your checking account, however, your money-fund shares are not insured. This should not worry you excessively. In the last 10 years, very few funds have ever run into difficulty. So you'd have to give money funds an A for safety.

The chief measure of safety is the quality of the investments that a fund makes with your money. In effect, the funds make short-term loans to federal, state and local governments as well as to corporations and banks. Generally, the higher the risk that a fund takes, the higher the yields that it pays.

Another gauge of safety is the so-called average maturity of the investments in a fund's portfolio — that is, the length of time a fund has to hold onto an investment before cashing it in. Most funds have an average maturity of 20 to 45 days. As a rule, the shorter the average maturity, the safer the fund.

If you are a cautious type who wears both a belt and suspenders, look into government-only money funds. They invest in nothing but federal securities. But you'll get a point or so less in interest payments for this rock-solid safety.

And if you are in the upper tax brackets, you are usually better off to put your cash in tax-exempt money funds. They lend short-term money to states and municipalities. If tax-exempt funds pay, say, 5%, that is the equivalent of 10% for someone in the 50% bracket and 7.35% for a person in the 32% bracket.

If you are shopping for a money-market fund, don't just dive into the one that currently pays the steepest interest. Look for a fund with yields that have been consistently above average for at least several years. (See also "Money-Market Funds.")

Savings

BANK MONEY-MARKET ACCOUNTS

Banks and savings and loan associations have been heavily advertising their new high-interest money-market deposit accounts and their so-called SuperNOW checking accounts ever since they came out late in 1982 and early in 1983. To tempt you to deposit money in their new accounts, some banks and S&Ls at first were offering to pay palm-moistening interest rates of as much as 25%. Of course, that was only a temporary come-on. Soon rates dropped down to the 8% to 10% range. But that was more than the 7% to 8% that the ordinary money-market funds were paying at the time.

Over the longer term, bank money-market accounts probably will yield the same or only slightly more than leading ordinary money-market funds. Banks have considerable overhead — all those tellers and big buildings — and that makes it hard for them to undercut the money funds by much.

However, if your savings have been idling in a bank or savings and loan passbook account yielding only 5¼% to 5½%, it makes sense to shift them into an insured, higher-yielding money-market deposit account at the same institution. You also should consider such an account if you want your money federally insured or you like the face-to-face service that banks and S&Ls offer.

Bank money-market accounts offer convenience. Some merchants are readier to accept local bank checks than those drawn on a money-market fund in Moose Jaw. And the money funds tend to restrict you to checks of $250 or more. Most banks will let you write checks for any amount, though some are planning to adopt new check-writing policies similar to those of the money-market funds.

If you are a safety-minded person, then federal deposit insurance on balances of up to $100,000 can make a bank money-market account or Super-NOW checking account look extremely attractive. Unlike them, ordinary money-market funds are not insured. But before you switch, ask yourself how important federal insurance really is to you. Only one money-market fund out of 295 or so has ever failed to pay in full — and that was half a dozen years ago. Its customers got back 93 cents on the dollar.

On the other hand, if you are invested in a so-called government-only money fund — the kind that buys U.S. government-backed issues — it might be worthwhile to switch to an insured bank money-market account. The government money funds earn about 1% less than regular money funds. Over the long term, a bank money-market account should do at least as well as a government-only money fund.

What about the SuperNOW checking accounts? They are likely to pay 1% to 2% less than either the regular money funds or the bank money-market accounts. That's because they are very expensive for the banks to administer. Don't open one unless you routinely maintain $2,500 in your checking account. Otherwise, you are better off in a regular checking account or a plain old NOW account.

Before you open a bank money-market account or a SuperNOW checking account, read all the fine print carefully. Among the possible catches: payment of simple rather than compound interest, frequent changes in interest rates, minimums on the size of the checks you can write and automatic loss of interest premiums for early withdrawal.

Sexes

PRENUPTIAL CONTRACTS

IF love is lovelier the second time around, marriage is messier. So more and more middle-aged and elderly people who are marrying for a second or third time are scurrying to lawyers for prenuptial contracts before taking wedding vows.

Typically, both the husband and wife bring property to the marriage that they wish to preserve for their own heirs. And the children naturally feel it's their right to share in their parent's estate. Some attorneys find that about a fourth of their older clients who sign agreements do so at the urging of their children.

Older people's burgeoning interest in prenuptial contracts also is due to leaping divorce rates. As a result, many couples sign agreements to keep their own assets from being divided if they divorce. A doctor, for example, may stipulate that his wife accept a lump-sum settlement instead of a share of his practice. In any case, it's a good idea for older marriage partners to have a prenuptial contract.

Shopping

CONTACT LENSES

W HEN shopping for contact lenses, your optical options are greater than ever. But so is the price you can pay.

Whether you pay a lot or a little depends largely on where you buy your contact lenses. They come in four distinct types. You can expect to pay $100 to $300 for your first pair of hard lenses, $125 to $350 for gas permeable lenses, $150 to $400 for regular soft lenses and $250 to $550 for the new extended-wear lenses.

Generally, optometrists' fees are lower than those of ophthalmologists, who are M.D.'s specializing in the eye. The Federal Trade Commission has found that optometrists working for high-volume retailers charge $30 to $50 less for an exam, fitting and follow-up than do optometrists in private practice, and $60 to $100 less than ophthalmologists in private practice.

Discounters working on high volume pose risks. They may be tempted to sell you the soft lenses that are easiest to wear so you don't come back complaining. But easy-wear lenses may not give you the best vision possible and they usually cost the most. Also, cleaning and otherwise maintaining your soft lenses costs about $120 a year, but those charges are only some $65 a year for hard lenses.

One way to gauge a practitioner is to ask how many kinds of lenses he offers. Having a complete selection shows he wants the lenses to suit you, not vice versa. Also find out whether the person who prepares your lens prescription will give you a copy of it. He has no legal obligation to do so. But once you are satisfied that your lenses fit comfortably and correct your vision properly, you may want to shop around for replacement lenses. Sometimes you can find them for as little as $35 at retail chains.

Shopping

EXERCISE EQUIPMENT

THE fitness phenomenon is moving Americans to spend weighty sums on home exercise equipment. And just as with any other important investment, there are some guidelines for sensible buying. Before you lay out anywhere from a few hundred to a few thousand dollars, you should decide what physical fitness benefits you want, so you can pick the right machine.

If you want aerobic exercise to increase the efficiency of your heart and lungs, then you will need a stationary rowing machine or bicycle. But if you are concerned primarily with body building and muscle toning, then you will want to work out with weight-training equipment in a so-called home gym.

It's wise to try out any apparatus several times before buying. You can rent bikes and rowing machines for a small fee at many sporting goods stores and surgical supply centers. You can try out weight-training equipment at your local YMCA or health club.

A top-quality rowing machine such as the Amerec 610 or the Finnish-made Tunturi will cost about $350. Whatever you buy, look for a machine that has a lightweight stainless-steel or aluminum frame, a cushioned seat that glides smoothly in its metal track as you row and smooth oar movements.

To get a well-constructed stationary bicycle, expect to spend at least $200. A top-of-the-line model, such as the Swedish-made Monark Trainer Ergometer or the Tunturi Ergometer, will cost $350 or $375. Make sure that the one you buy is welded, not bolted, together, that its wheel is solid steel or aluminum and steel and that its wheel tension is adjustable.

Finally, when you buy a so-called home gym for weight training, you will have to spend at least $1,500. But some of the machines exercise only one muscle group, say, your chest or shoulders or legs. So make sure that any you buy can work out and build up all the muscle groups you want.

Shopping

FUR COATS

W HEN the temperature soars and the humidity rises, that's the time to hunt for a bargain in fur coats. Late spring and summer are traditionally the seasons for sales on furs.

During those seasons, many fur retailers advertise savings of 20% to 30% off their regular prices. Wholesalers, who commonly sell to the public at discounts, offer additional spring and summer markdowns. For example, a fine-quality, full-length mink coat, which typically costs $8,000 or more, goes for about $6,400 at retail furriers and $4,500 at wholesalers. Mink accounts for about 60% of all fur sales, but most other furs cost less, of course.

Getting the best deal on a fur coat involves more than ferreting out the lowest prices. The density and silkiness of the fur, the suppleness of the underlying leather, the fit and style of the coat — all spell the difference between real and specious bargains.

The shopper's first challenge is making sure that the coat is well made with quality pelts. The best way for a woman to school herself is to try on lots of furs. Good pelts are silky; inferior ones are coarse, even whiskery. Sheared furs should be plush and even-textured; natural ones should have thick underfur and sleek, satiny outer hairs.

Dyeing fur weakens the skin and shortens the life of the garment; any new fur that is dyed is supposed to be labeled as such, but not all furriers are scrupulous about doing that. To be sure a fur has not been dyed, look for many gradations of color on the outer hairs and a paler underfur.

Shoddy workmanship also shows up inside the coat if the fur pokes through the seams. If you stretch the fur gently over your hand, and there are gaps at the seams, the coat is carelessly made.

Once you have gained some knowledge about furs, you're ready to tackle wholesale furriers. Well over half of them do an unofficial retail business on the side. They exist in many large cities, including Minneapolis, Chicago and Los Angeles; but the largest concentration of wholesalers is in New York. Some of them prefer shoppers to come recommended by former customers and to make an appointment. But if a customer looks right, most wholesalers will take a chance that she is serious and has money.

Shopping

SUN POTIONS

MILLIONS of people yearn to get a glowing suntan, but under an unpitying sun, the skin ages faster and can even grow cancerous. If you want protection, you are faced with a blinding array of sunscreens, quick-tanning preparations, moisturizing lotions and sunburn medications. Beware! Their cost is no gauge of their effectiveness. Some of these products are salubrious, some senseless and some potentially dangerous.

Their common enemy is ultraviolet radiation. Even mild doses of it can hurt skin cells. If you want to tan, do so gradually, and use a sunscreen. The crucial ingredient is an ultraviolet-absorbing chemical. Usually it's para-aminobenzoic acid, known as PABA. So be sure to look for PABA among the ingredients.

A four-ounce bottle of a common drugstore sunscreen sells for $4.49, but a cosmetic company's prestige package of only 3.5 ounces will run you $7.50. Both brands give the *same* protection.

Most sunscreens are voluntarily labeled with a sun protection factor, or SPF. The scale begins with minimum protection of SPF 2 and generally rises to SPF 15, though some products have higher ratings. Sunscreens with an SPF of 15 or more allow no tanning. (Sometimes the word "PABA" substitutes for SPF in the label.)

Besides sunscreens, few tanning products are markedly beneficial. Artificial tanning creams are little more than dyes. Tanning pills contain a pigment and food coloring and merely give the same effect as eating a lot of carrots. Expensive after-tan moisturizers may soothe skin dried by sun and wind, but they neither prevent the peeling that follows sunburn nor prolong your tan.

You can spend more than $4 for a small bottle of tanning oil. But such oils or lotions or butters are no more effective in accelerating tanning than perspiration or even plain water, which just make the outer layer of the skin more transparent so the sun can more readily penetrate. Since most of those tanning oils contain no sunscreens, they are for people who tan easily or are already brown.

Small Business

AVOIDING THE PITFALLS OF START-UPS

IT came to you faster than Federal Express, an idea more winning than Atari. You are going to start your own business. It will be the next IBM and you will be rich and famous. Maybe your dream isn't so far-fetched. Entrepreneurs *can* succeed in new enterprises if they plan now for the predictable hazards ahead.

When starting your own business, the first two or three years are the critical period. To survive them, you will need to anticipate the problems that accompany each stage of the business. You can avoid or conquer difficulty with sound planning, ample capital, solid management skills and, of course, a well-conceived idea.

When you get that idea, it may seem so stunning to you, so can't-miss, that your first impulse will be to quit your job, re-mortgage the house and kiss your spouse and kids goodbye while you devote yourself to your brainstorm. But don't do anything of the kind. Instead, you should evaluate your drive, dedication and experience in estimating whether you can turn a pipedream into a money-maker. Experience is the key.

Solid planning is also essential. You will need to draft a business plan itemizing the costs of developing your product or service, and projecting your company's share of market and sales over the next three to five years. This road map should be about 60 to 80 pages long and include weekly or monthly projections for the first two years and quarterly figures after that. Do the figuring yourself to become familiar with production, distribution and marketing. If you need help, invest $15.20 in a workbook called the *Business Planning Guide*, published by Upstart Publishing.

To find out if your plan for a new business is realistic, you will need outside and impartial advice. There are about 100 offices of the Small Business Administration where staff members and retired executives will work with you. The SBA also sponsors Small Business Development Centers at 23 colleges. Don't overlook your local banker or lawyer for a critique of your business plan, but the most qualified source may be the president of a similar business. It's amazing how accessible these chief executives are.

You may be considering starting a new business all by yourself, but it pays to remember that teams have better odds for success than individuals do. The right combination brings more management skills and more money than you alone can.

But where do you find the right people to be your partners? Building an enterprise simply on blood ties, friendship or a shared enthusiasm for golf can be dangerous. True, your relatives and chums may have money to invest. Yet starting a company is strain enough without the added trauma of firing someone dear who doesn't work out. Or, worse yet, having to keep him.

Everyone tends to hire people like himself, but you should seek those with complementary talents. An engineer who pairs up with a manufacturing or marketing person is better situated for success than a trio of engineers — even if their business is the next generation of computers. To ward off future difficulties, all partners should invest some capital in the business or at least forsake salary during the start-up phase. And you are much better off if you have worked with your new partners before.

Of course, money is supremely important when you start your business. Undercapitalization pits you against the clock in a losing race. To figure out how much capital you are going to need, hire an accountant — preferably one with experience in your industry. He can help show you how much money you would need either if heaven and Congress were on your side, or if Murphy's Law were in effect.

Even if you have the perfect partners and more than enough cash in the till, your new business still can be done in by poor record-keeping. Well before the day you first open, you will need to have sound financial information keeping you up to date on operating expenses, inventory costs, accounts receivable, debt obligations and income. Accurate financial records are an indispensable early warning system.

With all that, if your small business then can survive two or three years of growing pains, the odds for continuing success will be on your side.

Small Business

HOW TO RAISE MONEY TO START ONE

Next to a money-making idea, what you need most to get a new business off the ground is a talent for raising capital.

Even if your idea is brilliant, no backer will give you a dime until you have sunk in most of your own savings. So, the smart entrepreneur starts with as much of his own capital as possible, using all his or her sources of credit. If necessary, he will even remortgage his house. By maximizing his own stake in the business, he will impress other potential investors with his commitment. He also will retain tighter control of his enterprise.

When entrepreneurs need outside money, they begin by soliciting friends and relatives — and then go on to friends of friends and relatives. The advantage of family money is that it's patient. Close relatives usually are more willing than distant investors to wait for the profits to start rolling in.

Try to get this money as a loan rather than as an investment in return for a piece of your company. That way, you won't have to put up with Uncle Bill telling you how to run *his* business.

After you have approached friends and family, the best way to get names of potential investors you don't know is to ask accountants, bankers, lawyers, brokers and other business owners. They often know who has money to invest or lend. Local business groups like the Chamber of Commerce can provide more leads.

Once you have exhausted your individual financing sources, it's time to approach the institutions. If you need less than $100,000, the best sources are banks, savings and loans, commercial finance companies, the Small Business Administration and business development companies. When you have to go to those outside capitalists and bankers for money, you may be rather pleasantly surprised. Though real interest rates are high, money to finance promising new businesses is fairly plentiful. Banks are making loans to small businesses again. Professional venture capitalists are loaded with cash, and they even complain they can't find enough worthy enterprises to assist.

Venture firms like to invest close to home, and in amounts between $100,000 and $600,000. Sometimes they will lend the money. But more often than not, they want a piece of the business. No longer do venture capitalists concentrate their dollars on companies that have already proved that they will make it. Because of the unusual success of some recent new businesses, particularly in the realm of high technology and services, financiers are willing to take greater risks than just a few years ago — if they figure that they may also reap greater rewards.

For entrepreneurs in search of capital, a long, unblemished credit history is helpful. So is locating your business in California, Massachusetts, New York or Texas — because that's where 62% of venture-capital money goes.

Beyond friends, family members, banks, venture capitalists and the federal Small Business Administration, there are many other places to raise money for your new venture.

Among them, small-business investment companies, or SBICs, are private venture firms that borrow most of their funds from the Small Business Administration. Also, there are 130 minority enterprise SBICs that invest exclusively in concerns at least 51% owned by socially or economically disadvantaged people. That definition is broader than you might think. For example, Vietnam veterans are considered disadvantaged.

In about half the states, quasi-public business development corporations make loans to small businesses to create local jobs. You can get the details by asking your state's economic development agency where you can find a business development corporation, or BDC.

You also can turn to the little-known local development corporations, composed of local government officials and private citizens who borrow funds from the SBA and banks and then relend them to entrepreneurs in need of long-term financing.

Entrepreneurs searching for big bucks — say $500,000 or more for research and product development — should look into setting up limited partnerships. The people to speak with are local tax attorneys, accountants and brokers who have experience getting a group of high-bracket investors to invest money in a business in return for substantial tax write-offs.

You may even have to make a private offering of stock. The disadvantage is that it will reduce your stake in your own company. You could lose majority interest. The less you have to surrender, the more you can offer later to attract skilled managers and additional capital to your company.

In searching for financial help, be wary of firms that advertise that they are professional finders of money. Many of them charge high fees simply for sending out mass mailings to investors. But one reliable source of names of potential angels is the National Venture Capital Association. It will send you free copies of its membership directory if you write to the National Venture Capital Association, 1730 North Lynn Street, Suite 400, Arlington, Virginia 22209.

Plan to spend at least three months acquainting yourself with the sources of financing before you try to raise any substantial amount. Several books are especially useful, among them: *The Insider's Guide to Small Business Resources* by David Gumpert and Jeffry Timmons, published by Doubleday at $24.95. The bible for anyone planning to shop the venture-capital firms is the *Guide to Venture Capital Sources*, published by Capital Publishing,

P.O. Box 348, Wellesley Hills, Massachusetts 02181. Look for it in a good public library and save yourself the cover price of $90.

If you need help putting together your plan to start a small business, ask an accountant, lawyer or banker to refer you to a reliable professional consultant. Expect to pay your professional adviser at least $1,000. He may be able to show you how to use potential customers and suppliers as sources of financing and how to cut costs by leasing, rather than buying, equipment. So hiring a professional probably will be a sensible investment.

To increase your chances of raising money, start with the right source. If you want a bank loan, for example, call ahead to inquire whether the bank does the kind of lending you need. Then find out what your potential backers want — and deliver it. Ask a banker what it will take for him to lend you money. If you meet his standards, it will be hard for him to say no. Finally, if you are rejected, find out why. That way you can approach your next source with a better pitch.

Stock Market

HOW TO GET STARTED

Instead of splurging on a new stereo, many young people are setting aside part of their paychecks to invest in the stock market. That's partly because they can no longer assume that Social Security and a company pension will ultimately take care of their retirement needs. They also recognize that when you start investing while young, you can still afford to take some risks in search of great profits. But how best to go about it?

If you decide to invest in stocks, your first decision is whether to aim for income — that is, for high dividends — or for growth — that is, for stocks that pay little or no dividends but stand to rise in price. Most investment counselors agree that young people should choose a strategy of capital growth. As a start, you might consider investing in a mutual fund. For $1,000 or sometimes less, you can buy shares in a pool that is invested by the fund's professional managers in a wide range of stocks. That way you get a diversified investment that you probably could not afford on your own. Many funds grow nicely and, on the down side, few lose very much.

There are two basic types of funds: load and no-load. You buy load funds through brokers, and they charge you a sales commission, commonly 8½%. You buy no-load funds by mail or telephone, and you pay no commission for them. Since both kinds of funds perform about the same, it makes sense to save the cost of commission by buying the no-loads. (For more, see "Mutual Funds.")

A second way to lower your risks is to join an investment club. Since members jointly choose stocks to purchase, a club offers a good way to invest and to get experience in researching the market. Learning when to sell and when to hold onto a stock is another valuable lesson that can be learned in an investment club. Most members ultimately gain enough confidence to do their own investing. Studies show that after five years, 85% of members invest on their own as well as through the club. (For more, see "Investment: Investment Clubs.")

Once you strike out on your own, you probably can benefit from buying some sophisticated stock market information guides. A popular one is the Standard & Poor's *Stock Guide*, which gives the vital statistics on 4,200 companies and costs $68 a year. You can get still more in-depth information from *The Value Line Investment Survey* for $365 a year. To save money as well as earn it, just remember that these advisory service guides are often available at your public library. (See "Investment: Investment Advisory Services.")

But the most important advice is to start learning young about how to invest intelligently. In a time of rapid economic change, having no investment strategy is the worst strategy of all. Nobody knows, of course, which investments will surge, and which will slump, but you can develop a sensible investment strategy by following some basic guidelines:

— Keep a sharp watch on the world around you. International politics and economic policies will influence the prices of stocks and other investments more than ever before. Remember how much the markets fell in the 1970s on news of the foreign oil price increases and the rise in U.S. interest rates.

— Diversify your investments. Don't put all your money into just one investment, or you will stand to lose a bundle if it goes down. Eventually, you should aim to own a variety of securities and perhaps also some metals and a bit of real estate. But, as discussed, you might be wise to begin with a mutual fund that offers diversified investments. A list of both the best performing and the biggest mutual funds is published every month in *Money* magazine.

— Re-examine all your savings, and seek expert advice. Check again with your banker about just what interest rate you are collecting now, and investigate whether you could shift to some higher-yielding but still safe form of saving.

— Don't fall in love with any single stock or other investment. Be prepared to move quickly and to sell out if need be. If you try to wait to sell out at the very highest or buy in at the very lowest, you may well miss the boat. As they say on Wall Street: bulls make money, and bears make money — but hogs never make money.

Stock Market

REDUCING YOUR RISKS

AN investor, by definition, is a person who takes risks — but only sensible risks, the kind that will not endanger his or her financial health. And there are ways that you can reduce your risks in the market.

When you invest, as the late Wall Street writer Charles Rolo has observed, there are seasons for courage as well as for caution. So a strategy for all seasons must be one that decreases or increases your exposure to risk, depending on what kind of investment weather you expect. Managing risk does not mean dumping all stocks or other investments when you see storm clouds — or rushing in to buy at the glimpse of a rainbow. Controlling risk usually calls for making a few adjustments in your investments rather than for a sweeping change.

To develop a strategy for all seasons, you first must ask yourself a basic question about your investment goals: are you more interested in seeing your investments grow in value for the long-term, or in collecting immediate income from dividends and interest payments? Obviously, betting on future growth is riskier than collecting fairly well-assured dividends and interest payments.

The degree of risk that you choose to take should be determined by your age, family situation, current and prospective earning power, net worth, tax bracket — and temperament. A 30-year-old single person with bright career prospects can take larger risks than a middle-aged couple with children or retired persons living on their savings.

An aggressive investor who aims for high growth but does not demand immediate income from dividends might put all his money into high-growth, high-risk stocks. Or he could pick medium-risk growth stocks but simultaneously increase both his risks and his potential rewards by using leverage. That is, he borrows money from his broker to buy stocks on margin.

Meanwhile, a more conservative investor — one who is aiming for moderate growth combined with dependable income — might divide his investments almost equally among high-yielding blue-chip stocks, corporate or municipal bonds, and a money-market fund or bank money-market account.

When calculating how to manage risks, it pays to bear in mind that there are three kinds of investment risk:

First, the risk that is related to the overall behavior of the securities market is called, not surprisingly, *market risk*. The standard yardstick of a stock's market risk is its volatility — that is, the extent of its price fluctuations in relation to those of the Standard & Poor's 500 stock index. A stock that historically has risen or fallen more sharply than the Standard & Poor's index is considered riskier than the market as a whole. To find out a stock's historic record of volatility, ask your broker to look it up in *The Value Line Investment Survey*.

When you think it's time to be cautious, you can cut your market risk by reducing the portion of your assets that is invested in common stocks, eliminating the most volatile issues.

Second, stock prices also fluctuate because of industry and company developments. This type of risk is called *diversifiable risk* because you can reduce it if you diversify your investments. Small investors can achieve good diversification by owning only five stocks, provided they are in different industries that are exposed to different types of economic and political risk. For example, some stock groups that are not likely to behave in the same way at the same time are: airlines, banks, computers, cosmetics, energy exploration, gold mining and hospital management.

Third, investors also face what's called *interest-rate risk*. It stems from changes in interest rates and it applies primarily to bonds. But it can also affect the shares of corporations whose earnings are hurt when interest rates rise — and helped when they fall. These firms include utilities, banks, finance companies and savings and loans.

Ideally, you would buy these interest-sensitive stocks just before interest rates started to turn down — and then switch into money funds or Treasury bills just before the next uptrend begins. Calling the turns on interest rates right on target is an impossible dream, but anybody who reads the financial pages carefully should be able to get a handle on which way rates are likely to head.

Before you make any decisions about your investments, watch the relationship between short-term and long-term interest rates. The stock market always has trouble making headway when short-term rates, such as those available on Treasury bills, are higher than long-term rates, the kind offered on bonds. When short-term rates fall significantly below long ones, a bull market quite often follows in a few months.

However, if unexpected bad economic news sends the market down, then be sure to avoid companies with big debts. Look instead at large growth companies with low price/earnings ratios that are selling at low prices. Because of their low base, even a modest rise in price would mean a big percentage gain for you.

Stock Market

STRATEGIES FOR BUYING

THOUGH nobody can be sure whether the stock market will go up or down over the next few months, you should aim to recognize the few really major, long-term turning points in the market, such as the huge rebound that began in August 1982.

Stocks move in expectation of changes in the economy and in corporate profits. The market is always looking ahead. If both inflation and interest rates are heading down, as they have been recently, that's *bullish* news. But when the consumer price index and interest rates on Treasury bills show sustained increases, watch out. It's a clear and present danger signal.

The U.S. presidential election cycle also seems to foretell the market cycle. Since 1953, stocks have shown a clear pattern of declines in the 18 months or so after each quadrennial election. But then the market turns around and rises in the 30 months or so preceding the next election. That's because investors figure that politics induces Presidents to tackle tough, economy-jarring decisions early in their terms. Then, toward the end of their terms, they look ahead to the next election and take steps to stimulate the economy. According to the election cycle, the stock market should have turned up around the middle of 1982 — and it did, although just a few months late because of the economic recession. (For more, see "Investment: The Election Connection.")

Fortunately, your own decisions about the stock market do not have to be perfect to be profitable. Just watch for the major turns in the market. You can buy somewhere above the bottom and sell out some time after the market has hit its peak — and still make more money than the investor who ignores the market's long-term gyrations.

Stock Market

STRATEGIES FOR SELLING

For many investors, selling a losing stock is like shaking some bad habit. It's a painful step you know is good for you, but you keep putting it off. In fact, deciding when to sell a stock is harder — and more important — than deciding when to buy. If you don't buy a stock and the price rises, all you lose is an opportunity. But if you fail to sell a stock and then the price falls, you lose real money.

Here are some guidelines to help you decide what to do when the stock you love no longer loves you back:

First of all, cut your losses. Never hesitate to sell because you are behind. You could wind up further behind. Consider dumping a New York Stock Exchange issue if it declines 15% from the price where you bought it. American Stock Exchange and over-the-counter stocks are more volatile, so give them more rope. But sell them if they decline 20% to 25%.

If you bought a stock expecting favorable developments that then don't occur in a reasonable time, bail out. And if the expected does happen, but the price of the stock doesn't move, unload promptly.

Another sell signal is a sudden spurt in the price/earnings ratio of a stock. In falling markets, stocks with price/earnings ratios that have soared are likely to come tumbling down if earnings are at all disappointing.

If you learn of a significant deterioration in a company's sales growth or profitability or financial health, then it's time to kick the stock out. The same applies if the prospects for the industry that the company is in no longer seem so bright, or if the company itself loses its competitive edge.

Sometimes the behavior of the stock itself will tell you that your love affair with it is getting too hot not to cool down. One sign is if the stock market is rising and trading volume in the issue is heavy, but still it fails to advance in price. Another is when a stock is not making gains similar to those of others in its industry.

By shirking sell decisions, you're not playing it safe, you're taking the biggest risk of all. In the stock market, when the affair is over, there's no such thing as saying "Let's just be friends."

(For more, see "Brokers: Selling without a Broker.")

Stock Market

HIGH-TECH SHARES

Among the best clues to the quality of a high-tech stock is its price/earnings ratio. A technology company with earnings growth of 25% or more a year is often a reasonable buy at a stock price that is 25 times analysts' estimates for the coming year's earnings per share. The estimates are published by such investment advisory services as Value Line, whose reports often are available free in public libraries.

After you own a stock, you usually should seriously consider selling if the price/earnings ratio rises by 50% — for instance, from 20 to 30. That's especially true if you see potential trouble ahead for the stock market as a whole.

In selecting a technology stock, pick a company that dominates or is a clear leader in its particular market. You can measure a small company's financial strength by two telling clues. One is a very low amount of long-term debt. The other gauge is an annual return on equity that's very near 20% or better. You arrive at that number by dividing a company's net income by its net worth — but it's much easier just to ask your broker.

Remember, though, that even today's most attractive small technology companies could suddenly hit unforeseen disaster. For example, a technology breakthrough by a foreign or American competitor could quickly make a company's products obsolete. So, even if you are a young and daring investor, you need some diversification. You need a variety of stocks that could not all be clobbered by the same development.

If you want to get in on high-tech growth but don't want to pick your own stocks, then consider buying into mutual funds that concentrate on high-tech shares. Among those that invest chiefly in such stocks are the Nova Fund (303 Wyman Street, Waltham, Massachusetts 02154), Fidelity Select-Technology (The Fidelity Group, P.O. Box 832, Boston, Massachusetts 02103), the Nautilus Fund (24 Federal Street, Boston, Massachusetts 02110) and T. Rowe Price New Horizons (100 East Pratt Street, Baltimore, Maryland 21202).

Stock Market

THE PLEASURES AND PITFALLS OF NEW ISSUES

INVESTORS seem to be passionately eager to get in on the hot new issues of stocks that are coming to market for the first time. No wonder. In 1982, Standard & Poor's index of new issues leaped 84%. Some initial offerings still present bright opportunities, but before plunging in, examine them closely. Offering prices are often inflated, and companies that are too questionable to get the financial support of blue-ribbon underwriters have little trouble finding unexacting sponsors. As one long-established underwriter warns: "Anyone who ventures into new issues needs to be rigorously selective. A lot of real junk is being brought to market, and that's scary."

On the other hand, quite a few companies of real substance are marketing their issues to the public for the first time. The new issues market is presenting the public with a chance to invest in some youthful companies that are trailblazers in applied technology. Out of such companies will emerge the top growth firms of the mid-1980s and 1990s. Again, the key is selectivity.

Getting information about new issues is not difficult. Some brokerage houses publish weekly calendars of forthcoming offerings. Most brokers subscribe to the *Investment Dealers' Digest,* a weekly that covers the new issues market. But the prospective investor should also ask his broker for the stock's prospectus, the so-called red herring, and scrutinize it carefully.

Look for the passage that lays bare the holdings of the top officers of the company that is selling its stock to you. If they are unloading a lot of their own shareholdings, then you should shun the issue.

Check the prospectus to see that the underwriter of the issue is a well-established firm. Even the best underwriters make occasional errors of judgment, but they will not knowingly market the stock of a company that's likely to damage their reputation.

See who is providing the venture capital financing. Strong backing by venture-capital entrepreneurs suggests that the company has been well groomed to go public and probably has genuine promise.

Examine the balance sheet in the prospectus. Are the company's finances strong enough to keep it going even if profits do not meet expectations — or, if profit growth is on target, to provide capital for continued expansion? If you don't trust your own judgment on these matters, don't invest in new issues without reliable professional guidance.

If a broker is particularly eager to sell you a new issue, don't buy it without checking it out especially carefully. Worthwhile stocks do not need a hard sell. Be prepared to do a good deal of homework. Spread your risk over several issues, even if that means buying a small number of shares in each one.

If you can't get an alluring issue at its offering price, then be a contrarian. That is, instead of chasing after it when it is selling at more than 30 times per-share earnings, have the courage to wait — and buy it after the market takes its next nosedive. In the past, three-quarters of the new issues have fallen back to their initial offering price or even lower within a year. That was because of temporary business problems or a general stock market decline.

In fact, Norman Fosback, the editor of *New Issues* newsletter, has calculated that over the long term, investors who waited and bought these stocks after such declines did just as well as those who got in on the ground floor.

Stock Market

HOW TO FIND TAKEOVER CANDIDATES

T ENS of thousands of investors have been blessed with bonanzas from the surge in corporate mergers and takeovers. Because the stocks of the acquired companies have been bid up to giddy highs, many investors now are trying to guess which firms will be acquired next — so they can buy those companies' stocks and ride them up.

In a takeover deal, the acquiring company typically pays a premium of 50% or even more over the market price for each share of the company it wants to acquire. So it's small wonder that many investors are rushing to buy the stocks of companies that they think are candidates for takeovers. According to the late Wall Street writer Charles Rolo, here are some guidelines for finding them:

First, look where the bargain-hunting corporations shop. Acquirers prefer companies that have large cash holdings. The buying company then can recover part of the purchase price by using the selling company's very own cash. Acquisition-minded corporations also look for stocks selling appreciably below book value — that is, total assets minus total liabilities per share.

Second, look where owners may want to sell. Deal makers often search out companies whose principal owners have reasons to want a merger — for example, if they are elderly, own the controlling interest and have most of their eggs in that one corporate basket. A sellout would enable them to diversify their holdings and perhaps get some stock that is more readily marketable.

Third, look where merger activity is already strong. It is expected to become intense among companies in life insurance, machine-tool manufacturing and oil production.

If you already own a stock that has soared following an offer of merger or takeover, you have a difficult decision to make. Should you cash in right away on the windfall or wait for larger gains if the deal reaches the finish line? In the case of a tender offer — that is, a solid cash offer with a set expiration date — the smart policy is not to tender or sell your stock until the deadline is near. That way, you will not miss out on a further gain if another big corporate buyer announces yet a higher bid.

Stock Market

STOCK SPLITS

W HEN the stock market soars, it's time to watch for stock splits. A company subdivides its stock to keep it attractive to investors. They generally prefer shares in the $10-to-$40 range. If a stock rises to, say, $60, then the company may issue three new shares in exchange for two old shares. That usually brings the price per share down to about $40.

A New York Stock Exchange study shows that stocks splitting at least three shares for two between 1963 and 1980 rose an average 2½ times more than stocks that did not split. The study compared prices three years before the split with those three years after it.

Firms most often declare stock splits when their earnings are strong. Splits thus can be good news for shareholders, bringing increased dividends and favorable growth prospects. So it may be wise to ask a broker for his recommendations of stocks that seem likely to split.

Taxes

WHAT IF YOU CAN'T PAY ON TIME?

ALMOST one out of three people who owe the government taxes on April 15 can't pay. What should you do if you can't pay your taxes on time?

Don't panic. What you should do is file your tax *return* on time and send in whatever amount you can. Otherwise, you will be stuck with stiff penalties.

First, you will be fined at least 5% of your tax liability *each month* for late filing of your form plus ½% *each month* for late payment. Second, you will be charged 11% annual interest, compounded *daily*.

You can ask for an extension. Use IRS Form 4868. With the extension, you can mail in your return as late as August 15 without incurring the 5%-a-month failure-to-file penalty. However, to avoid the late payment penalties, you must send a check for 90% of your taxes by April 15.

Make every attempt to borrow money to pay off your bill as fast as possible. If you can't raise the money on time, about the best you can hope for is that the IRS will let you pay off your bill monthly over the next year or so. However, the IRS grants less than 10% of the requests for installment agreements.

Still, there's no harm in asking. Just be sure to visit your local IRS office immediately after receiving the first delinquency notice instead of waiting for the fourth and final notice about three months later. The IRS gets tougher with each passing day. If you have a professional tax adviser, bring him along. He probably will charge you at least $100, but he can get the IRS to agree to better terms than you can.

Several hundred delinquent taxpayers each year manage to persuade the IRS to reduce the amounts they owe. But such deals are reserved for people whom the tax collectors think will never be able to pay their bills in full. For example, an elderly person with few assets and little chance of earning much might be a candidate for such a compromise.

Once this ordeal is over, make a point of preventing it from happening again. If you are a wage-earner, take fewer withholding allowances at work so more money for taxes will be deducted from your pay. If you are self-employed, increase your quarterly estimated tax payments.

Taxes

HOW TO SURVIVE AN AUDIT

IF you become one of the 1,800,000 or so unfortunate taxpayers who are audited each year, keep cool. The damage probably will be minimal, unless you have engaged in outright fraud.

After that dreaded audit notice arrives in the mail, try to get some idea of how extensive the examination is going to be. One way is to phone the IRS and say you want to schedule an appointment on a day when no one will be rushed. If the IRS agent responds that the interview should not take longer than a couple of hours, relax. It is likely to be a hasty one-hour job. That is the kind most people get. But if you are told to set aside a week, then you know it is going to be a serious review — and you have trouble.

Always bring a professional tax preparer along to help explain your return. Insist the audit take place at the office of your preparer or at the IRS, but not at your own home or office. There is no point in giving the tax collector a more complete picture of your economic station than he will get from your written return.

Your attitude will do a lot to determine how tough or lenient the auditor will be, so be polite. Answer all questions simply and directly, but never volunteer any information. If the auditor assigned to you is abusive, you have the right to demand another.

If you find that you are repeatedly audited for the same deductions — say, higher than average dental bills — and these deductions have been allowed in the past, have your tax preparer write to the IRS to ask that the latest audit be canceled. When he points out that in past years these deductions have been allowed, you have a better than 50% chance of avoiding an audit this year.

In an audit, the best defense is a good offense. If possible, ask for additional *deductions* at your audit. If you can document them, you may improve your overall bargaining position.

Taxes

TAKING YOUR CLAIM TO COURT

Have you ever tried to take the Internal Revenue Service to court to fight out a tax dispute? The IRS has tallied its won and loss records in court cases for one recent year — 1980 — and the results are not encouraging for complaining taxpayers. But you *can* beat the tax collector — if you go to the right court with the right kind of case.

If you have a really serious dispute, you can fight the IRS in a U.S. tax court or in a U.S. district court or in the U.S. Court of Claims. In any of them, you stand less than a 50–50 chance of winning a complete victory. Even so, you have a better chance in some courts than others.

Your worst shot would appear to be in the district courts. In 1980, taxpayers won complete or partial victories there only one-third of the time. Chances aren't much better in the U.S. tax courts. There, taxpayers won completely only 10% of the time, although they had partial victories in 38% of the cases.

Statistically, your best chance at beating the tax collector would seem to be in the Court of Claims. It decided close to half of its cases fully in favor of the taxpayer.

Alas, statistics don't tell the whole story. While the U.S. Court of Claims may seem to be the most appealing place to tangle with the IRS, it has several drawbacks. Fighting a tax case there requires you to make a trip to Washington. If you lose, you rarely can appeal. Before your case even is heard there, you must pay the taxes in dispute and any interest and penalties. Yes, you do get a refund if you happen to win. But only when you can afford the cost and inconvenience should you resort to the Court of Claims.

Surprisingly, the best place to take your suit against the taxman may be in the U.S. tax court — *if* your case is strong. While only one in 10 complaining taxpayers won full victories there in the year studied by the IRS, some lawyers say that that was because many cases brought in the tax courts are frivolous — but that the odds of winning strong cases indeed are better than the statistics indicate. On the other hand, if your case is legally shaky but the kind that's sure to win sympathy from other taxpayers, you might be wise to take it to a U.S. district court. There it will be decided by a jury of your peers — and guess whose side they're on.

Taxes

HOW TO GET QUICK ANSWERS

I F a tax question has you stumped, here is a quick way to get answers:

Now you can call the Internal Revenue Service's new Tele-Tax Service on a pushbutton phone. You simply punch out the number code that correlates to any one of 140 tax topics — for example, the tax treatment for renting your house to a relative. An informative recording summarizes the law on the subject.

The service's local phone numbers and tax-topic codes are listed in the IRS's free Publication Number 910, titled *Taxpayer's Guide to IRS Information and Assistance.* This handy guide is available at IRS offices and most public libraries.

It also ranks the 10 most common errors taxpayers make. Number one is using the tax table incorrectly. Happily, IRS Publication 910 suggests ways you can avoid these errors.

Taxes

USING AN EASY NEW FORM

IF you have no dependents, you might want to consider using a new tax form called the 1040 EZ. And easy it is — it has half the number of lines of the 1040A short form.

But be careful. You cannot fill out the EZ if your taxable income — that is, your income after subtracting all deductions — was $50,000 or more in the year for which you are filing. You also are not allowed to use the new form if you had stock dividends, if you invested in a money-market fund or an Individual Retirement Account, or if your interest income was more than $400 during the year.

Like the regular 1040A short form, the EZ will not let you claim itemized deductions or the child-care credit. Also, it does not give married couples some deductions, exemptions and exclusions that 1040A filers get. But if you are young, single and just starting out in the work force, the EZ might be just the form for you.

Taxes

STATES THAT TAX MOST AND LEAST

No matter what you have to pay in state and local taxes, you probably think it's too much. In 1980, the latest year for which figures are available, American taxpayers forked over an average $2,414 in such state and local taxes. But the tax bite is much deeper in some states than in others.

If you are looking for tax relief, head for Wyoming. That's where individual taxpayers had to lay out the lowest state and local levies. Wyoming residents paid on average only $890 in state and local taxes in 1980. Other states in the bottom 10 were Louisiana, $1,002; Nevada, $1,062; Tennessee, $1,132; Florida, $1,173; Texas, $1,186; Washington, $1,258; North and South Dakota, about $1,400 each; and Indiana, $1,480.

States with rock-bottom state and local taxes generally raise much of their revenues from captive businesses. Wyoming, Louisiana and Texas, for instance, tax the extraction of their plentiful oil, gas, coal and other natural resources. Alaska has actually repealed its personal income tax and lives largely on its oil revenues.

The worst state for taxes is New York — you had to part with $4,088 on average in the Empire State in 1980. Next is Massachusetts, at $3,364. And third from the top is the District of Columbia at $3,260.

Next in the top ten are, in order, Maryland, Wisconsin, Minnesota, Michigan, Delaware, New Jersey and Rhode Island. All tax residents between $2,800 and $3,100. These states can't afford to shift the burden onto businesses. They would chase away too many jobs — and taxable revenues.

Tax Advisers

HOW TO GET THE BEST ONE FOR YOU

Do you want a really reliable adviser to help with your income taxes? Here are some tips on how to get one:

Suppose you are salaried, earn less than $30,000 a year, perhaps own a little stock and pay a mortgage. Chances are your tax profile is simple. If so, you should be able to handle your own forms with the help of a do-it-yourself tax preparation book. Or you can take your forms to one of the national storefront chains such as H & R Block or Beneficial Income Tax Service. They all charge set fees, depending on the complexity of your form. The average price of a Block preparation comes to only $40.

If your personal finances are more complex — say that in the past year you have sold a house, started a business or had active stock trades — you will find that no professional is better trained to handle your taxes than a certified public accountant. It's best to hire a CPA who specializes in taxes, rather than one who does general accounting. Accountants charge, on average, $50 an hour. Merely having your forms filled out probably will cost at least $100.

If your income is large enough to warrant an accountant's help, you probably will need tax planning, too. At one of the so-called Big Eight accounting firms, that could include estate planning, several meetings with a personal adviser on tax strategies and shelters, updates on relevant IRS rulings, monthly projections of your taxes and an array of tax reports. The cost is generally more than $3,500. But an experienced CPA in a small firm should be able to approximate this royal treatment for $300 to $500.

One group of professionals who offer expertise in areas where even accountants fear to tread is tax attorneys. They are great for handling specialized tax problems such as those related to divorce and the sale, purchase or start-up of a business. These lawyers usually work for taxpayers in, or close to, the 50% bracket who want to shelter part of their income. Tax lawyers can argue your case before the IRS and into tax court. Their rates typically are $200 an hour.

Whoever you choose to prepare your taxes, he or she should sign your return. He should be willing to visit the IRS, if necessary — unequivocally willing — since in technical matters it is a mistake for an amateur to appear alone.

How can you evaluate the quality of help you will get from an accountant or tax lawyer or storefront tax preparer whom you are contemplating hiring? Start by asking what kind of clients his firms handles. See if its members are experienced with people in your shoes. Beware of firms that operate on a "pool arrangement" in which your tax forms float among a number of accountants, each of whom handles a few lines.

Listen to the questions the tax adviser asks *you.* If he neglects to inquire about the basics of your tax situation — whether you own a home, have a pension plan or contribute to an IRA — you've drawn a dud. Be particularly suspicious if he starts steering you into such esoteric tax shelters as jojoba bean partnerships without first finding out your needs. He may be trying to sell you a product rather than providing a service.

Although the code of ethics of the American Institute of Certified Public Accountants forbids those professionals from accepting fees from the sponsors for selling you tax shelters, many accountants do so. Yet the fact that an accountant is paid for selling you a shelter is no indication that he is giving you bad advice. What can tell you a lot about the quality of the shelter — and of your tax adviser — is the size of his commission or fee for the shelter. Commissions greater than 10% of your investment drain needed capital from the shelter and suggest that it's not set up to make money for its investors. If a reasonable commission is not clearly stated in the prospectus, dump the shelter and, perhaps, the tax adviser.

The vast majority of tax professionals are competent and honest, but the number of incompetent, negligent and fraudulent tax preparers is much higher than the Internal Revenue Service's estimate of only a few thousand, out of roughly 200,000 in the country. According to the government's General Accounting Office, the IRS is not doing enough to find or penalize the wrongdoers.

How can you tell if your tax preparer might be a problem? Watch out for one who demands a percentage of your tax refund as his payment. Especially steer away from a preparer who guarantees you a refund. Also, avoid anyone who says he will give you a refund right away and will later endorse and cash your IRS check himself. That is illegal — and subject to a $500 penalty.

Tax Savings

HOW TO CUT YOUR TAXES

Almost anyone now can reduce his or her taxes by using some techniques that the rich have been using for years. You do not have to be wealthy to take advantage of them. But don't wait until next April to think about ways to save on your taxes. Start looking now for deductions and credits that will cut your tax bill for this year — and future years. The earlier you act, the most you stand to save.

You can, for example, give money and other assets to your children. They will pay taxes on any income from those assets at far lower rates than you will. It also helps to defer income from the current year to the next one. You might, for example, wait to take a profit on stocks or bonds, or receive installment payments on the sale of a house over several years. Such delaying tactics are perfectly legal.

Of course, it won't pay to increase your tax write-offs if you don't itemize your deductions. So, the first thing to do is add up any expenses that you can write off for the year. The IRS automatically gives you deductions of $2,300 if you are single and $3,400 if you are married and filing jointly. If your total deductions top that, then it pays to itemize.

Congress also has provided plenty of investments that legally and quite effectively shelter you from taxes. Municipal bonds offer tax-exempt current income. Utility stocks pay some tax-deferred dividends. Oil drilling and real estate shelters can offer both immediate deductions and future income payments that will escape taxation.

But anyone mulling over investments that will save taxes is a little like a teenager pondering marriage: you had better be sure that the lust to avoid taxes isn't leading you into a disastrous long-term commitment.

Your personal financial situation will determine which tax-avoiding investments are right for you. If you are an employed person with few work-related deductions, you should consider tax shelters that offer large deductions to cut your current tax bills. On the other hand, if you are in business for yourself, you may have plenty of immediate tax breaks related to your company. You could be better off investing in tax shelters that concentrate on future tax-sheltered income rather than current deductions.

If you want to set up a tax-saving Individual Retirement Account for this year, you can do it any time before you file this year's tax return — that is, as late as April 15 of next year. On the other hand, self-employed people who want to set up a tax-saving Keogh plan have to do it by December 31 of this year — or their Keogh contributions this year won't be tax-

[311]

deductible. But here is a further wrinkle: once you have opened your IRA or Keogh, you can make contributions to either one as late as April 15 of next year. (See "IRAs" and "Keogh Plans.")

Taxpayers can take write-offs for rooms in their homes that are used exclusively for a second business. So now might be a good time to set up a home office. You also can take deductions for the purchase of office supplies, phone bills, and other operating expenses and depreciation for such assets as file cabinets, desks, typewriters and computers.

If you use your car while on the job, you can write off your costs on your income taxes. And you can fatten your deductions even more by keeping conscientious records. Your regular commuting costs to and from work are not deductible. But if you drive your car on business — say, to make sales calls — the IRS lets you deduct 20¢ a mile for the first 15,000 miles and 11¢ for each additional mile. Unfortunately, this can fall far short of what it costs to keep your car running. But you can deduct your actual auto expenses — so long as you have the proper documentation.

Start by keeping a log of the miles you drive for business purposes and note your total mileage for the year. Also, keep track of your outlays for gas, repairs and insurance. Then figure out what proportion of your driving is on business. Finally, deduct that percentage of your costs.

Make a resolution to keep better records this year of all your tax-deductible expenses. Remember: pack rats always pay less. Silly little deductions have a way of becoming impressive big ones. Keep even your grocery receipts when the purchases are for business entertaining.

If you are getting a refund this year, you gave the IRS an interest-free loan last year. To prevent that from happening again, you might have your employer increase your number of exemptions to lower the withholding on your salary.

If you make estimated payments of state income or property taxes, send in your fourth-quarter installment in December instead of January when it's due. This way you can deduct it from your tax bill for the current year. Make any charitable contributions before the year is over. Deductible expenses charged on a credit card in November or December can be written off this year even though you don't pay the bill until January. If you are itching to change jobs, be aware that travel and other expenses connected with your job search are deductible as long as you are seeking employment in the same field of business you're already in.

Tax credits are much better than tax deductions. Deductions only reduce the adjusted gross income on which your taxes are calculated, but credits reduce your actual taxes, dollar for dollar. So if you have a chance to accelerate any credits, seize it. For example, if you insulate your house, you can take a residential energy credit of 15% of the cost up to a maximum credit of $300.

If you need a tax loss and are determined to boot out a few dogs among your investments, there is a way to do it without altering your overall investment strategy. Swap lagging bonds for similar ones you think will rise soon. You also can do the same with stocks, but it's harder to find shares that are almost identical to ones you already hold. Generally, you make these swaps late in the year. But whatever you do, don't wait until the last days of December to swap. It will be hard then to find what you want.

Mutual-fund investors can consider taking a few losses, too. What you do is redeem only those shares that are worth less than you paid for them. You will need to go over your records of purchases, with their dates and prices, carefully, and it's drudgework. Pick out the losers and send a list of them to the bank that serves as the fund's transfer agent, instructing the bank to redeem only those particular shares.

Remember: there is nothing wrong with employing legal tax-avoiding tactics. Every one of them was put into the tax code by act of Congress or judicial decision for some purpose — to encourage Americans to save, invest and become homeowners, which in turn enables businesses to start, to grow and to expand employment. As the late Judge Learned Hand said in a 1947 tax decision: "Nobody owes any public duty to pay more than the law demands: taxes are enforced exactions, not voluntary contributions."

Tax Savings

USING A COMPUTER TO HELP

You can save money on your income taxes by using a personal computer. A few new software programs give you help year-round with forecasting, planning and record-keeping — all of which can reduce your bill.

The idea of being able to do year-round tax planning on your own home computer has been slow to develop. Even now, most of the programs that you can buy just help you do the calculations needed to fill in your 1040 form at the last minute. But there are a few that allow you to update and store financial records month by month, and others that can assist you in devising tax strategies. Unfortunately, no one program does both.

The programs that help you update and store your financial records include Home Accountant, Checkmate Plus, Financial Wizard, Radio Shack's Budget Management and the Financier Personal Series. There are a handful of other programs that let you feed tax data into them at any time of the year and play "What if." As in: What if I sold my stock to pay for my vacation — or would it be better for tax purposes to *borrow* for the trip? Among the choices here are Taxmode, Aardvark's Personal Tax Plan and the Financier Tax Series.

Taxmode is rather sophisticated, but its clear instructions make it useful for the intelligent layman. The Financier Tax Series is a good general aid that wisely assumes you have not mastered the tax code. Aardvark's Personal Tax Plan allows you to deal with 37 different items, such as medical deductions or the childcare credit, and analyze five possible courses of action at the same time. All of these programs are updated as the tax law changes, but ask about this before you buy one. Updates usually do not come free.

Computers are great organizers and calculators, but the value and the accuracy of the result depend on the quality and consistency of the data that *you* feed them. And if you are ever audited, you can bet that any errors will — in the eyes of the IRS — be purely human.

Tax Savings

GIVING MONEY AWAY

FOUR years of college can easily cost $40,000 these days, but careful tax planning can cut your cash outlay by up to 50%. You can save a lot of taxes if you give money to your children while they are young. That way, the interest and dividends paid on that money have many years to compound at the youngsters' low or nonexistent tax rate. A parent who invests for his child's future without transferring the money to him or her is just letting the government take an unnecessary share of it.

Similarly, any adult who owns stocks or bonds with appreciated value and sells them to pay for a child's education is just plain foolish. Instead, give the securities to the child, and let *him* sell them. Profits from the sale will be taxed at the child's tax rate rather than your much higher one.

An occasional gift of money can work wonders. Invest $3,000, tax-free, at 10% interest now, and in 15 years your little genius will have over $12,500 to pay for freshman year. That's not a bad introduction to Economics 101.

The easiest way to give money to a child is to set up a custodial account under the Uniform Gift to Minors Act. You just get a Social Security number for the child, then ask a banker, broker or mutual fund manager to open an account in the child's name.

Whoever is custodian of the money can spend it for any purpose that benefits the youngster, usually including private school, summer camp or violin lessons — but not for something frivolous like a trip to Disney World. You also lose the tax break if you spend the child's money on anything that constitutes an ordinary parental obligation — such as clothing or food and shelter, except in the case of college room and board. (See also "Children: The Cost of Kids.")

Tax Savings

COMPANY THRIFT PLANS

W<small>HEN</small> bureaucratic-sounding memos come around explaining your company's profit-sharing or stock purchase plans, do you just file them in the wastebasket? If you do, you are making a big mistake.

You get a big tax break on company thrift plans. Taxes are deferred on all contributions your company makes to your account and on all the earnings on your account. You don't pay any taxes on them until you withdraw the money when you quit or retire. And then you often can cut the taxes due by using the ten-year averaging payment system.

One type of company thrift plan is profit sharing. The company makes deposits in employee accounts based on the size of corporate earnings. And employees may be able to make voluntary contributions of their own.

Usually you have a choice of investing the money in stocks or bonds and perhaps an interest-paying account. Happily, some companies now offer a family of mutual funds as an alternative. Stock mutual funds have, on average, earned more than the bank trust departments and investment counselors who usually manage profit-sharing funds.

Another type of company plan is the stock purchase program. In this, you might have the option of contributing between 3% and 7% of your gross salary. Often the company will kick in one dollar for your two. All funds go to buy stock in the company itself. You may have to wait three years or more to become vested, that is to have title to the stock bought by the company matching funds.

Thrift plans aim to provide for your retirement, but you often can withdraw the money much sooner if you need to, without upsetting the tax deferral on the earnings.

If you have a choice of several company plans, the best place to park your voluntary contributions is where the company puts in the highest proportion of matching funds. How heavily you want to contribute to a company stock plan will depend on how optimistic you are about your employer's future. Beware of buying company stock so heavily that most of your assets wind up in that one issue. A reverse in the company's fortunes could jeopardize both your nest egg and your job.

Tax Savings

SALARY REDUCTION PLANS

IF you like your Individual Retirement Account, you'll love a new plan with the rather misleading name of the salary reduction plan. Actually, it could cut your income tax bill.

You can use salary reduction in addition to or instead of an IRA. With such a plan, you can elect to have up to 10% of your salary deposited in an investment account, with no taxes due on either the contributions or earnings until you make withdrawals. You often can put aside more tax-deferred savings this way than with an IRA. That's why several hundred major corporations have adopted such programs, including RCA, Mobil, FMC, Ford Motor, Honeywell and Westvaco. More are expected to offer them to their employees in the near future.

Salary reduction plans have several advantages over IRAs, in addition to the potentially larger annual tax deferral. Companies often partially match employees' contributions. In a typical situation, you might be permitted to defer between 2% and 10% of your gross salary. The company then would match half your contributions up to the 6% level. When the company gives you one dollar for every two you put in, you have a 50% return on your money before it's even invested.

With salary reduction, you don't have to take a deduction on your tax return; your contribution simply never shows up on your W-2 form as income. When you withdraw money accumulated in a salary reduction plan — as you retire or leave the company for other reasons — you can use an especially favorable formula. It calculates your tax as if the money were paid out in equal annual amounts over the following 10 years. But this 10-year averaging cannot be used with IRA funds.

Tax Savings

SIDELINE BUSINESSES

PARTICULARLY if you are a young adult, you should be looking for ways to increase your income rather than merely avoiding taxes. In that case, you might start a small sideline business of your own. It can be both a sound investment and a tax haven. Look to your hobby for something you really enjoy doing — and turn it into a spare-time occupation. As tax expert Paul Strassels notes, "it could be anything: chartering a fishing boat, dealing in antiques, selling real estate, catering."

If you launch a business, you immediately create many deductions for equipment, entertainment, travel and car expenses. Most important, a spare-time enterprise eventually may turn into a profitable full-time venture.

A sideline business has another major tax advantage. If it loses money, the loss is deductible from income that you earn elsewhere, say, from your full-time salaried job. As a rule, the IRS will let you deduct such losses if you report a profit in only two out of five years. But be careful. If you report only minuscule profits, the IRS could assume that you are not serious about making the business succeed. So, keep meticulous records. They will help you show that you spend a great deal of time and effort looking for clients and making the business go.

Unfortunately, the IRS audits the owners of small businesses more than any other taxpayers. So don't get carried away and deduct too much for your sideline. And the taxmen are especially watchful for such cardinal sins as failure to report income or to pay withholding taxes.

Tax Shelters

WHAT TO LOOK FOR, WHAT TO AVOID

Just mention tax shelters, and many people get anxiety attacks. No wonder. Limited partnerships all too often fail to deliver on their bright promises. Still, if you are in a fairly high tax bracket, it *is* worth the effort to seek out those shelters where tax deductions and cash returns combine into a sound investment.

You can buy shelters through brokers, financial planners and accountants. It's safest to stick with publicly registered limited partnerships. The Securities and Exchange Commission requires the sponsors to disclose their records, and your chances of an audit are less than with so-called private placements. The price of public deals usually starts at $2,500 or $5,000. Private partnerships want bigger chunks of your cash.

A shelter is an investment where many people just like you put up some money to finance oil and gas drilling, or a big real estate purchase, or some other investment that Congress has deemed is both productive enough and risky enough to deserve special — but totally legal — tax breaks. Shelters are usually set up as limited partnerships. The sponsors, who are the general partners, are responsible for all business decisions. And the investors, who are the limited partners, put up most of the money. That gives them the right to take tax credits or deductions based on the partnership's business expenses. If the venture makes money, the investors get to share in the profits. If it fails, their liability is limited to the amount they have agreed to invest.

Lately, slow times in the real estate market have made real estate shelters attractive. Much the same difficulties in the oil-drilling industry have made oil and gas programs enticing. Because shelter partnerships can acquire oil reserves or office buildings at fairly reasonable prices today, they could pay you a high income in years to come.

In real estate shelters you get write-offs for depreciation, mortgage interest and other expenses. These deductions can equal 70% of your investment over the first four years or so of the program, when expenses run high. In addition, you collect rentals. On a good shelter, they should pay you an average 5% or so annually before taxes. After anywhere from five to 15 years, the shelter sponsor sells the properties and distributes the profits, if any. Each investor's after-tax share might equal twice what he originally put into the shelter. Adding everything up, somebody in a high bracket might well collect a 25% average annualized return on his investment. (See "Tax Shelters: Real Estate.")

Oil and gas shelters use your money to lease drilling equipment and land. These shelters usually last about 15 years. They give you most of your tax deductions in the first year or two and income after that. A successful drilling program might pay out a total annualized after-tax return of 20% a year: an especially successful partnership might pay much more. (See "Tax Shelters: Oil and Gas.")

In general, avoid any deal promising first-year deductions of two or more times your investment. And if you're scouting for a shelter, the old rule is truer than ever: make sure it is a strong investment with solid prospects for offering future profits as well as immediate tax benefits. Here are some do's and don'ts to help you evaluate a shelter:

— Never consider any investment proposed in a classified ad or by an unknown caller on the telephone.

— Avoid any deal that promises you will get 50% or more of your money back from the investment tax credit. The value of the property on which the credit is based is sure to be inflated, and the deal will cry out for an audit, disallowance and fine.

— Reject any program that fails to provide detailed information on the sponsor's prior performance. It's prudent to have an accountant or financial planner scrutinize the prospectus or the offering memorandum to see if you are dealing with an experienced, reputable shelter sponsor. Examine closely the performance records of the sponsors — that is, the general partners — to make sure that they have a proven, successful history.

— Check the prospectus to see that the general partners get their share of the profits at the same time as you, the limited partners, do. You want to make sure there is no skimming.

Several monthly newsletters evaluate public tax shelters and sponsors, and they can point you in the direction of reliable programs. Two are written by CPAs and assess specific deals of all types as well as tax-planning strategies. They are *Brennan Reports*, Suite 245, P.O. Box 882, Valley Forge, Pennsylvania 19482, and *Limited Partners Letter*, P.O. Box 1146, Menlo Park, California 94025.

You can ask brokers or financial planners for prospectuses, but many sell partnerships only from concerns they know well. If you contact the general partners directly — you can find their names in the newsletters — they will sell you a shelter or direct you to a broker or planner.

All shelters are chancy ventures, but some offer safer tax deductions and surer profits than others. To recapitulate how you can increase your return and reduce your risk in tax shelters:

Determine whether you want to buy into a so-called public partnership or a private partnership. The public ventures have to be registered with the Securities and Exchange Commission, and rules governing them tend to be stricter. A private partnership, by contrast, might offer you the comfort of dealing with your own family lawyer or accountant. But just because someone is a savvy accountant does not mean that he or she is an expert in the ups and downs of real estate or oil and gas drilling. Impartial experts tend to agree that the most consistently successful results come from investing in public programs.

Ask your broker what public shelters he or she might recommend. Dealing with a solid broker helps you to avoid jerry-built shelters. Study closely the prospectus covering the shelter. It will help tell just what you are buying and whom you are buying from.

Examine the financial picture of the general partners. Be very careful if their net worth is less than one-tenth of the amount that they are seeking to raise for a real estate project. The ratio can be lower for oil and gas ventures because they tend to require less capital.

Look for the section in the prospectus on prior performance. It's a bad sign if the sponsors of real estate deals have waited more than a year to start the cash distributions. On oil and gas ventures, payouts should begin within two years.

Look for unusually high or low fees. High charges mean that you will get less investment for each dollar that you put up. On the other hand, suspiciously low charges up front may disguise inflated operating costs or other expenses later on. But don't worry if 80% or preferably 85% of your money is actually being invested.

Tax Shelters

REAL ESTATE

REAL estate limited partnerships can take immediate advantage of low prices for solid commercial properties that produce high rental income. Some 65 companies manage these public partnerships. You can buy pieces of these partnerships from financial planners and stockbrokers, usually in minimums of $2,500 or $5,000. Some new partnerships tailored for Individual Retirement Accounts go for $2,000, the most you can put into an IRA in any one year.

Investors in these deals get rental income that should be around 5% a year, plus big tax write-offs. After five to 15 years, the buildings usually are sold, and each limited partner then collects a proportion of the capital gains — or losses — from the sale. A successful sale can greatly increase the investor's average annual return from the shelter.

You can invest in basically two kinds of real estate partnerships. The more conservative of the two buys older properties. Your first-year tax deductions are relatively small, but in addition to them, you can expect fairly predictable cash payouts from the rental income. The smoothest flow of cash comes from partnerships that emphasize long leases. On the other hand, short leases can provide a better hedge against inflation because rents can rise every time the lease is renewed.

A less conservative tax shelter invests in new buildings. In these, the tax benefits may outweigh the immediate income. That's because it can take time for new buildings to become fully occupied, so rental income may be low in the early years of the investment program. But construction costs and accelerated depreciation can produce big tax write-offs.

When you are shopping around for a broker from whom to buy any tax-sheltered investment program, consider this: the ability to weather slumps generally gives large real estate companies the edge over smaller competitors. Major brokerage houses can put you in contact with several large firms that specialize in public partnerships in real estate.

Before you invest, look into the partnership organization's success with past deals. That tells you as much as you can know about its prospects. In a survey of the performance of 33 major partnership organizations from 1970 through 1981, three firms stood out. They were: Robert A. McNeil Corporation of San Mateo, California; Fox and Carskadon, also of San Mateo; and JMB Realty of Chicago.

If you would like to invest in real estate without having to tie up money for several years, then buy into a real estate investment trust. Most so-called REITs are publicly held companies whose shares are traded in the stock market. They invest in property or mortgages and distribute the income as dividends. A portion of those dividends may be nontaxable. If the properties appreciate handsomely, the market will probably bid up your shares, giving you a capital gain.

Like any stocks, REITs go down as well as up in value. During the mid-1970s, they fell like houses of straw under the cold breath of recession. But in the 12 months through mid-1983, Standard & Poor's REIT index surged 42%.

Tax Shelters

OIL AND GAS

Oɪʟ and gas have been the source of some of the most lavish personal fortunes, and even small investors can get in on tax-sheltered energy ventures. But there are many risks to watch out for and some guidelines to follow.

Several types of tax-sheltered oil and gas partnerships are on the market:

Ventures that offer the largest tax write-offs and the highest returns are called *drilling* partnerships. These are investments in the search for new wells. Trouble is, that also makes them the riskiest of the energy tax shelters. The dollars that you spend on drilling may turn up merely a dry hole and worthless dust.

One of the safest shelters is called an *income* partnership. It shares in the income from already established wells. But the relatively high cost of leases on producing wells makes your cash payout from them lower than from other types of oil and gas partnerships, and there are no huge offsetting tax deductions.

Many experts think that the best energy shelters for people who want tax deductions without too high a risk are the so-called *developmental* partnerships. They invest in drilling sites near wells that are already proven.

Risks can be reduced further by diversifying among several oil and gas shelters. People who can safely invest $5,000 or so would be wise to stick with large tax shelter investment companies. They spread out your money among several drilling sites, so if some wells are dry, one or more others may strike energy.

Remember: no matter how carefully you select, any tax shelter remains a high-risk investment. One Wall Street broker who is an enthusiastic promoter of shelters keeps a miniature oil rig on display near his desk. Push a button and it plays "The Impossible Dream."

If you are looking for a relatively safe tax shelter, you can get recommendations from financial planners, lawyers or accountants. The best source of advice is probably a national brokerage house, or a regional broker that has oil and gas shelter specialists on its staff. Shelter analysts at brokerage firms screen hundreds of prospectuses each year and discard those that look legally or financially questionable. About 90% of all deals go into the wastebasket. That's a gigantic piece of work done for you.

The surest deals generally are those in which the sponsors have some of their own cash at risk. So, when examining an oil and gas shelter prospectus, look to be sure the general partners — and not just the limited partners — will lose money if the hole turns up dry. Beware of sponsors who are raising several times as much as they did for past drillings. One other caution: Commissions and fees run high on shelter investments — 15% is not uncommon. Be suspicious of any proposition that costs you much more than that.

Here's a list of successful oil and gas shelter sponsors as selected by *Money* magazine in mid-1983:

Callon (300 Franklin Street, P.O. Box 1287, Natchez, Mississippi 39120; 800–647–6752); Columbian Energy (First National Bank Building, 1 Townsite Plaza, Topeka, Kansas 66603; 800–255–3569); Dyco (1100 Shelard Tower, Wayzata Boulevard at Highway 18, Minneapolis, Minnesota 55426; 612–545–2828); Hawkins Exploration (320 South Boston Building, Tulsa, Oklahoma 74103; 918–585–3121); HCW (Church Green, 101 Summer Street, Boston, Massachusetts 02110; 800–343–9132); Samson Properties (2700 First National Tower, Tulsa, Oklahoma 74103; 800–331–2618); and Woods (National Foundation West Building, 3555 Northwest 58th Street, Oklahoma City, Oklahoma 73112; 405–947–7811).

Tax Shelters

RESEARCH AND DEVELOPMENT SHELTERS

A LITTLE-KNOWN tax shelter lately has begun offering investors bright new advantages. It's called a research and development limited partnership. "R & D" may conjure up fantasies of daring scientific breakthroughs, but these deals more often finance fairly mundane improvements in existing technology.

The shelters usually are partnerships limited to 35 investors each. In the past, the investors have been very rich, because each one has had to put up $100,000 or more. But Merrill Lynch in 1981 brought out an R & D partnership for people with $10,000 to invest. It raised $50 million to finance the development of several new computers — and similar deals have followed.

If you are looking for an R & D shelter, ask a well-established brokerage house that has carefully screened a number of deals. Typically, you can deduct 80% to 90% of your investment from your taxes in the very first year. That's higher than in real estate deals. And, unlike real estate shelters, you can put your money in toward the end of the year and still take a full year's write-off. If the R & D project is commercially successful, royalties from any sale of the patent rights usually are taxable as capital gains, at a maximum of 20%.

The catch is that a lot of R & D deals are quite risky. To identify the most solid and promising ones, search for a project in which the general partner — that is, the organizer — has successfully worked on similar projects in the past. Look also for an R & D shelter that spreads investments over several projects. That reduces the risk of total failure. And avoid projects that are on the frontiers of exotic technologies. As one financial planner says: Stay away from R & D projects where most of the "R" still has to be done. Instead, concentrate on the "D," which is the development.

Tax Shelters

BEWARE OF BURNOUT

W HEN you buy any tax shelter, watch out. The kind of shelter that gives you huge deductions for a modest cash outlay may solve your immediate tax problem, but in a few years it can give you much greater headaches.

Avoid tax shelters that provide big write-offs now but hit you with hefty tax bills in the future. Be especially wary of jumping into exceptionally high-write-off limited partnerships such as some in real estate and equipment leasing.

These shelters can succumb to what accountants call burnout. A burned-out shelter not only stops generating tax write-offs; it also starts piling up paper profits that increase your taxes but don't produce enough real cash for you to pay the taxman.

Here's how burnout happens. In a shelter's early years, it produces large paper losses that you can deduct on your tax returns; in its later years, it produces large paper gains, on which you have to pay taxes.

The shelter has income from such items as rents on an apartment building. That income is more than offset by the shelter's expenses, primarily depreciation and interest payments on the building's mortgage. But as time goes on, the depreciation dwindles, and the principal repayment part of the mortgage bill increases. The principal repayment is not tax-deductible. As a rule, when principal payments exceed depreciation, your shelter has burned out. Even though it isn't taking in more money than it is spending, the taxman treats your shelter as if it were earning a profit for you.

Many sheltered investments don't burn out — ever. The big three in this league are municipal bonds, Individual Retirement Accounts and a new kind of shelter called tax-advantaged limited partnerships. Those last mentioned pay you a fairly steady if modest stream of cash rather than offer you spectacular tax deductions in the early years. (See "Tax Shelters: Income-Oriented Shelters.")

To avoid burnout, ask some questions of anybody who tries to sell you a tax shelter. Find out what year burnout is scheduled to occur. If the term "burnout" makes the shelter salesman gag, use the more polite word, which is "crossover." The tax shelter's prospectus also should contain enough information for you to determine when the investment is likely to burn out. Five years or so is typical. It's wise to get an impartial lawyer, accountant, broker or financial planner to read the prospectus and tell you whether — and when — burnout will strike.

[327]

Tax Shelters

INCOME-ORIENTED SHELTERS

O NE new investment that is gaining popularity is a tax shelter that does not have all the high risks and the high write-offs found in traditional shelters. The new shelters emphasize steady payments of cash to you. They are called *tax-advantaged* shelters, and you don't have to be rolling in money to make use of them.

The tax-advantaged deals are tax shelters for the timid. You can buy them from many stock brokers and financial planners for $2,500 to $5,000 — and sometimes less than that. Just like old-style shelters, they typically concentrate on real estate, oil and gas and equipment-leasing ventures. But the resemblance pretty much ends there.

The new shelters aim to produce steady tax-free income for you more than deep deductions. Instead of generating write-offs that reduce taxes on your salary or on your income from other investments, the newer shelters use depreciation and other deductions to offset income produced by the shelter itself.

These investments offer you the chance to earn tax-free yields equal to or higher than the yields available from intermediate-term municipal bonds. But unlike bonds, these shelters don't guarantee to pay you either a fixed rate of interest or even to return the money you invest. Still, the risks are far lower than with traditional shelters, whose tax advantages can run out in early years, leaving you with a walloping tax bill.

The difference between the old and new shelters is largely a matter of the size and timing of the write-offs. Old-style shelters pass along to investors the expenses of, say, drilling for oil, allowing investors to deduct all their stake in the first couple of years. In the new-style shelters, the deductions are spread in small installments over five to 10 years.

For people who want more than merely deductions, the attraction of the new income-oriented tax shelters has never been stronger. That's because the tax law enacted in 1981 lowered the top tax brackets and thus made deductions *less* attractive than before. At the same time, lower taxes and faster depreciation allow investors to keep more of whatever income the shelter produces.

Of all these new tax-advantaged deals, the ones best suited to conservative investors are real estate shelters. They might pay you about 5% a year from rental income. Depreciation keeps this income tax-free for about five years. Then the sponsors of the shelter typically start selling off properties and investors also share in any profits. One problem is that those profits may not be as much as you expect because real estate probably will not appreciate as fast in the mid-1980s as it did in the 1970s.

You also can invest in a tax-advantaged deal that buys producing oil wells — and that has many advantages. Yet there *are* risks. Even with the best technical expertise, you are still guessing at the extent of reserves and at future oil prices.

Telephones

CUT-RATE LONG-DISTANCE SERVICES

IF your AT&T long-distance bill averages $25 or more a month, consider subscribing to an alternative phone company. You may cut your long-distance charges by as much as 50%, depending on where and when you call.

Four major companies are competing with AT&T. They are MCI Communications, Southern Pacific's Sprint, International Telephone and Telegraph and Western Union. But you will pay a price for cut-rate long-distance service. Subscribers sometimes complain about fade-out and false busy signals.

All these companies charge a monthly fee, ranging from $5 to $10. Rates per call vary from service to service. For example, in mid-1983 for a 10-minute call from Chicago to Dallas made during night hours, AT&T would have charged you $1.79. MCI would have billed you $1.38, Sprint, $1.27, Western Union's MetroFone, $1.21 and ITT's Longer Distance, $1.05.

Television Repairs

HOW TO FIND A SERVICEMAN

GETTING your television set repaired does not have to be as suspenseful or traumatic as an episode from "As the World Turns." Well-trained, reliable TV repairers abound, and here are some tips for finding a reasonably priced one.

Although TV sets are generally sturdy, they probably will malfunction once or twice during their average 10-year life span. If your set's problem is covered by a warranty, it must be repaired by one of the manufacturer's authorized service dealers. Their addresses usually come with the TV. But only a small percentage of TVs need repairs during warranty periods; that's normally 90 days for labor, one year for parts and two years for the picture tube.

Sometimes you can extend the free repair service by buying a service contract. It can cost up to $235 for 33 months of home service. But you are gambling that breakdowns will occur in the first few years and not later on.

Even if your warranty has expired, it's wise to use an authorized dealer for repairs because he stocks parts for your set and he has experience in fixing TVs like yours. You can find authorized dealers in the Yellow Pages under "Television Service" or "Television Repairs." If you can't locate an authorized service dealer, make sure the repairer you choose has a place of business — not just a truck and phone number. Some fly-by-night operators pick up sets and are never heard from again.

Membership in groups such as the Electronics Technicians Association, International and the National Electronics Service Dealers Association provides some evidence that the repairer is competent, as well as interested in maintaining a reputation for reliability.

If possible, take your TV set to the repair shop to save on the house-call service charge. Ask for a written estimate of costs in advance.

When a repairer finishes work, he should give you an itemized bill and guarantee his work for at least 30 days. He should also return to you all parts he replaced, except the picture tube.

Above all, don't try to repair your TV yourself. For one thing, opening the back of your set can be dangerous because color picture tubes release electrical voltage for hours after the set has been unplugged.

Theft

WHAT TO DO IF YOU ARE RIPPED OFF

WHEN your pocket has been picked, you are left with a purseful of problems. But there are ways to help your recovery from a rip-off.

Some 16 million Americans are victims of personal larceny each year. If you are one of them, chances are slim that your property will ever be recovered. Still, you should quickly inform the police about the theft. You will need a police report to prove your loss to the IRS, to your insurer and perhaps to your bank.

You also should notify your bank and any of your credit card issuers immediately. A thief can swiftly begin using your checks and credit cards, and a few hours' delay increases the chances that he will get away with it. If you know the numbers of any stolen checks, your bank can stop payment. If not, you probably will have to close your account and open a new one. You are not liable for checks written by a thief, but if the signature closely matches your own, you will have to spend time proving to the bank it was a forgery.

Once you report the loss of your credit cards, you are not liable for any subsequent changes. If the thief gets away with using your cards before you report the loss, your liability is limited to $50 a card. But that amount adds up quickly if you have several cards. Many credit card issuers have operators available around the clock. They also may provide toll-free numbers or will accept collect calls.

One precaution is to sign up with a credit card protection service offered through banks and credit card firms. For $9 to $12 a year, a service will immediately contact all of your credit card issuers after you notify it of your theft. The service pays any liabilities incurred after you call. Some services will even wire you money if you are robbed while traveling.

Another piece of plastic you may carry is a debit card used to operate the automatic teller machine at your local bank. Your liability is $50 if you notify the bank within two business days after theft; it jumps to $500 if you take three to 60 days. After that, liability is unlimited.

Tipping

ADVANCE PAYMENT HELPS

T HE word "tip" is widely held to mean to insure promptness. But in many restaurants, nightclubs and stadiums, you can get more than promptness by giving a tip *before* you get the service. It takes only a few dollars paid in advance to send the red carpet rolling, ensuring you choice seats, superior service and the real — though possibly ignoble — thrill of bypassing a long and footsore line.

Advance tipping seems to work best in big cities that have a fluid social structure. In such places as New York, Chicago and San Francisco, money talks more commandingly than family name does. Tipping gets you less far in Boston or Minneapolis, Atlanta or Washington, D.C., where what counts is breeding, charm or connections.

Some gestures are self-defeating. It's gauche to try to tip the owner of a restaurant. One tip to tippers: owners usually dress more casually than employees. So look for the man in the tuxedo: he works there. It's also boorish to try to sneak in a $1 bill in place of $5 or $10 for immediate seating at a good table in a top restaurant. And don't overtip: $20 doesn't get you a table twice as good as one for $10.

Another bastion of benign bribery is the parking garage. In many cities, a couple of well-placed dollars can open a garage that is said to be full up. Usually you give the money to the dispatcher. He's the fellow sitting in the little glassed-in booth.

And at sports events, ushers usually can tell when a season-ticket seat will remain empty that day. To trade up, look for the usher about 20 minutes after the game has started, and ask whether any seats near yours are vacant. As you do this, hold a $5 bill where it's visible but not flagrant.

Even in cities where advance tipping is rare, nightclubs are often an exception to the rule of first come, first served. In Las Vegas, the first act of most shows is the so-called Captain's Waltz, which starts with a visible $20 bill in the palm. Some people start with $50 or even $100. But that's just showing off.

Travel Agents

HOW TO FIND A GOOD ONE

Iᴛ you're planning a trip, a knowing travel agent can help guide you through the complexity of fares and the many package deals available. But how do you pick a good travel agent?

A travel agent, after all, is a double agent. He is engaged by you, the traveler, but he is paid by the airlines, hotels, tour operators and other travel services, which give him commissions — usually 10%. Thus, most travel agents prefer writing expensive international tours to planning a car trip to the nearest beach. Some may push hotels that offer better commissions than they do rooms, or package tours that are easier to arrange than customized itineraries.

But many travel agents do put their clients' needs first. For one thing, they thrive on repeat business and recommendations. The problem is not how to find an honest agent. What's most difficult is discovering one who is expert and experienced enough to guide you. You might test to see if his taste is compatible with yours by asking him for his favorite hotels and sights in places that you have visited and are well acquainted with.

Just about anyone can set himself up in the business. Window decals that boast affiliations with national travel agent associations guarantee that the agency meets some standards, but not very high ones. If the agent himself has completed a two-year course given by the Institute of Certified Travel Agents, he can use the initials CTC after his name. This label at least suggests above-average commitment.

But the best guarantee to a competent agent is word of mouth. If you're trying an agent on someone else's recommendation, then tell that agent just who sent you. Agents work harder if they have to please old customers as well as new ones.

Solid professionals are interested in the outcome of trips. They usually take the initiative to call customers on their return. If you have complaints that are well founded, travel agents can help you get at least some of your money back.

Before settling on a travel agent, interview two or three on the telephone. Ask where each one has traveled in the past year. A conscientious agent can share first-hand experience of the places and services he recommends. He probably takes two or three week-long trips and several weekend excursions a year — just to keep his information up to date.

If an agent is unfamiliar with a destination, he should be willing to refer you to a colleague or another customer who has recently been there. You can tell an agent knows a place fairly well if he speaks authoritatively without continually consulting guidebooks and maps.

Don't hesitate to prod the agent to find the lowest fare. You will know he is really digging if he suggests times or dates that would result in cheaper tickets. On the other hand, be sure to investigate carefully any extremely low-priced package tours. Sometimes they cut so many corners that the hotel and meals aren't anything you would care to remember.

Travel agencies range from hometown mom-and-pop operations to the giant chains like American Express or Thomas Cook. Customers who want personal service often do better with small agencies with local reputations to protect. But large chains and agencies frequently offer a wider selection of services and a staff that knows about more areas of the world. Volume also breeds influence. Agencies that send planeloads of travelers to a destination can get scarce hotel rooms more easily in peak seasons.

Customers with particular travel needs should seek out specialized agents. Some are expert in exotic travel, in rail travel or freighter cruises, still others in the needs of singles or business travelers. Travel guidebooks are the places to find such specialists. And foreign airlines or national tourist offices also can be an invaluable guide to agencies familiar with their countries.

Urban Homesteading

BARGAINS IN INNER-CITY HOUSES

Everyone has heard about intrepid couples with moderate incomes who bought houses in decaying urban neighborhoods for a few thousand dollars 10 years or so ago. They fixed them up — and now they have homes worth $300,000. Believe it or not, you still can get terrific housing from that kind of do-it-yourself urban renewal in most U.S. cities. But bargains may be harder to find now, so it makes sense to buy these houses because you love them and want to fix them up — not because you want to make money.

When you hunt for a homestead on the urban frontier, look only in neighborhoods that show signs of being on their way back. Seek out areas bordering on ones that already have revived, so you can benefit from the domino effect of spreading affluence. The neighborhood also should be near a bus line or other mass transit. It's ideal if it has some natural attraction such as a river, a lake or a park.

Don't try to judge an old house by the condition of its paint, plaster, plumbing or wiring. They are likely to be in wretched shape anyway, and amateurs can't spot the real problems. Hire professionals to examine any property you are thinking of buying for three fatal flaws: extensive termite damage, decayed sills — sills are the wooden base the house rests on — and excessive settling of the foundation.

If you need a loan to pay for rehabilitating your inner-city house, you're best off applying to a local bank for it. These days, bankers view rehabbers as desirable customers. The federal government has put pressure on banks to invest some of their deposits in neighborhood businesses and housing.

In fact, banks are more than willing to give loans for the construction as well as mortgages. Construction loans are important because the cheapest thing about any dilapidated house you buy may well be its purchase price. Charming 19th-century hardwood floors, stained glass windows and plaster moldings generally are accompanied by not-so-charming plumbing, roofing and wiring.

Typically, in mid-1983 you could get a 30-year conventional mortgage at 13%, and if you qualified for an FHA loan, the rate would be one point less. Your bank also may be able to give you a 15-year FHA-insured renovation loan of up to $15,000; in mid-1983, the rate was 16% — a full point lower than for conventional home improvement loans. In addition, the government makes low-cost loans to inner-city home buyers whose incomes are less than 80% of the median for the area. Check with your local community development office to see if you qualify.

[336]

There are tax incentives if you rent out any part of a house that the National Park Service certifies as historic. You can take a credit of as much as 25% of the cost of renovating the rented rooms, but the Park Service has to approve the work. The government generally approves fix-ups that preserve the facade, so don't try to put a sliding glass door in your bay window or a skylight in the mansard roof.

Few lenders are willing to finance shells of houses, unless you have an architect's plan for the renovation. But with blueprint in hand, you should be able to get a so-called "value after repair" mortgage covering the price of the renovation as well as the property.

Finally, beware of doing so much renovation that you price your house right out of the resale market. It doesn't make much sense to buy a house for $50,000 and pour $150,000 worth of work into it only to sell it for $175,000.

Utilities Stocks

TAX SAVINGS PLUS HIGH DIVIDENDS

ONE of the simplest, safest ways to save on taxes is to invest in the shares of electric utilities. To help these power companies attract investor capital, Congress has given their stocks novel appeal as a shelter. Now when you buy shares in most of the large electric utilities, you can reinvest dividends automatically, often in stock the company offers at a 5% discount. The Internal Revenue Service lets you exclude up to $750 a year of these reinvested dividends from your taxable income, or $1,500 a year for a married couple filing jointly. There is no tax on the dividends until you sell the stock.

And if you hold your shares for more than a year, the earnings are taxed at the long-term capital gains rate. That's only 40% as much as the ordinary-income rate that usually applies to dividends.

There is more to recommend utility stocks than preferential tax treatment. In most states, the regulators have eased up a bit in recognition of the companies' need to earn more profit, and the moderation in oil prices and interest rates should further energize the stocks. Utility dividends in mid-1983 averaged 10% of their share price — a considerably better return than you could get on taxable money-market funds.

But you can't pick a utility stock with your eyes shut. A troubled power company strapped with costly construction projects usually pays high dividends — up to 12% in mid-1983. You can get substantially more peace of mind by settling for a bit less current return.

Another way to plug into the utilities' high dividends without fueling up your tax bill is to invest in so-called tax-managed funds. These funds are sold through brokers. They are similar to mutual funds, except that they reinvest all dividends and capital gains and make no distributions to shareholders. You take your profits in the form of an increased share price when you sell out. If you hold your stock for more than a year, the profits are taxed at the low capital-gains rate.

Vacations

BED-AND-BREAKFAST GUEST HOUSES

V ACATIONERS find that staying in a big city hotel can easily cost $100 a night. But there is a fast-growing new alternative: guest houses that offer bed and breakfast. They have the comforts of home at truly down-home prices.

Many of the large new hotels are marvels of chrome and glass — but whatever became of charm and personal attention? Both are alive and well, and for far less than hotel rates.

More and more private houses throughout America take in paying guests. Like the well-known European homes that offer tourists bed and breakfast for nominal fees, these guest houses flourish in many cities, towns and resort areas where they cater mostly to travelers who have given up on hotels because of their champagne prices and no-fizz accommodations.

These guest houses rent out an average three rooms, and rates for a couple can range from $10 a night at a mansion in Geneva, New York, to $80 in Arroyo Grande, California. Breakfast and free parking are almost always part of the deal. There is no guilty fumbling for tips; hosts rarely accept them.

Most offer the kind of hospitality that is rare at hotels, eagerly sharing with you insiders' insights on fine restaurants and shopping bargains. But you may miss some amenities available at even moderately priced hotels. You probably won't have a TV or phone in your room. You may have to share a bathroom.

You can find a listing of 500 bed and breakfast hosts in a book, *Bed & Breakfast U.S.A.* by Betty Revits Rundback and Nancy Ackerman. It costs $6.95. To find out where to get it, if it is not readily available at your local bookstore, you can write to the Tourist House Association of America at Box 355-A, R.D. 2, Greentown, Pennsylvania 18426.

Bed & Breakfast U.S.A. includes a chapter on how to start your own and lists over 100 bed-and-breakfast reservation agencies. They usually send free brochures describing members' houses and an application asking for your itinerary, how long you plan to stay and whether you insist on comforts such as air-conditioning. Sometimes you can choose your house; other times you are assigned to one. These booking agencies may take a week or two to confirm reservations, so plan your trip in advance.

Vacations

DUDE RANCHES

IF you're looking for a moderately priced family vacation, you might consider spending a week at one of America's 150 dude ranches. Each can offer a private cabin, three hearty meals and a companionable horse for the price of just a room in a big city hotel. A week at a ranch typically costs around $350 to $500 per adult — with 10% or more off for children. The ranches are mostly in the open spaces of the West, but the East and South have a sprinkling of smaller spreads.

Many of the ranches still raise cattle for profit and let visiting dudes help round up the herd, brand a steer or lend a hand with chores. But the emphasis is on horseback riding. Ranches offer easy, medium and fast rides. Other activities can include fishing, hiking and swimming. The newest breed of ranches couples conventional resort fare such as tennis with an Old West setting. But the more frills a ranch offers, the more expensive it is likely to be.

To find a dude ranch, write or phone the tourist office in the state or states you'd like to visit. If you're interested in the West, write the Dude Ranchers' Association at P.O. Box 471, LaPorte, Colorado 80535.

Figuring your budget is simple because the rates are inclusive. You need add in only your transportation costs. It can cost less than $150 to outfit you from head to toe for a dude ranch. The biggest and most important investment is for cowboy boots. They start at about $60. You'll also need a couple of pairs of jeans, flannel shirts, and a warm jacket for cool morning or evening rides. A snug cowboy hat will shield your eyes from the sun and dust. The cheapest is about $20.

A warning about dude ranches: don't expect luxurious rooms and gourmet meals. Both are simple and basic.

Vacations

GETTING GOOD VALUE ON PACKAGE TOURS

ALMOST every would-be tourist has heard horror stories about package tours. But you don't have to swear off those bargain deals if you want your vacation to go smoothly. You can get top value for your money if you know how to examine your package tour in advance. Here are some of the questions you'll want answered:

— Does the package include an inexpensive and convenient charter flight? Regular fares are down so much on some routes that you could wind up saving only about $25 on round-trip charters from New York City to London. When the savings are substantial, make sure that you don't have to stop en route in two or three other U.S. cities before heading for Rome — via London and Brussels.

— What do "first-class" accommodations really mean? The best European hotels are rated "deluxe." All that first class gets you is a clean bedchamber with a private bath. You can determine if you're going first class or fleabag by looking up the amenities of your hotel in two books. One is *The Official Hotel and Resort Guide,* and the other is *The Hotel and Travel Index.* Both are available at travel agencies and libraries. The guide and the index also list the price you'd pay for the room if you booked on your own. If the daily cost of the hotel on your package tour is *less* than the hotel's usual room rate, you know you're getting a deal.

— Will the meals consist of foie gras and roast pigeon, or tomato juice and roast chicken? Tour operators won't tell you what you will eat at meals included in the package, but they will give you hints. If you find you are to eat in hotel restaurants, remember that they seldom are great gastronomical palaces.

— What happens if you have to cancel? Read the brochure's fine print carefully. You will probably lose your hotel deposits, typically the cost of one to three nights. But most tour operators will refund the rest of your money, minus a fee of $20 to $100 depending on how close to the departure date you back out.

Vacations

HOLDING DOWN COSTS OF FOREIGN TRAVEL

THE value of the dollar has risen so much lately against the French franc, the British pound, the Italian lira and most other foreign currencies that travel abroad has become affordable once again. You can get bargains even in Paris — for the first time in memory. Still, to prevent any unexpected blows to your pocketbook, it pays to prepare a sensible travel budget in advance.

Before you go, it's wise to read (or at least skim) one or two up-to-date guidebooks. They will help you arrive at a reasonable estimate of what your trip will cost. At least half a dozen travel newsletters also offer reliable cost information tailored to specific clients, such as retired travelers or singles. You can find out where to subscribe to them from travel agents, travel magazines and your own special interest groups.

After you have done your homework, sit down and make a daily budget. Add up the estimated costs of hotels, food, tips, taxis and incidentals. Then tack on at least 25% more for the unexpected.

Don't plan to spend the same amount each day. Try the "budget-splurge" method of travel. Cut back on certain days by eating cold cuts in the park for dinner. Then you can afford a really terrific restaurant the next day.

Prepay as much of your trip as possible before you leave. That avoids budget-busting surprises.

Package tours are surely the cheapest way to travel. But some stripped-down tours have more hidden costs than France has churches. Hotel and restaurant managers may ask you to pay extra charges for items you thought had been taken care of well in advance. You will have a hard time trying to collect when you get back home. You are much better off to be sure of exactly what you are paying for before you leave.

The surest way to save money is to plan a trip as far ahead as possible. That way, you can get the cheapest air fares, which you often have to reserve weeks ahead of time. Also, news of bargain hotels tends to travel fast. So you may have to book as much as six months in advance to get reservations.

Plan to pay for your expenses abroad with a combination of travelers' checks and credit cards. Don't carry too much cash because hotel thefts are on the rise. In a pinch, you usually can cash personal checks at top hotels and the offices of credit-card companies. But you need to have a credit card to do it.

If you enjoy train travel, one of the world's last great bargains is the Eurailpass. It allows you to travel first class as much as you want in sixteen European countries for $260 for 15 days. Children under 12 go half price; under four years old they ride free. Britain is not covered by the Eurailpass but has its own version, which allows an adult 14 days of unlimited travel by railroads all over England, Scotland and Wales for $219.

European trains are usually fast, clean, comfortable — much better than most of their American counterparts. They are also good for stretching out and sleeping in — which is a clever way of saving a bundle on a hotel room every now and then.

Just about everywhere, you can save money by avoiding the costly capital cities and trekking off to the provincial centers and the countryside. For example, rural Britain is not only charming but also far less expensive than swinging London. But wherever you decide to go, you might follow the advice of the most savvy and seasoned travelers: take half of what you pack and twice as much as you've budgeted.

Vacations

HOW TO SURVIVE CUSTOMS INSPECTIONS

YOU'RE just back from a great trip overseas, and the only obstacle between you and your waiting family is a cold-eyed U.S. customs agent. How can you best survive that customs inspection of your baggage?

Even before they leave home, smart travelers write or visit an office of the U.S. Customs Service and get two of its leaflets. One is called *Know Before You Go*, and, among other things, it lists the articles you cannot legally bring home. The second booklet tells about goods that are duty-free if they are made and bought in any of 140 developing countries and territories. That leaflet is titled *GSP & the Traveler*. GSP stands for Generalized System of Preferences.

A few items are duty-free no matter where they are bought. Among them are paintings, antiques, cut diamonds and binoculars.

Each returning traveler, even an infant in diapers, is allowed $400 in duty-free merchandise. A family can pool their allowances. For example, a family of four — mom, dad and two children — get a total allowance of $1,600. If you go above your total, you are charged a flat 10% duty on the next $1,000 and up to 40% on everything else.

Customs agents are not easily fooled. They have price lists for popular goods such as French perfume or Scottish woolens. They can spot amateurishly stitched American labels on clothes — a sure sign that somebody bought the garment abroad.

Inspectors are tougher at some gateways than others. The easiest entry into the country is often from Canada, since there is less concern about contraband traffic from the North. The toughest entry points are from the Orient, the Caribbean and South America because that's where the drugs come from. So it's small wonder that Honolulu and Miami have a well-earned reputation as the roughest U.S. customs checkpoints.

When you go through customs, you invite suspicion — and a search — if you act nervous or belligerent or carry something bizarre, such as a fur coat in summer. If an examiner finds an item you have not declared, he can charge you a fine equal to its wholesale price or six times the duty, whichever is less. On top of that, he can confiscate the item.

So the best advice, of course, is to do your homework, keep your bills straight, tell the truth — and if you've overstepped your $400 per-person limit, be prepared to pay your duty, which, after all, probably won't be very large.

Vacations

RESORT DISCOUNTS

MANY owners of rental houses and apartments in popular vacation spots give big discounts to pilots and flight attendants stranded between trips. But you don't have to work for an airline to get the same cuts. You can qualify by joining the Airline Discount Club-International for $45 a year.

Members receive four quarterly issues of *Vacation Times*. It lists available houses and apartments in Hawaii, Florida, Bermuda, the Bahamas and elsewhere — at 30% to 40% off regular rates. The club keeps a computerized reservation list so that members who call or write can find out immediately if a place is vacant. A deposit of $50 to $100 is required within seven days. For more information, write to Airline Discount Club-International, P.O. Box 616, Parker, Colorado 80134.

Vacations

ROMANTIC HOLIDAYS

THOSE lavish honeymoon packages at hotels and resorts aren't just for newlyweds. Many times they are offered to anniversary celebrants as well — and it's a rare hotelier who will demand that you celebrate your wedding on its anniversary. Next time you book a room for two, simply ask for the hotel's anniversary or honeymoon rate.

Just one example: the Westin Hotel on Michigan Avenue in Chicago in mid-1983 was offering a one-bedroom suite any night of the week. Guests got champagne on arrival, two crystal glasses from Tiffany's to take home with them and breakfast the morning after. The cost: $185, compared with a regular rate of $305 for the suite alone.

Places outside the U.S. are equally hospitable. For example, Sam Lord's Castle Resort in Barbados has a $474 eight-day package that saves you $156 on the room alone. So, have a happy honeymoon — or whatever.

Vacations

SWAPPING HOMES

IMAGINE a week-long stay in a furnished condominium with a view of the Pacific, or at an island retreat at Hilton Head, South Carolina — rent-free. If you happened to own either place, you could probably swap it temporarily for the other through a vacation-home exchange club.

Such organizations sell directories that list homes for exchange. Property owners pore over the books for a house in the right spot and then negotiate trades with each other. Most clubs give advice on contracts, insurance and other details but otherwise aren't involved in exchanges. All of these clubs allow members to advertise their homes for rent as well as exchange.

The largest of them, Vacation Exchange Club, lists about 6,000 homes in two general directories published during the year. For information, write to the club at 350 Broadway, New York, New York 10013. About half of its listings are in the U.S. and Canada, and the rest are in Europe, Australia and New Zealand, with British swappers particularly plentiful. It costs $22.70 to get both editions of the directory and to list your house in one of them. For $15 you get the directories without a listing; owners of Hawaiian beach houses, for instance, often prefer to initiate trades rather than list their homes and have to respond to sacks of mail.

Among the other clubs:

— Holiday Exchanges (Box 878, Belen, New Mexico 87002) will send you 12 monthly newsletters for $20. A year's listings total about 1,200 American and foreign properties.

— InterService Home Exchange (Box 87, Glen Echo, Maryland 20812) lists about 1,000 mostly foreign properties in semiannual directories. Cost: $24 a year with a listing, $18 without one.

— Hideaways International (Box 1459, Concord, Massachusetts 01742) focuses on U.S. and Caribbean resort areas. Three directories and four supplements a year, with 1,500 listings, cost $39.50; a quarter-page spread on your home, including photos, is $65 more. Hideaways also runs ads for vacation-home rentals, as well as for yacht and houseboat charters.

Vacations

TAX-DEDUCTIBLE ADVENTURES

THOUSANDS of Americans will vacation in exotic parts of the world this year. They will swim with dolphins in Hawaii or survey an Inca citadel in Peru or photograph an ancient cathedral in Russia — and their expenses will be tax-deductible.

You can write off on your income taxes the costs of your vacation if you volunteer for nonprofit scientific research expeditions. The Internal Revenue Service will allow you to deduct your air fare, food and lodging as a contribution, so long as the sponsor has tax-free status in the U.S.

Many trips are sponsored by Earthwatch, the Massachusetts-based field research organization, and by the University Research Expeditions Program at the University of California. Participants range in age from 16 to 60. Only a few projects demand very long hours or herculean strength, but work is involved in all of them. Among other things, volunteers build animal traps, use surveying devices, monitor bumblebee behavior and compile experimental data.

For example, on an Earthwatch trip to Rumania, you will explore the caverns beneath the Transylvanian Alps to study ecological damage. You will live in a primitive chalet and cook over a wood fire. The cost? About $1,200 plus air fare to Bucharest — most, if not all, of it tax-deductible.

For information about tax-deductible adventures, contact Earthwatch, 10 Juniper Road, Box 127, Belmont, Massachusetts 02178 or the University Research Expeditions Program, University of California, Berkeley, California 94720.

Beyond that, the Archaeological Institute of America, 53 Park Place, Room 802, New York, New York 10007 acts as a clearinghouse for excavations around the world and publishes the annual *Field Work and Opportunities Bulletin* ($5 for nonmembers, $3.50 for members). It lists 50 to 60 projects that need volunteers. And from time to time, a few universities and museums will directly accept helpers on their own projects.

Vacations

TIME SHARES

Time sharing can offer great low-cost vacations. But if you don't choose carefully, your bargain can become a burden.

Some 300,000 Americans have been swept up in the vacation time-share boom. It began during the mid-1970s, when many builders of resort condominiums adopted the European idea of dividing expensive real estate among many buyers. Developers learned that they could double their profit by selling 52 weekly shares in every apartment. Each share entitled the buyer to one week in the apartment, at the same time, year after year.

The time-share concept quickly spread to hotels and motels as well as to yachts and campgrounds. Meanwhile, exchange services sprung up that enabled buyers to swap their time shares in one resort for vacation weeks at another resort.

Prices of time-share vacation units vary from $2,000 for one week in a studio apartment in Myrtle Beach, South Carolina, to nearly $20,000 for a week in a luxurious Hawaiian hotel. The average cost is $5,500. Most buyers are middle-aged and middle-income, but many resorts attract other people. For example, time shares in Aspen are popular among young professionals while those in the Florida Keys appeal to wealthy, older couples.

Competition for time-share customers is fierce, high-pressure sales are common, and many states do not have adequate protection for customers. True, most time shares are fairly sold and most buyers are happy with them. Some, however, grow tired of spending year after year at the same place.

If you buy a vacation time share but later become bored with visiting the same old resort, you have two options. The first is to exchange your time share for a share in another place at another time. Two services — Resort Condominiums International (9333 North Meridian Street, Indianapolis, Indiana 46260), and Interval International (7000 Southwest 62nd Avenue, Miami, Florida 33143) — work to find someone to trade with you. But you can't swap an off-season week at an unknown beach resort for a snow-season week at a top ski resort. Swapping a time share can be tough unless you have one that is in a popular place at a desirable time of year.

The other alternative when you want to unload your time share is to sell. But selling the wrong season and the wrong resort may be next to impossible. So it's smart to think about the possibility of having to sell before you even buy. Some builders offer resale brokerage offices, but they charge commissions of around 15%. The commission — coupled with closing costs of $250 to $500, paid by the seller — can make it difficult to turn a time-share unit into a profitable investment.

So, if you are thinking of buying a vacation time-share unit, be sure to satisfy this all-important test: find a place you will love to be in that same time year after year. Here are some guidelines to picking the right time share for you:

If you buy a time-share unit in fee simple, which means you own it outright, brokers recommend you pay no more than 10 times the going rate for a comparable week in a hotel or rental apartment.

If you buy the right to use, which in effect is a lease of 12 to 60 years, then divide the price by the number of years you get to use the property. If the amount is less than the cost of an equivalent rental unit, then the price is right.

Buy one- or two-bedroom units. They are easier to resell than very small or very large ones.

Buy time during the peak season at a popular area. This enhances your chance of swapping, renting or selling.

Buy in a place that cannot be overbuilt because of geography, local building codes or moratoriums on further time shares.

Buy your time share from an experienced builder. You will be less likely to wind up with poor maintenance, bad management or unforeseen liabilities. Also, big developers are more likely to help you rent or resell your time share.

Buy in a place that is easy to reach. If it isn't, that may discourage potential swappers or buyers.

If you make the right choice — but only if you make the right choice — then chances are you will have the double pleasure of regular access to a nice vacation spot plus a sound investment.

Vacations

TRAVELING ABROAD WITH CHILDREN

Y ou don't have to wait until your children have graduated from college to take a vacation in Europe. You can go now and take the children with you without breaking the bank at Monte Carlo. The money-saving trick is to stay away from places like the bank at Monte Carlo.

Peter Carry, an assistant managing editor of *Sports Illustrated*, who has spent several summers in Europe with his wife and their young children, advises that the first rule of international travel with the under five-foot-tall set is: don't travel. Rent a house and stay put except for family day trips and the occasional parental overnight. Hauling youngsters from one hotel to another and in and out of restaurants calls for the resources of the Aga Khan and the forbearance of Mother Teresa.

The key part of planning a family trip is finding the rental house. Avoid cities and well-known resorts. In a small town or village, your rent is likely to be relatively inexpensive, the chances will be good that you will have friendly neighbors and you can absorb local culture that isn't gussied up for the tourists.

The least expensive arrangement is to house-swap through an organization such as the Vacation Exchange Club. If you have a lot of lead time, it is worth investing $22.70 for a listing in the club's biannual guide. Write to the Vacation Exchange Club, 350 Broadway, New York, New York 10013.

If you want to rent a house on fairly short notice, comb the classified ads in the Friday edition of the *International Herald Tribune.* You can buy it at major newsstands in large cities. The national tourist office of the country you want to visit, its consulate in your area or its embassy in Washington can also point you in the right direction.

When all else fails, get a guidebook to the country you like to visit and select half a dozen or so towns that sound appealing. Then write to the local tourist office in each — most good guides like the Michelin include those addresses. You also can have your travel agent put you in touch with a rental agency. But once you have found your house, be sure to ask for photographs and a list of the contents before you consider renting.

Your largest single expense probably will be plane fares. But there are ways to hold down these and other costs.

Sometimes the country where you will be staying isn't necessarily the one you should fly to. For example, if you are traveling to the south of France, you may be wise to check to see if there is a specially inexpensive New York

[351]

to London fare, and then pay extra to fly from London to Marseilles. Or you might want to fly to Barcelona because it is often cheaper to rent a car in Spain than in France.

But before you buy tickets on any cut-rate plane flights, be sure they have reduced-cost seats for children. Some of them do not. So more than ever, when flying to Europe with your family, you have to shop around.

You can carry more weight on a transatlantic flight than used to be allowed because most carriers have replaced the 44-pound maximum with a system that limits each passenger to two bags of certain dimensions plus a carry-on. This is a tremendous advantage if you are renting a house abroad.

Though the strengthening of the dollar against European currencies means that food, drink and rental houses are less expensive than in recent years for the American traveler, many products remain much more expensive in Europe than at home. That decidedly includes plastic and paper household products. So stuff all your leftover luggage capacity with them, if you are renting a home for several weeks. And if you are traveling with infants, remember that an army duffel bag can hold more than 200 disposable diapers.

Consider springing for another plane ticket — and bring a baby-sitter along with you. That's right. If you usually have a mother's helper at home or often use baby-sitters, you probably can buy a seat to Europe for the same amount as these services cost. And because there seems to be an endless supply of bright, responsible American teenagers who will baby-sit in exchange for a chance to go to Europe, you need not pay more than expenses. A mother's helper means freedom for mother — and father — to get away, if only for an hour at the local café for coffee and a *digestif.*

Vacations

WHAT TO DO IF YOUR BAGGAGE
IS LOST

THE best laid travel plans can be spoiled if your baggage is lost on an airline trip. Here's what to do if that happens to you — and some advice on how to prevent it from happening.

The reassuring news is that less than 1% of all luggage is lost, even temporarily, and almost all bags that go astray are found, usually within a few hours. If you cannot locate your bag, your first step is to report the loss to the airline's representative immediately; the bag may still be on the plane you came in on. If a search turns up nothing, you will be given a form to fill out. Don't leave the airport without handing in the form — and keep a copy for your records.

If you will be bagless overnight, most airlines will give you either a toilet kit or the money to buy one. The airlines are stickier about replacing clothes. Many a week-long vacation has been hampered, if not ruined, because an airline did not pay for clothes until the vacation was almost over. Even then the carrier might pay only half the cost.

When luggage is lost, the airline is liable for damages, usually up to $750. Commuter lines are not liable for even that much, though many would pay anyway. If your luggage and its contents are worth more than $750, you can buy excess-valuation insurance from the airline when you check in. Most carriers charge $1 for each $100 worth of coverage — up to $5,000. Even so, some airlines may refuse to insure breakable items, including jewelry and antiques.

Once your bag has been missing four or five days, you should file a claim form. Extensive dickering over the worth of goods is fairly common. Settlements are figured on the depreciated value, not the full replacement cost. Count on waiting six weeks for the payment. If you don't feel the settlement is fair, take the matter to small-claims court — before cashing the airline's check.

The major causes of missing bags are mix-ups when they are moved from one place to another, failure to remove old airport tags and theft — usually by someone hanging around the baggage carrousel. To avoid loss, always pull old airport tags off a bag before checking it; that avoids confusion about where it is heading. Learn the tag code letters for airports to which you often fly so that you can be sure your bag is properly ticketed. Make sure your name, address and phone number are marked on the outside of any checked luggage. If you don't have baggage tags, the airline usually will give you stick-on labels. In sum, bright, clear identification is your best guarantee that your bags will get to their destination.

Venture Capital

HOW TO INVEST IN NEW BUSINESSES

O NLY rich people used to be able to put up the venture capital that got new companies going. But you can invest in beginning businesses, too, and you don't have to be a millionaire to do it. Instead of pumping large sums of money directly into a new company, you can invest in start-ups indirectly. You do that by buying publicly traded shares in small business investment companies or venture capital concerns. Or you can buy units in limited partnerships assembled by brokerage firms and other money managers.

There are 363 small-business investment companies, or SBICs. Most are owned by banks or groups of private individuals, but there are a few whose shares can be bought or sold over the counter or on the American Stock Exchange. The best recent performer among SBICs has been Narragansett Capital, traded over the counter. From mid-1982 to mid-1983, its net asset value per share jumped 114%.

SBICs concentrate on small business that creates jobs. They are regulated by the Small Business Administration, which lends them up to $4 for each $1 of private capital they raise. Some of their money is invested in start-ups that offer little more than potentially workable concepts. The rest is in second- and third-round financings to help spur the growth of companies that are already marketing a product or have moved solidly into the black.

Quite a few SBICs prefer to cut out as much risk as possible. They invest only in companies that are mature enough to provide some current income, which they pay out to their shareholders in dividends.

What kind of SBIC you invest in depends on whether you want immediate income or longer-term capital gains. But whatever kind you select, ask yourself two questions. Do you think that the companies supported by the SBIC are sound businesses? And, what is the investment record of the SBIC's manager? You can draw much of this information from the fund's quarterly and annual reports.

Another way to get in on promising new businesses is to buy shares in public venture capital companies. They are traded mostly on the American Stock Exchange and over the counter. They invest aggressively, and so they are not for the fainthearted. Before you plunge in, read the annual and quarterly reports carefully. You want to know what new companies they are financing and what is the past performance of the manager doing the investing. The top performer among capital companies in the first half of

1983 was Heizer Corporation. Its shares, traded on the American Stock Exchange, rose 41% from January through midyear.

Lately, Merrill Lynch brought out a public partnership that invests in new businesses. It cost $5,000 a unit and you had to pay an 8% sales commission. Unfortunately, there is no place where you can sell your units if you suddenly should need the money. All Merrill Lynch will do is try to match up sellers with buyers.

You also can try to buy the shares of new companies, when they first go public. It is not easy to get in on a popular new issue. And the price may shoot to the stratosphere when all the people who couldn't buy it try to pick it up from those who could. But within a year, *three-quarters* of all new issues have slipped back to their offering price — or gone even lower. Investors who wait for such a decline usually have gains as big as those who got in early.

If you want to buy a company that's going public, ask a broker for a prospectus. See who is doing the selling. If all the original backers are now backing out, beware. The public offering of stock may be bailing them out of a bad investment. But if the original investors are hanging onto their shares, that could be a sign the company has a very bright future.

Which fields are most likely to produce the next generation of successful new companies? If you ask venture capitalists, business school professors, bankers and owners of small enterprises for their list of the potentially fastest growing areas of the economy in the coming years, they will most likely recommend these:

First, data processing: The future looks bright for companies that make or service computers and software. Retail outlets for equipment and programs are especially promising businesses to get into.

Second, health: Americans spend over $200 billion a year on health and medical services. One reason for this high bill is that it costs so much to stay in a hospital. So there will be plentiful opportunities for making, selling or servicing medical equipment for use in the home.

Third, genetics: Some of the best possibilities for smaller firms are in support fields — for example, manufacturing lab equipment or producing enzymes for use in genetic research.

Fourth, communications. Opportunities can be great for entrepreneurs who make, sell or service cable TV and satellite transmission equipment.

There are, of course, still more opportunity areas. For example, extracting valuable metals from materials before disposing of it, or helping companies become more productive and efficient. The needs abound; the choice of investment is up to you.

Wedding Costs

THE NEW, SENSIBLE SHARING

Nowadays, couples are back to marrying, or remarrying, in old-fashioned ways, even if they have been living together for years. This return to basics, alas, makes a considerable dent in the family's finances.

Traditional weddings, with white satin gowns and three-tiered wedding cakes, are in style again, but it is expensive to let them eat cake. The cost for dinner, drink and dancing — along with flowers, invitations, clothing and church or synagogue fees — comes to an average of close to $5,000. More than half is spent at the reception. The cost of a dinner or buffet ranges from $12 to $50 a person; add 50% for kosher catering. That's just for food. If you want an open bar, figure on another $3 to $10 per guest, plus up to $30 for each bottle of champagne. So it is not hard to spend close to $100 a guest.

Sensible planning can help keep those costs down. Some couples getting married on the same day agree to share the cost of flowers at the scene of the ceremony. Others save a few hundred dollars by skipping such reception giveaways as printed matches and napkins. Friends can contribute their photographic or musical talents, or even their cake-baking and flower-growing abilities.

Traditionally, members of the wedding paid for their own dresses and tuxedo rentals. Now some couples and their families sensibly handle these bills instead of giving their attendants expensive gifts of jewelry as a keepsake of the wedding.

Even pre-wedding festivities are more practical. Gone are the days of a group of women giggling over a sexy negligee at a bridal shower. Today friends often give "couples showers." Guests are expected to bring gifts that both members of the pair can use, like gardening tools. Couples who start out willing to share gardening chores can probably count on sharing many years together.

It used to be that the wedding bills were paid by the father of the bride. But now that old etiquette is giving way to the new economics. It is becoming increasingly common for the families of the bride and the groom to split the costs.

Often the expenses are divided four ways — among both sets of parents and the bride and groom. Splitting the costs seems natural to many of today's career-minded brides. After all, their parents paid for educations that were intended to prepare their daughters to pay their own way — or at least a good part of it.

So, parents of the bride can take heart: You may be losing a daughter, but at least you are not obliged to pay the whole bill.

Widows

MANAGING WHEN ALONE

IT is sad but true that more than ten million American women are widows. Those who are in the best financial shape are not necessarily the ones with the largest inheritances. Rather, they are the women who regularly discussed family finances with their husbands and, more important, what to do with their legacies if their husbands died first.

Because women live much longer than men, widows outnumber widowers by five to one. New widows are, on the average, only 56 years old and, unless they remarry, they face two decades of life on their own. Yet the overwhelming majority of them have never thought much about how to handle the family's assets or how their own economic needs would be met. In fact, one widow in four exhausts her husband's life insurance within two years of his death.

By contrast, the widows who cope the best are those who taught themselves — well in advance — how to manage money. The *wrong* time to start asking, say, the difference between money-market funds and stock-market mutual funds is when a woman has to start managing the family assets alone.

Wives should insist on periodically reviewing their family assets and liabilities with their husbands. Lynn Caine, author of the book *Widow*, suggests that a couple set aside an annual "contingency day" to assess what the surviving spouse would inherit and consider what he or she should do with it. They should discuss whether she — or he — ought to sell the major inherited assets, such as their house or art collection or business. The couple should also re-examine their wills *every* year and discuss where the widow — or widower — should seek financial advice.

Every married couple should update and put in writing all the information that can help the survivor and an executor settle the estate. This should include such basic facts as the names and phone numbers of the family attorney, accountant, stockbroker and insurance agent; also, the locations of bank accounts and safe-deposit boxes and important documents, such as wills, deeds and partnership agreements; and a list of assets and debts. Of course, all this information should be kept in one safe and convenient place.

Every married woman should regularly read the financial pages in the press. That is a necessary first step in planning for the possibility that someday she may have to direct her own financial affairs. A wife also should handle her own checking account, pay the bills periodically and take an active part in meetings with any of her husband's professional advisers, such as the stockbroker or insurance agent.

The first priority of a widow should be to preserve her inheritance. For instance, it may be foolish to sell off the family house, which is probably the best place for her to live today and may well be worth more tomorrow. She may be able to delay paying some bills so that the money can earn bank interest. To guard against mistakes and con men, a new widow would be wise to double check whether questionable bills already have been paid.

She ought to wait six months or a year before considering investing her inheritance in anything that isn't safe and liquid. Quite often, she will not be thinking straight before then. Until the widow is ready to absorb the counsel of professionals and decide how to diversify her investments, any insurance money and other inherited cash can be kept safely in certificates of deposit, money-market funds or those mutual funds that invest in conservative stocks.

A new widow can get good counsel from a pamphlet called *What Do You Do Now?* It is available for $1.30 from the Life Insurance Marketing and Research Association, Order Department, P.O. Box 208, Hartford, Connecticut 06141. She also can get advice on additional sources of financial and emotional counsel by writing to The THEOS Foundation, 410 Penn Hills Mall, Pittsburgh, Pennsylvania 15235.

Remember this: eventually, a widow must assume responsibility for financial decisions. The sooner any married woman prepares for widowhood, the better. A much better legacy than money is knowing how to manage it.

Wills

DRAFTING YOUR MOST IMPORTANT DOCUMENT

INFLATION has pushed up the dollar value of your assets, so there is new teeth in the old saw that you are probably worth more dead than alive. Because you will have more than you expected to leave to your heirs, it is increasingly important that you have a carefully prepared will. There is no way without a will to leave your heirs exactly what you intend to leave them.

You do not have to be super rich to need a will. If you are middle-class, the value of your house, pension and personal property could easily run between $350,000 and $450,000 — or more. You need a will to dispose of any property that is not jointly owned or that does not have a named beneficiary, as an insurance policy does. Only in a will can you appoint a guardian for your children or pass along grandfather's favorite watch or make special provision for an aging relative or a handicapped child.

If you put off preparing and signing a will, then the state will carve up and parcel out what you leave — and quite possibly not the way you want to leave it. Usually the state gives one-third to one-half of your after-tax estate to the surviving widow or widower and the rest to the children. If you have no surviving spouse or children, then your estate goes to your parents, brothers and sisters and other blood relatives — or if you have none, then to the state itself.

Most states do not accept wills that have not been vouched for by witnesses. Don't ask a beneficiary to be a witness; the will may be legal, but the beneficiary could lose his legacy.

It is wise to have a lawyer draft your will — and your spouse's. Only a lawyer knows what constitutes a valid document in your state. Some lawyers at legal clinics will draw up your will for as little as $50, but $200 is average. The cost depends on the complexity of your finances. Don't be shy about interviewing a prospective lawyer and getting the cost in writing.

Lawyers admit that wills are loss leaders, and they hope to be made executors for the estate. Fees for them typically are 2% to 5% of the gross estate. But you are under no obligation to do more than pay your lawyer for the will.

Once the will is drawn, sign only one copy and leave it with your lawyer. You can make minor changes with amendments at any time. Don't put your will in a safe-deposit box. Some states require safe-deposit boxes be sealed on the holder's death and it takes time to get the will released.

[361]

When drawing up a will, people often make the mistake of trying to control their beneficiaries after they themselves have gone. For example, some time ago, one man set up a trust in his will but specified that the trust could hold only assets that yielded 4% to 8%. That was a reasonable return when the will was written — and anything above 8% was considered dangerously speculative. But as interest rates roared up, the trust manager was forced by the terms of the will to sell off many sound and high-yielding investments.

A sensible guideline when making bequests in a will is to use percentages rather than dollar amounts. If you do not, a lot can go wrong. Take the sorry case of a man who had a $100,000 estate and left all of it to his beloved sister, except for $10,000 that he willed to his nephew. But when the man died after a long illness, medical bills had shrunk his estate to only $12,000. The nephew got his promised $10,000, but the unfortunate sister collected only $2,000. The man would have been far wiser to have left his nephew 10% of the estate. In that case, the sister would have collected $10,800.

Dissolution of a marriage automatically cancels any rights your ex-mate might have to your estate. But should you die before a separation agreement is signed, your soon-to-be-ex will still inherit. And people will think it was very sporting of you not to hold a grudge.

Review your will periodically, and keep it up to date. Be sure to revise it if you move, particularly from a common law state to a community property state or vice versa. In a community property state, any assets acquired during marriage are jointly owned by both partners — except for gifts and inheritances. But in a common law state, assets are owned by whoever buys them.

Surely if you get your will in order, you can save your family lots of bitterness. No family situation brings more stress than divvying up Dad's estate. In fact, one academic study shows that where there was no will, arguments among the heirs were four times as likely to occur.

Windfalls

HANDLING UNEXPECTED WEALTH

THE odds that one day you will receive a windfall are gradually improving. Most sudden money comes from inheritances and court settlements, but 17 states now have lotteries, and the jackpots are huge. The problem is, what do you do with your new fortune?

Unless you already have considerable money and know how to manage it, sudden wealth will require a new financial strategy. Your goal should be to preserve that hefty capital and make it work for you. Taking big risks with your riches is not only unnecessary, but also unwise.

When that first check arrives, stash the cash for six months or so in a money-market fund, a Treasury bill or some other short-term investment. There it will remain, liquid and safe, while you sort out your options.

Your first priority is minimizing taxes on your treasure. All windfalls are taxable as ordinary income, except inheritances and unsolicited awards and prizes. To reduce Uncle's take, use what is called five-year income averaging on your tax return. That will spread out your windfall, for tax purposes, as if it were earned over five years. Set up an Individual Retirement Account so you can deduct $2,000 from your taxable income each year, and if you are self-employed, start a Keogh account to defer taxes on up to $15,000 a year, or $30,000 beginning in 1984.

When investing your hoard, the main rule is diversify, so that you don't blow the whole wad on a single mistake. Consider a mix of no-load mutual funds, Treasury bills and either municipal bonds or real estate limited partnerships where tax deductions can shelter investment income. Seek out professional help. You will probably need an accountant for tax advice and a financial planner to devise a strategy for conserving your money and making it grow.

Many of the suddenly rich feel uneasy, not to say guilty, about their new wealth. Others make the mistake of quitting their jobs in euphoria, and some suffer by changing too much about their lives too soon. A windfall can catapult you from one economic position to another, but attitudes, values and behavior change more slowly. So, ease into your new status gradually.

Postscript

T‍HIS book begins with a look ahead to America's next ten years. It concludes in the present, with an examination of America's assets. The material is drawn from an article by the author that was published in *Money* magazine of March 1981, and then was broadcast by him in five programs on the CBS Radio Network. These broadcasts won the first place award for network radio that year in the Champion Media Awards for Economic Understanding, administered by Dartmouth College's Amos Tuck School of Business Administration. Some of the statistics have changed over time — the originals are reproduced here — but the conclusions remain the same.

American Assets

INVESTING IN THE NATION'S UNDERVALUED
STRENGTHS

THE stock market has been doing rather well lately, and many people wonder why it suddenly looks strong. Well, maybe it's because so many folks at home and abroad are taking a close look at America's real assets — those basic resources and attributes that will determine the future of investments — and they like what they see.

A smart investor will shrewdly size up both the assets and the liabilities of what he invests in, whether it's stocks or bonds or real estate or a private business. So, before putting your money into any investments, it might be worthwhile to investigate the assets and liabilities of the country in which they are located: the United States. In short, if the country does well in the future, investments in its land and businesses also stand to do well.

The remarkable fact is that, for all its flaws, the United States has unique and sometimes undervalued assets. Much the same could be said about our strong, friendly neighbor to the north — Canada.

Foreigners often see these visible advantages more clearly than we do, and so they are investing in America as if it were a high-growth stock. In record numbers, Europeans, Latin Americans and Asians are putting their money into apartments in New York, into houses in California, condominiums in Florida, beach fronts in Hawaii, factories in South Carolina, farms in Iowa, mines in Colorado and much more.

Investments by foreigners in America have more than doubled in the past five years, to a total $456 billion dollars. That's billions — not millions. Middle-class Latin Americans, worried about revolution, have opened so many bank accounts in Miami that Dade County is now a major center of international finance.

And foreigners are increasingly investing their lives in the United States. Immigration visa applications since 1978 have jumped 32%. Many of the newcomers are not only the oppressed from Russia and Cuba, Poland and Nicaragua, but also educated, affluent people from all over.

What these investors and immigrants are telling us should be clear: America is a stable, free land with the prospect of great future wealth, and Americans who have some money to save might well invest it in that future.

*　*　*

An immigrant from Greece who's built a prosperous restaurant in New York has put a big sign in his window. It says this: "I'm sick of seeing

[365]

America run down." Many other Americans feel the same way. And anybody who is investing his money, his career, his life in this country ought to take stock of some of its often undervalued assets.

You don't have to be a chauvanist to see — and to value — America's material strengths. They are strengths that will help your investments grow in the future.

For example:

Enviable communications and transportation systems link 17,700 cities, towns and hamlets spread over 3,600,000 square miles. To anyone who has experienced the frustrations of foreign phones, Ma Bell and her proliferating competitors are wonders of speedy reliability. Telephone rates in the U.S. are the least expensive in the world. And airplane fares are usually the world's lowest.

Though it might not be easily recognized by anyone waiting in line 20 minutes to deposit a paycheck, the banking system is supremely effective. It clears about 32 billion checks a year, up 32% since 1970. Depositors need not worry about bank failure because the Federal Deposit Insurance Corporation protects them. Since its founding 47 years ago, 568 banks have failed, but not a single depositor has lost a cent.

The brokerage business is also a model of modern efficiency — good news for all you investors. In an instant, you can trade stocks, bonds and commodity futures contracts. Modern electronics allow the New York Stock Exchange to handle more than 90 million shares a day, with none of the back-office snarls that forced some brokerages into bankruptcy in a few successive 20 million share days in the 1960s.

The United States has by far more computers per capita than any other nation — one for every 181 citizens. While some of you may think these electronic brains to be a mixed blessing, they do permit you to make not only those instant brokerage transactions and immediate airline reservations, but they also provide remarkably error-free credit card and department-store billings.

❁　❁　❁

Beyond its many resources of machines and computers, the United States possesses a fabulous amount of raw materials, and they are bound to pay rewards in the future for the investors of today.

All of us worry about the energy shortage, but sometimes we overlook that the United States is the Saudi Arabia of coal, with 300 years' supply at current rates of use. Because that use is destined to rise, some of the country's most economically deprived regions, such as Appalachia, could surge in the future. The Intermountain West has the world's largest reserves of oil shale and much of its uranium and coal — and thus a boom ultimately may come to such unlikely places as Rifle, Colorado, and Vernal, Utah. So much methane gas is locked in the Tuscaloosa Trend under the Gulf of Mexico and the Anadarko Basin in Oklahoma that entrepreneurs are investing huge sums in them, anticipating the rise of secondary sources of energy.

It's often said that America is running out of basic metals and other non-energy resources, but it has a treasure of supplies that can be made available by alternative methods of recovery. Among them are platinum mixed with other valuable minerals in Alaska, phosphate ores buried deep in northeast Florida, zinc, manganese, lithium, iron and lead from superheated water in California's Imperial Valley. Extracting these minerals is far too costly now, but it will become economically feasible — indeed, absolutely necessary — as a demanding world runs out of easily utilized supplies in the future.

America's richest resource is that ultimate energy — food. The United States is by far the largest exporter of agricultural products: corn, soybeans, wheat and cotton, as well as tractors, combines and other farm machinery. In 1980, the nation's food and fiber sales to the world grew by a bin-bursting 16 million metric tons, to 163 million metric tons.

And the productivity revolution on the farm keeps rolling right along. Back in 1940, one American farmer fed 10.7 people at home and abroad; in 1980, he fed a remarkable total of 65 people.

*　*　*

If you are worried that America is falling behind in the global economic competition, you might be comforted by one startling fact: many products of American technology are still the most sought after in the whole world. And this demand should help your investments in American business to grow in the future.

The exports of many American industries climbed smartly in 1980: to $7.5 billion worth of computers and parts for electronic equipment, $10 billion worth of heavy construction machinery and $14.1 billion of civilian aircraft and parts. Even the battered automobile industry had exports of $15.9 billion.

The export demand stems in part from the surprising reality that American productivity, though flat for the past several years, remains the world's highest. In terms of output per hour, the American worker produces 17% more goods than the West German — and 49% more than the Japanese.

Of course, the Japanese are ahead — far ahead sometimes — in efficiently manufacturing steel, cars, cameras, handheld calculators and TV sets. But Japan has built all these industries afresh after World War II, with the most modern equipment. Still, the Japanese and nearly everybody else are behind the United States in both productivity and quality in agriculture, computers and software, aircraft, mining equipment and many other industries.

Living standards are significantly higher in the United States than in any other major industrial nation, despite some statistics in the past purporting to show that Americans rank tenth in per capita income. Those figures were based on distorted currency values. In fact, the average American house-hold has 1.6 telephones, 1.5 television sets and 1.4 cars in the garage. The average West German family has only eight-tenths of one telephone, eight-tenths of one auto and 1.3 TV sets.

✻ ✻ ✻

If you are thinking about investing in stocks or bonds or land or any other of this country's assets, consider this: It is not in industry or agriculture that America has made its boldest advances. It is in society — and that societal progress stands to greatly enhance the nation's human capital.

Altogether, 12 million Americans are now attending universities. That works out to one in every 2.5 people aged 18 to 24, versus only one in six in West Germany and one in eight in Britain. When they graduate, many of these students will go into business, industry and the sciences and may well increase the value of your investments.

The United States will also gain a significant advantage in the intensify-ing global competition because so many American women are at last be-ginning to be admitted to positions of leadership. The United States already leads the world in terms of women managers in banking, brokerage services, computer sciences, advertising, insurance and a host of other enterprises. And that list will grow fast tomorrow. One student in four studying for an advanced degree in business is a woman. Simply put, with a larger pool of talent to choose from, we stand to choose better leaders.

We are entering an era when the countries that possess the rare combina-tion of human *and* material resources will prosper and inherit the future. In this environment, one can reasonably conclude that the United States and Canada are among the very few nations that have all the necessary ingre-dients for success.

America has the resources. What it has lacked is the will, the methods and the procedures to productively exploit those human and material re-sources; also, the skill to rally its people and the resolve to surmount indi-vidual interests for the benefit of all. If it can achieve that, then the future of the country — and all those who invest in it — should indeed be remark-able.

Index

[370]